THE CAMBRIDGE BIBLE COMMENTARY

NEW ENGLISH BIBLE

GENERAL EDITORS

P. R. ACKROYD, A. R. C. LEANEY
J. W. PACKER

RUTH, ESTHER, ECCLESIASTES
THE SONG OF SONGS, LAMENTATIONS

THE BOOKS OF
RUTH, ESTHER
ECCLESIASTES, THE SONG OF
SONGS, LAMENTATIONS

THE FIVE SCROLLS

COMMENTARY BY

WESLEY J. FUERST

Associate Professor of Old Testament
Lutheran School of Theology at Chicago

CAMBRIDGE UNIVERSITY PRESS

CAMBRIDGE

LONDON · NEW YORK · MELBOURNE

Published by the Syndics of the Cambridge University Press
The Pitt Building, Trumpington Street, Cambridge CB2 1RP
Bentley House, 200 Euston Road, London NW1 2DB
32 East 57th Street, New York, NY 10022, USA
296 Beaconsfield Parade, Middle Park, Melbourne 3206, Australia

Library of Congress catalogue card number: 74–82589

hard covers ISBN: 0 521 20651 0
paperback ISBN: 0 521 09920 x

First published 1975

Printed in Great Britain
at the University Printing House, Cambridge
(Euan Phillips, University Printer)

GENERAL EDITORS' PREFACE

The aim of this series is to provide the text of the New English Bible closely linked to a commentary in which the results of modern scholarship are made available to the general reader. Teachers and young people have been especially kept in mind. The commentators have been asked to assume no specialized theological knowledge, and no knowledge of Greek and Hebrew. Bare references to other literature and multiple references to other parts of the Bible have been avoided. Actual quotations have been given as often as possible.

The completion of the New Testament part of the series in 1967 provides a basis upon which the production of the much larger Old Testament and Apocrypha series can be undertaken. The welcome accorded to the series has been an encouragement to the editors to follow the same general pattern, and an attempt has been made to take account of criticisms which have been offered. One necessary change is the inclusion of the translators' footnotes since in the Old Testament these are more extensive, and essential for the understanding of the text.

Within the severe limits imposed by the size and scope of the series, each commentator will attempt to set out the main findings of recent biblical scholarship and to describe the historical background to the text. The main theological issues will also be critically discussed.

Much attention has been given to the form of the volumes. The aim is to produce books each of which will be read consecutively from first to last page. The introductory material leads naturally into the text, which itself leads into the alternating sections of the commentary.

The series is accompanied by three volumes of a more general character. *Understanding the Old Testament* sets out to provide the larger historical and archaeological background, to say something about the life and thought of the people of the Old Testament, and to answer the question 'Why should we study the Old Testament?'. *The Making of the Old Testament* is concerned with the formation of the books of the Old Testament and Apocrypha in the context of the ancient near eastern world, and with the ways in which these books have come down to us in the life of the Jewish and Christian communities. *Old Testament Illustrations* contains maps, diagrams and photographs with an explanatory text. These three volumes are designed to provide material helpful to the understanding of the individual books and their commentaries, but they are also prepared so as to be of use quite independently.

P. R. A.
A. R. C. L.
J. W. P.

CONTENTS

THE FOOTNOTES TO THE
N.E.B. TEXT

The footnotes to the N.E.B. text are designed to help the reader either to understand particular points of detail – the meaning of a name, the presence of a play upon words – or to give information about the actual text. Where the Hebrew text appears to be erroneous, or there is doubt about its precise meaning, it may be necessary to turn to manuscripts which offer a different wording, or to ancient translations of the text which may suggest a better reading, or to offer a new explanation based upon conjecture. In such cases, the footnotes supply very briefly an indication of the evidence, and whether the solution proposed is one that is regarded as possible or as probable. Various abbreviations are used in the footnotes.

(1) Some abbreviations are simply of terms used in explaining a point: *ch(s)*., chapter(s); *cp*., compare; *lit*., literally; *mng*., meaning; *MS(S)*., manuscript(s), i.e. Hebrew manuscript(s), unless otherwise stated; *om*., omit(s); *or*, indicating an alternative interpretation; *poss*., possible; *prob*., probable; *rdg*., reading; *Vs(s)*., Version(s).

(2) Other abbreviations indicate sources of information from which better interpretations or readings may be obtained.

Aq. Aquila, a Greek translator of the Old Testament (perhaps about A.D. 130) characterized by great literalness.

Aram. Aramaic – may refer to the text in this language (used in parts of Ezra and Daniel), or to the meaning of an Aramaic word. Aramaic belongs to the same language family as Hebrew, and is known from about 1000 B.C. over a wide area of the Middle East, including Palestine.

Heb. Hebrew – may refer to the Hebrew text or may indicate the literal meaning of the Hebrew word.

Josephus Flavius Josephus (A.D. 37/8–about 100), author of the *Jewish Antiquities*, a survey of the whole history of his people, directed partly at least to a non-Jewish audience, and of various other works, notably one on the *Jewish War* (that of A.D. 66–73) and a defence of Judaism (*Against Apion*).

Luc. Sept. Lucian's recension of the Septuagint, an important edition made in Antioch in Syria about the end of the third century A.D.

Pesh. Peshitta or Peshitto, the Syriac version of the Old Testament. Syriac is the name given chiefly to a form of Eastern Aramaic used by the Christian community. The translation varies in quality, and is at many points influenced by the Septuagint or the Targums.

Sam. Samaritan Pentateuch – the form of the first five books of the Old Testament as used by the Samaritan community. It is written in Hebrew in a special form of the Old Hebrew script, and preserves an important form of the text, somewhat influenced by Samaritan ideas.

Scroll(s) Scroll(s), commonly called the Dead Sea Scrolls, found at or near Qumran from 1947 onwards. These important manuscripts shed light on the state of the Hebrew text as it was developing in the last centuries B.C. and the first century A.D.

Sept. Septuagint (meaning 'seventy'); often abbreviated as the Roman numeral (LXX), the name given to the main Greek version of the Old Testament. According to tradition, the Pentateuch was translated in Egypt in the third century B.C. by 70 (or 72) translators, six from each tribe, but the precise nature of its origin and development is not fully known. It was intended to provide Greek-speaking Jews with a convenient translation. Subsequently it came to be much revered by the Christian community.

Symm. Symmachus, another Greek translator of the Old Testament (beginning of the third century A.D.), who tried to combine literalness with good style. Both Lucian and Jerome viewed his version with favour.

Targ. Targum, a name given to various Aramaic versions of the Old Testament, produced over a long period and eventually standardized, for the use of Aramaic-speaking Jews.

Theod. Theodotion, the author of a revision of the Septuagint (probably second century A.D.), very dependent on the Hebrew text.

Vulg. Vulgate, the most important Latin version of the Old Testament, produced by Jerome about A.D. 400, and the text most used throughout the Middle Ages in western Christianity.

[...] In the text itself square brackets are used to indicate probably late additions to the Hebrew text.

(Fuller discussion of a number of these points may be found in *The Making of the Old Testament* in this series.)

THE BOOKS OF

RUTH, ESTHER, ECCLESIASTES, THE SONG OF SONGS, LAMENTATIONS

✻ ✻ ✻ ✻ ✻ ✻ ✻ ✻ ✻ ✻ ✻ ✻ ✻

THE FIVE SCROLLS

In the Hebrew Bible there are gathered together in one collection near the end several small books which in Western traditions have been placed at different points in the Old Testament. These books – Ruth, Esther, Ecclesiastes, Song of Songs, and Lamentations – are called in Hebrew the Megilloth, which means the 'Scrolls'. The earliest record of the location of these books in the Old Testament comes from the oldest complete Greek manuscripts. In the fourth-century manuscript Codex Vaticanus, Ruth follows after Judges, Lamentations after Jeremiah, Ecclesiastes and the Song of Songs after Proverbs, and Esther (along with Judith and Tobit, both now in the Apocrypha) is placed just before the prophets. This order probably reflects the earliest associations of the books with material that was historically linked or traditionally related; it belongs to a period not long after the era when the books' authority and sanctity were decided and accepted in Judaism and in Christianity.

Over the course of some centuries, these five small books gradually came to occupy a special place in Hebrew tradition as selected readings for major festivals, and accordingly in the Hebrew manuscripts they were brought together to form a group of five scrolls (after the analogy of the five books of the law, Genesis to Deuteronomy, and the five books of the Psalms). The major festivals and the associated scrolls which were read in connection with them are: the Passover,

I

celebrating the Exodus – Song of Songs; the Feast of Weeks, marking the end of the harvest season and remembering the giving of the law on Mount Sinai – Ruth; the Ninth of Ab, in memory of the fall of Jerusalem in 587 B.C. – Lamentations; the Feast of Tabernacles, six months after Passover and celebrating the grape harvest – Ecclesiastes; Purim, the festival of national deliverance and victory over enemies – Esther. In Hebrew manuscripts and printed editions the Five Scrolls are placed in this same order, and follow the Hebrew calendar of festivals for the year beginning with Passover in the first month of the Hebrew year.

The Five Scrolls offer a fascinating variety of material, including a short story (Ruth) and a historical novel or festal legend (Esther), speculative wisdom (Ecclesiastes), poetry (Song of Songs), and lamentations and dirges (Lamentations). They all come down to us in their present form from rather late in the Old Testament historical period, although some portions or underlying strata of tradition may well be centuries older. Each book is very different from the others, bringing its own unique message and viewpoint, and reflecting a distinct faith.

It was about several of the books in the final third of the Hebrew Bible, including the Scrolls, that debate took place on the authority and holiness, that is, the canonicity, of certain parts. Esther, Ecclesiastes, and the Song of Songs were all questioned at some time or other by famous rabbis. The Scrolls therefore represent a kind of frontier for the Old Testament, and they pose some of the thorniest problems in interpretation.

The oldest records of debates about whether these books were holy or not are from the Mishnah and the Talmud, documents from Judaism in the second and following centuries A.D. which collected teachings and sayings from the rabbis, as well as reflections on scriptural meanings and stories from Jewish tradition. Although it must be taken for granted at the outset that prevalent opinion favoured these books, some weighty uncertainty must have existed for a long time. Regarding Ecclesiastes, the strict school of Rabbi Shammai opposed it but the liberal school of Rabbi Hillel accepted it as holy; they disagreed in the same way over Ecclesiasticus, which ended up in the Apocrypha outside the collection of Jewish holy books. Debate over Ecclesiastes and the Song of Songs is recorded from the early second century A.D., and even much later it was still declared by some rabbis that Ecclesiastes did not 'defile the hands' (see below) because it was the human wisdom of Solomon, and that Esther was not given from the Holy Spirit.

The word 'canon' means measure, or standard, and was applied to the body of holy books centuries later in Christendom. But it is a useful term to use for understanding the earlier discussions because they were based on certain criteria, or standards, for determining whether a book was holy or not. An early date associated with a book was important; this applied however to literature in general in an era when the traditions were taken to be so important, and therefore many books written during the last centuries B.C. and the first centuries A.D. bore titles with the names of ancient figures like Solomon, Moses, and Enoch. Another measurement for canonical status was whether the book was orthodox in its teaching, agreeing with the Torah (the Law, the five 'books of Moses', Genesis to Deuteronomy) and consistent within itself and with the revelation in the Torah.

Still another measurement was described in the expression already used: whether a book 'defiled the hands', which probably included elements from the other criteria but which also said something in addition. In ancient thinking, holiness was regarded as a substance as well as a quality; it could be physically transmitted. When a person held and read what was really a holy book, holiness was held to pass to the person's hands; this kind of holiness could be a dangerous thing, and the hands therefore needed to be cleaned afterwards. So when a rabbi said that Ecclesiastes does not defile the hands, he meant that he did not feel that he had to clean his hands after reading it. This was a psychological as well as an intellectual matter; either one was moved by the scroll, emotionally, spiritually, and intellectually, or one was not. So personal as well as collective judgements were applied to the books.

What is remarkable about the canonizing process in Judaism, which took place actually over a long period of time, with many fluctuations and in the process of using the books, is not its legalism but its openness and liberality. Ruth of course was a lovely story from the early days, with a very traditional message. Lamentations was a hard and painful book, but from a climax in Israel's history and with a striking word of prophetic truth. Esther did not offer discourses about God and his work, but did speak of vital national experience, and was beloved by the people. But Ecclesiastes bore a very difficult message, challenging the foundations of the traditional beliefs and of orthodoxy; and the Song of Songs was enjoyed, but was not understood, at least as a religious or theological book. That these books were kept is a sobering testimony to the vigour of a process which could accept and tolerate variety, difference, and challenge.

Our reaction to these books is confronted with the same test. We are asked also to weigh their messages against the whole of the traditions which we have received, as well as the whole of our faith. But we must also let them speak to us about their religious experiences, faiths, observations of the world and life and God, and their conclusions.

✻   ✻   ✻   ✻   ✻   ✻   ✻   ✻   ✻   ✻   ✻   ✻

RUTH

* * * * * * * * * * * * *

THE NATURE OF THE BOOK

The book of Ruth is a story about people, their problems, and their deepest concerns. It is told primarily through conversations which are clustered around six scenes and which reveal a deep and complicated network of common human experiences, desires, and reflections. The account is of one piece, without any seams or other signs of the combining or adding of traditions, except for the last few lines (4: 18–22).

It tells the story of a family in Bethlehem, and of how Ruth the daughter-in-law who was from Moab came to a full and happy life, and through this brought about new life for the family, by meeting and marrying Boaz. The book does not relate a major incident in the history of Israel; rather, with sensitivity and strict artistic control it exposes the question of human need and how that need is met under divine providence.

Ruth is a short story, comparable with Esther and other such closely-knit narratives in the Old Testament. It is often compared with the Joseph story in Gen. 37–50; many scholars use the technical term 'novella' for this kind of short story. But the similarities with the Joseph story exist more in content or in issues affecting the content of the stories than in their literary form. Scholars have observed a remarkably symmetrical design in the structure of the book; this design demonstrates the great artistry of its composition.

HISTORICAL REFERENCES AND SETTING

At the outset the book establishes the setting in which the story belongs: 'in the time of the judges'. Thereby Ruth has been associated with the book of Judges, and placed beside it in the Greek manuscripts of the Old Testament. Judges ends with the observation, 'In those days there was no king in Israel and every man did what was right in his own eyes' (Judg. 21 : 25), and its last chapters depict the chaotic and law-less situation when 'no king ruled in Israel' (Judg. 19: 1). Ruth fits into this context, but bears an impression – serene, charming, pastoral – which is very different from those times.

The book exhibits an easy familiarity with ancient customs, although it should not be assumed that we have anything like photographic detail from the period of the judges. The ancient institution of levirate marriage, whereby a man assumed res-ponsibility for the wife of his dead brother (or, in an early form, other near male relative) and for raising children by her in the name of the deceased (see under 1 : 8–14 and 4: 5 below), is represented only in Ruth and in Gen. 38, though the law is set forth in Deut. 25: 5–10. Gen. 38 is referred to in Ruth at the end of the book. The genealogy of Perez (Ruth 4: 18–22), and therefore of David and of Jesus, included both these levirate marriages: Judah and Tamar (Gen. 38), Boaz and Ruth (Ruth 4). In Ruth this practice is combined with the old Hebrew provision for the role of *go'el*, that is, the next-of-kin who acts as a 'redeemer', that is, one who keeps intact the property and name of the family, by recovering land (cp. the story in Jer. 32: 6–12) and ensuring the continuance of the line (as in Ruth and in Gen. 38).

Bethlehem is the location for the story, and no doubt the place where the tradition was handed down. It was the home of David's family, and the town where Jesus of Nazareth was born; otherwise there was little of distinction in its history.

Moab is mentioned already in the wilderness traditions in Numbers, in the efforts of Balak son of Zippor the king of Moab to persuade Balaam to curse Israel (Num. 22–4). Old Testament references to it include oppression of Israel by Eglon king of Moab and Israel's deliverance by Ehud the judge (Judg. 3), hostilities against King Saul of Israel (1 Sam.

14: 47), subjugation under David (2 Sam. 8: 2), and finally
freedom from Hebrew rule when King Mesha of Moab revol-
ted from Ahaziah the son of Ahab of Israel (2 Kings 3: 4–5).
The Moabite language was closely related to the Hebrew, and
Moabite and Hebrew political fortunes alternated from
mutual enmity to co-operation against some more powerful
foreign aggressor.

HOW THE BOOK CAME TO BE

Speculation concerning the date of the book's composition
has ranged from the days of Samuel (who, according to Jewish
tradition in the Mishnah, was its author) to a time long after
the exile. Arguments based on alleged late Hebrew expressions
and Aramaic words in the book have been adduced to support
a theory of final composition after the exile; but this evidence
is meagre, and its conclusiveness is debatable. A recent proposal has suggested three stages in the origin of Ruth: (1) an
old poetic tale, perhaps transmitted in oral form, coming from
the days of the judges; (2) a version written in prose in the
ninth or eighth centuries; (3) a final edition of the material
into its present form after the exile. Another recent view
maintains that there are no serious objections to the idea that
the book of Ruth was written in the time of Solomon. There
is of course no direct evidence to prove such a date, and no
final conclusion is possible.

The text contains a number of words not found elsewhere
in the Old Testament, and it is written in a classical form of
Hebrew. Severe textual problems and radical textual variants
are not numerous.

In later Judaism Ruth was read at the celebration of the
Feast of Weeks, the festival observed seven weeks after the
Passover, which marked the end of the harvest of wheat in the
agricultural calendar.

WHAT THE BOOK WAS MEANT TO SAY

Despite scattered efforts in the past to see behind the book a Canaanite religious festival celebrated at Bethlehem, there is general agreement that Ruth was intended to tell a story about simple folk from the early days of the Hebrews. It has been argued that Naomi, and not Ruth, is the principal character in the book; Naomi is indeed an important person in the narrative, but Ruth is really the central character.

The story is about all three principal characters, Ruth, Naomi, and Boaz, and about what happens as their lives intertwine. The hand of God does not intrude explicitly in their lives; they rather experience his presence, will, and action as they try to live faithfully with each other and confident of his promise and blessing. If the book is also designed to say something about the Hebrews and their neighbours – in this case the Moabites – and so to present a wider outlook than some of the strongly nationalistic stories in Judges, it is done incidentally and without emphasis (cp. the comments on pp. 10 and 30).

✳ ✳ ✳ ✳ ✳ ✳ ✳ ✳ ✳ ✳ ✳ ✳ ✳

Naomi and Ruth

NAOMI'S MISFORTUNES

1 LONG AGO, in the time of the judges, there was a famine in the land, and a man from Bethlehem in Judah went to live in the Moabite country with his wife and his two
2 sons. The man's name was Elimelech, his wife's name was Naomi, and the names of his two sons Mahlon and Chilion. They were Ephrathites from Bethlehem in Judah. They arrived in the Moabite country and there they stayed.

Elimelech Naomi's husband died, so that she was left ₃ with her two sons. These sons married Moabite women, ₄ one of whom was called Orpah and the other Ruth. They had lived there about ten years, when both Mahlon and ₅ Chilion died, so that the woman was bereaved of her two sons as well as of her husband.

✽ The story of Ruth begins with a very compact and condensed summary of the details which provide the background to the drama. The stage is set in order that the reader may understand Naomi's plight: without husband and sons, she is now about to migrate once more in order to seek some measure of shelter and security in the land of her youth. All the main characters except one, Boaz, are quickly introduced into the plot, and the meanings linked to their names suggest the mood of the story.

1. *Long ago, in the time of the judges:* is literally in the Hebrew, 'and it happened in the days when the judges judged'; the word for 'to judge' in this instance can also signify 'to govern'. The narrative mood of the story may suggest a tale from 'long ago', but the text itself does not explicitly say that.

Time of *famine* was the occasion for other stories in the Old Testament; for example, Jacob and his sons had been forced to emigrate to Egypt years before (Gen. 42–7) by just such a famine in Palestine. *Bethlehem* is a town located about 6 miles (nearly 10 km) south of Jerusalem on the Judaean hills, and the name means literally in Hebrew, 'house of bread' (*Beth-Lehem*), an ironic note during a famine. The journey to the *Moabite country*, which is visible across the Dead Sea from the heights east and south of Bethlehem, was not a long one, and a 40- or 50-mile trip (about 64–80 km) from Bethlehem would bring the sojourners around the north end of the Dead Sea, through the country of the Ammonites, into Moab.

2. Commentators feel that the names are suggestive of

foreboding, or are meant to convey at least something about the characters. *Elimelech* means 'God is king', a name suggestive of a sure confession of faith in God. *Naomi* means 'my pleasant one', or 'my darling'. But *Mahlon* and *Chilion* are traced to Hebrew words meaning 'to be sick' and 'to be weakening', although other explanations have also been proposed; these names correlate well with the fate of the young men, adding to the effect of the story. All the names except Mahlon are found in the Canaanite texts from Ugarit (Ras Shamra, on the coast of modern Syria) belonging to the fourteenth century B.C.; this may indicate that the names were simply old ones, and widely known.

Ephrathites here refers to members of a family or clan dwelling around and in Bethlehem; compare Mic. 5: 2, 'But you, Bethlehem in Ephrathah, small as you are to be among Judah's clans, out of you shall come forth a governor for Israel.' Elsewhere (cp. Judg. 12: 5) it refers to a member of the tribe of Ephraim.

3–4. Even within the brief compass of the introduction to the book there is room for a dramatic change in fortune. The husband dies, bereaving Naomi; but her sons marry, opening the possibility of new hope and fulfilment in grandchildren. Any rules or feelings against Moabites, such as one encounters in Deut. 23: 3, may have been non-existent and therefore not at issue when this story originated. Some scholars believe that the book of Ruth was deliberately written against such discriminatory rules and practices in the days of Ezra around 400 B.C. Most probably however the story of Ruth is simply older than the discriminatory rule, and comes from a time when the Hebrews were not so concerned with purity of race. The matter is discussed further at the end of the commentary (p. 30).

Scholars have identified the name *Orpah* with an ancient word for 'cloud', or with words meaning 'to drip, to trickle', or 'nape of the neck', and therefore signifying someone who is stubborn or obstinate. Although the matter remains uncertain, the name *Ruth* has been associated with a word which means 'friend'.

5. Naomi's hopes for the future are dashed when both of her sons die, with no offspring. She is now alone, without husband or sons to defend her in a world where such were the first and sometimes last lines of defence, and she is a foreigner, living where she has no family and no traditional ties. From the standpoint of that day, she is in a desperate situation, being needy and at the same time extremely vulnerable. ✲

RUTH RETURNS WITH NAOMI

Thereupon she set out with her two daughters-in- 6
law to return home, because she had heard while still in the Moabite country that the LORD had cared for his people and given them food. So with her two 7
daughters-in-law she left the place where she had been living, and took the road home to Judah. Then Naomi 8
said to her two daughters-in-law, 'Go back, both of you, to your mothers' homes. May the LORD keep faith with you, as you have kept faith with the dead and with me; and may he grant each of you security in 9
the home of a new husband.' She kissed them and they wept aloud. Then they said to her, 'We will return with 10
you to your own people.' But Naomi said, 'Go back, my 11
daughters. Why should you go with me? Am I likely to bear any more sons to be husbands for you? Go back, my 12
daughters, go. I am too old to marry again. But even if I could say that I had hope of a child, if I were to marry this night and if I were to bear sons, would you then wait 13
until they grew up? Would you then refrain from marry-ing? No, no, my daughters, my lot is more bitter than yours, because the LORD has been against me.' At this 14

they wept again. Then Orpah kissed her mother-in-law and returned to her people,*[a]* but Ruth clung to her.

15 'You see,' said Naomi, 'your sister-in-law has gone back to her people and her gods;*[b]* go back with her.'
16 'Do not urge me to go back and desert you', Ruth answered. 'Where you go, I will go, and where you stay, I will stay. Your people shall be my people, and your God
17 my God. Where you die, I will die, and there I will be buried. I swear a solemn oath before the LORD your
18 God: nothing but*[c]* death shall divide us.' When Naomi saw that Ruth was determined to go with her, she said no
19 more, and the two of them went on until they came to Bethlehem. When they arrived in Bethlehem, the whole town was in great excitement about them, and the
20 women said, 'Can this be Naomi?' 'Do not call me Naomi,'*[d]* she said, 'call me Mara,*[e]* for it is a bitter lot
21 that the Almighty has sent me. I went away full, and the LORD has brought me back empty. Why do you call me Naomi? The LORD has pronounced against me; the
22 Almighty has brought disaster on me.' This is how Naomi's daughter-in-law, Ruth the Moabitess, returned with her from the Moabite country. The barley harvest was beginning when they arrived in Bethlehem.

✻ The picture painted here in the opening scene is one of deep personal heartbreak and misery. Ruth's decision to come with Naomi might seem to be a decided improvement in the situation. But the real state of affairs is disclosed by the word-

[a] and...people: *so Sept.; Heb. om.*   [b] *Or* god.
[c] I swear...nothing but: *or* The LORD your God do so to me and more if...
[d] *That is* Pleasure.   [e] *That is* Bitter.

play on names which is the keynote in this section, and
Naomi's bitterness is revealed in her resentful and ironic comment about her name (verse 20). Naomi has lost her position
as a wife, and as a mother of sons; now she must return to her
home bereft, and like a beggar. Ruth's presence with her
means just that the two beggarly women can at least look
after each other.

The large proportion of dialogue and conversation in this
section is characteristic; dialogue occupies more than half of
the book. The conversation accentuates the personal, individual quality of the story.

6. The play on words from verse 1 is resumed; the woman
from *Beth-Lehem*, the 'house of bread', who left because of
famine, hears that 'the LORD had cared for his people and given
them bread'. 'Bread' is really the word translated *food*; in
Beth-Lehem, the 'house of bread', there is now plenty of food.

8–14. The words spoken are mainly Naomi's; she under-
lines what is at stake – should one, for the sake of personal
loyalty and commitment, forsake home and family, hope of
husband and children, and the security and fulfilment which
they ensure? Naomi, out of human considerations, says 'No',
'*Go back, my daughters.*' She can no longer be a source of hope
for anyone. In the so-called levirate marriage the young
widow could expect that her dead husband's brother would
get children by her, which would perpetuate the family and
name of her deceased husband. But Naomi has no more sons
for Orpah and Ruth, and cannot expect to satisfy them with
new brothers-in-law in the future. She is too old to expect a
new husband, and then sons for her daughters-in-law, and
finally grandchildren from them.

Orpah accepted her fate and *returned* (verse 14) to her
mother's home (verse 8), where she might at least expect
something from the future for herself. But Ruth staunchly remained with Naomi, and cast her lot with her mother-in-law.

security (verse 9): the word combines the concepts of 'place
of rest' with 'security' and 'fulfilment'.

15. Naomi's words to Ruth prepare for Ruth's well-known response in verse 16. Orpah's allegiance is not only to her people but also to the god of the Moabites, who was called Kemosh (cp. Jer. 48: 13). It is noteworthy that the story does not disparage Orpah's choice or belittle her act of allegiance; the eventual gain of Naomi and Ruth is not at the expense of Orpah or with scorn for her decision.

16–17. Ruth's reply to her mother-in-law has justly become famous, although the context is frequently forgotten or ignored. Her commitment to the older woman is to involve every aspect of her life: in going, in staying, *people*, *God*, dying and burial. She fastens her fate to that of Naomi, dramatically and completely. Most remarkably, she binds her oath with the name of Naomi's God, 'Yahweh', translated here as LORD.

20. Naomi's request that her name, 'my pleasant one' or 'my darling', be changed to *Mara*, 'bitter one' (cp. N.E.B. footnotes), typifies the mood of this section. The book faced a practical and real problem: does God provide for his people, especially when life seems impossibly difficult and the faithful person is constrained to say that 'the LORD has brought me back empty' (verse 21)?

21. *Almighty:* this word for God, in Hebrew *Shaddai*, is noteworthy. It is found in the priestly passages of Genesis–Deuteronomy, in Job, in two Psalms, and in Ezekiel and Isaiah. It was an ancient title perhaps meaning 'God of the mountain'; the famous passage in Exod. 6: 2–3 is important in showing how in the Old Testament tradition the term was used: 'God spoke to Moses and said, "I am the LORD. I appeared to Abraham, Isaac, and Jacob as God Almighty. But I did not let myself be known to them by my name JEHOVAH" (Yahweh).'

22. The harvest season began with *barley*, in early May in the area around Bethlehem; it marked the beginning of a season which ran for several weeks. A major agricultural event and festival in pre-Israelite days in Palestine, it became identi-

fied in the Hebrew religious calendar with the Feast of
Unleavened Bread which was one name used for the
Passover. ✢

Ruth and Boaz

RUTH WORKS IN THE FIELDS OF BOAZ

N OW NAOMI HAD a kinsman on her husband's side, **2**
a well-to-do man of the family of Elimelech; his
name was Boaz. Ruth the Moabitess said to Naomi, 'May 2
I go out to the cornfields and glean behind anyone who
will grant me that favour?' 'Yes, go, my daughter', she
replied. So Ruth went gleaning in the fields behind the 3
reapers. As it happened, she was in that strip of the fields
which belonged to Boaz of Elimelech's family, and there 4
was Boaz coming out from Bethlehem. He greeted the
reapers, saying, 'The LORD be with you'; and they
replied, 'The LORD bless you.' Then he asked his servant 5
in charge of the reapers, 'Whose girl is this?' 'She is a 6
Moabite girl', the servant answered, 'who has just come
back with Naomi from the Moabite country. She asked 7
if she might glean and gather among the swathes behind
the reapers. She came and has been on her feet with hardly
a moment's rest[a] from daybreak till now.' Then Boaz said 8
to Ruth, 'Listen to me, my daughter: do not go and
glean in any other field, and do not look any further, but
keep close to my girls. Watch where the men reap, and 9
follow the gleaners; I have given them orders not to
molest you. If you are thirsty, go and drink from the jars

[a] *Prob. rdg.; Heb. adds* in the house.

10 the men have filled.' She fell prostrate before him and said, 'Why are you so kind as to take notice of me when

11 I am only a foreigner?' Boaz answered, 'They have told me all that you have done for your mother-in-law since your husband's death, how you left your father and mother and the land of your birth, and came to a people

12 you did not know before. The LORD reward your deed; may the LORD the God of Israel, under whose wings you have come to take refuge, give you all that you deserve.'

13 'Indeed, sir,' she said, 'you have eased my mind and spoken kindly to me; may I ask you as a favour not to

14 treat me only as one of your slave-girls?'*a* When meal-time came round, Boaz said to her, 'Come here and have something to eat, and dip your bread into the sour wine.' So she sat beside the reapers, and he passed her some roasted grain. She ate all she wanted and still had some

15 left over. When she got up to glean, Boaz gave the men orders. 'She', he said, 'may glean even among the sheaves;

16 do not scold her. Or you may even pull out some corn from the bundles and leave it for her to glean, without reproving her.'

17 So Ruth gleaned in the field till evening, and when she beat out what she had gleaned, it came to about a bushel*b*

18 of barley. She took it up and went into the town, and her mother-in-law saw how much she had gleaned. Then Ruth brought out what she had saved from her meal and

19 gave it to her. Her mother-in-law asked her, 'Where did you glean today? Which way did you go? Blessings on the man who kindly took notice of you.' So she told her

[a] may I...slave-girls?: *or* if you please, treat me as one of your slave-girls.   [b] *Heb.* ephah.

mother-in-law whom she had been working with. 'The
man with whom I worked today', she said, 'is called
Boaz.' 'Blessings on him from the LORD', said Naomi. 20
'The LORD has kept faith with the living and the dead.
For this man is related to us and is our next-of-kin.' 'And 21
what is more,' said Ruth the Moabitess, 'he told me to
stay close to his men until they had finished all his
harvest.' 'It is best for you, my daughter,' Naomi 22
answered, 'to go out with his girls; let no one catch you
in another field.' So she kept close to his girls, gleaning 23
with them till the end of both barley and wheat harvests;
but she lived with her mother-in-law.

* Each chapter in this small book advances the story one
distinct phase. Ch. 1 tells the story of Naomi's misery
and introduces Ruth as the faithful Moabite daughter-in-law,
who totally committed herself to Naomi and to a share in
Naomi's future; it closes with the scene of Naomi's return to
Bethlehem. Ch. 2 moves the action forward more subtly;
there are no outstanding events like deaths or migrations, or
even profound and dramatic personal decisions and commit-
ments. This chapter is full of dialogue and the kind of action
which takes place in dialogue. In the plot, Ruth meets Boaz
who is attracted to her and gives her special privileges among
the gleaners, and in this simple and idyllic relationship the
weeks pass from barley harvest to wheat harvest.

In the dialogue the characters of the principal people are
displayed and their relationships are developed. Ruth is am-
bitious, eager to work (verses 2 and 7), gently aggressive
(verses 10 and 13), grateful (verse 10), and steady and persis-
tent (verse 23) in her work habits and in her care of Naomi.
Boaz is generous and solicitous of Ruth, whom he likes (verse
8), expresses respect for her honourable behaviour towards
Naomi (verses 11f.), grows more friendly (verse 14), and

finally becomes lavish in his generosity to Ruth. Naomi is now in the background, giving advice and providing information (verse 20).

1. The role of *Boaz* is designated by his name, which means something like 'strength (is) in him'; Boaz was also incidentally the name for one of the two pillars standing before the entrance to Solomon's temple (1 Kings 7: 21). He is presented as a close *kinsman* of Elimelech, Naomi's husband, and therefore he enjoys the special relationship to Naomi which is mentioned later in verse 20 and which turns out to be decisive for the ending of the story. He is furthermore *well-to-do*, a 'mighty man, or gentleman, of means'.

2. Ruth asks permission to follow the reapers in the fields, to hunt for heads of grain which they overlooked or had dropped; it was customary for land-owners to afford this thin measure of opportunity to the poor for gathering something from the harvest. The custom is referred to in Deut. 24: 19–22, where 'the alien, the orphan, and the widow' are specifically named; these categories of the traditionally helpless and vulnerable in ancient Near Eastern society apply strikingly to Naomi and Ruth.

3. *As it happened:* is expressed rather deliberately, and could be translated, 'as fate or chance should have it'. This concept of fate or chance applied to that quality of God's providence which seemed to be accidental or random in the experience of man.

5. *Whose girl is this?* In the story Boaz notices Ruth immediately, perhaps because she was very attractive, or because she was obviously a foreigner, or for both reasons. He is interested in her identity, and to whose household she belongs.

7. The meaning and wording of the end of the last half of the verse are uncertain both because the versions have important variants and because the Hebrew text is not clear. But the present translation is a good solution of the problems.

8–9. Boaz urges Ruth to remain in his fields; the account sweeps together many elements into one little conversation,

and somehow between his question in verse 5 and his statement in verse 11, perhaps behind the summary remark in
verse 6, he has learned much about her. His solicitude may
have been the result of understanding what Ruth had done.
The special measures taken to ensure Ruth's safety suggest
something of the dangers faced by a lonely young woman in
the field.

10. *fell prostrate:* a common gesture of subjection, and
courtesy. Her question to Boaz is a play on words behind *take
notice* and *foreigner*; it is analogous to saying 'notice the un-
noticed one' or 'bring in the outcast'.

11–12. The blessing of Boaz foreshadows the ending of the
story. The fuller title for God, *the LORD* (in Hebrew,
'Yahweh') *the God of Israel*, signifies Ruth's new religious
commitment. *give you all that you deserve* literally translated is
'make your wages full'. *wings:* a commonly used figure of
speech for God's over-arching and protective presence in the
Old Testament. The Hebrew words in Ps. 91: 4 for 'find
safety beneath his wings' are exactly the same as those in this
text in Ruth.

13. The second half of the verse has proved to be very
difficult. The Septuagint read it, 'And behold, I shall be as
one of your slave-girls.' Other attempts to translate it range
from 'Oh that I were one of your servant-girls' to 'I do not
claim to be like one of your servants.' Perhaps the sense is
clearer if we translate, somewhat more literally, 'You have
comforted your servant, even though I am not like one of your
servants.'

14–16. Boaz adds generosity to his mercy; he invites her to
eat with the working men and share their provisions, and
finally guarantees that she can gather all she wants.

17–18. Ruth is thus able to bring home to Naomi an extraordinarily large amount for one day's gleaning, and even
left-overs from lunch!

20. The theme of Yahweh's providence, forecast by Boaz
in his blessing in verse 12, is made more explicit by Naomi;

God has not forsaken his covenantal love with either the *living* (Naomi) or the *dead* (Elimelech, Mahlon, and Chilion).

next-of-kin: literally, 'he is one of our next-of-kin'. The term for next-of-kin in Hebrew is *go'el*, the root meaning of which is 'to redeem or to buy back' and 'to avenge or to vindicate'. In the Old Testament the term is used more often of God's activity for Israel, but it was a common expression in society and in civil law for the near relative whose role and responsibility were to avenge the wrong done to his kin, or to restore family property and rights. A shock wave of hope and relief passes over the story at this verse when in one breath God's covenantal loyalty and love for the living and for the dead are remembered, and we are also informed that the powerful and wealthy Boaz, already obviously much taken with Ruth, is Naomi's *go'el*.

21-2. *Ruth the Moabitess*, as the narrator pointedly continues to call her, is urged by Naomi to continue in the fields of Boaz. *catch you* may connote 'find you', but it can also mean 'molest you, or meet you with hostility'.

23. The weeks of harvest pass by, happily it would seem, from the barley to the wheat harvest. Ruth resides with her mother-in-law, we are carefully told. No great events have occurred; but the reader is now expectant. ✳

RUTH GAINS THE COMMITMENT OF BOAZ

3 One day Ruth's mother-in-law Naomi said to her,
2 'My daughter, I want to see you happily settled. Now there is our kinsman Boaz; you were with his girls. Tonight he is winnowing barley at his threshing-floor.
3 Wash and anoint yourself, put on your cloak and go down to the threshing-floor, but do not make yourself known to the man until he has finished eating and drink-
4 ing. But when he lies down, take note of the place where he lies. Then go in, turn back the covering at his feet and

lie down. He will tell you what to do.' 'I will do what- 5
ever you tell me', Ruth answered. So she went down to 6
the threshing-floor and did exactly as her mother-in-law
had told her. When Boaz had eaten and drunk, he felt at 7
peace with the world and went to lie down at the far end
of the heap of grain. She came in quietly, turned back the
covering at his feet and lay down. About midnight 8
something disturbed the man as he slept; he turned over
and, lo and behold, there was a woman lying at his feet.
'Who are you?' he asked. 'I am your servant, Ruth', she 9
replied. 'Now spread your skirt over your servant,
because you are my next-of-kin.' He said, 'The LORD has 10
blessed you, my daughter. This last proof of your loyalty
is greater than the first; you have not sought after any
young man, rich or poor. Set your mind at rest, my 11
daughter. I will do whatever you ask, for, as the whole
neighbourhood knows, you are a capable woman. Are 12
you sure that I am the next-of-kin? There is a kinsman
even closer than I. Spend the night here and then in the 13
morning, if he is willing to act as your next-of-kin, well
and good; but if he is not willing, I will do so; I swear it
by the LORD. Now lie down till morning.' So she lay at 14
his feet till morning, but rose before one man could
recognize another; and he said, 'It must not be known
that a woman has been to the threshing-floor.' Then he 15
said, 'Bring me the cloak you have on, and hold it out.'
So she held it out, and he put in six measures of barley
and lifted it on her back, and she*a* went to the town.
When she came to her mother-in-law, Naomi asked, 16
'How did things go with you, my daughter?' Ruth told

[a] *So many MSS.; others* he.

17 her all that the man had done for her. 'He gave me these
   six measures of barley,' she said; 'he would not let me
   come home to my mother-in-law empty-handed.'
18 Naomi answered, 'Wait, my daughter, until you see
   what will come of it. He will not rest until he has settled
   the matter today.'

* The story of Ruth has unfolded in distinct scenes: (1)
Naomi's decision to return to Bethlehem and Ruth's decision
to accompany her, (2) the arrival in Bethlehem, and (3) Ruth's
day of gleaning in the field owned by Boaz. This chapter contains the fourth scene, where Ruth comes to Boaz on the
threshing-floor.

The harvest is over. We await what is to happen to Naomi
the widowed mother-in-law, to Ruth the faithful Moabitess,
and to Boaz the wealthy *go'el*, next-of-kin.

1–5. Naomi has made her plan, and now instructs Ruth
what to do. The weeks of harvest are past, and it is time to
remind Boaz about Ruth, but in such a way that desire super-
sedes duty.

1. *One day* is perhaps too casual; the Hebrew has the simple
connective which is most often translated by 'and' or 'then'.
happily settled is an unusual form of the word which in 1: 9 is
translated as 'security'. It is the responsibility of the mother-
in-law, in lieu of the natural parents, to care for such matters.

2. The *threshing-floor* was a hard, flat surface, of smooth
rock or pounded earth, located where a good breeze could be
counted on. After flailing the stalks of grain, or dragging a
sledge over them, in order to remove the kernels from the
husks, the labourer used a kind of fork to throw the grain into
the air; the wind blew the chaff and straw to the side, while
the kernels which are heavier fell back directly to the floor.
(This may still be seen in the Near East, cp. *Old Testament
Illustrations* in this series, p. 126.) The work was hard, but
joyful in time of good harvest; at the day's end, after a hearty

meal, sleep came quickly. Boaz would remain there sleeping, in order to guard the grain. *Tonight:* in the sense of 'evening', taking advantage of the evening breeze which ceases about sun-down.

6–9. Naomi's plan, full of practical wisdom and conditioned by the patterns of acceptable behaviour in her society, is carried out to the letter. When Boaz awakes, Ruth straightforwardly asks him to *spread* his *skirt* over her (verse 9) as a sign of matrimony, for he is *go'el*, next-of-kin. The word for *skirt* is the same in Hebrew as that for God's 'wings' in the blessing of Boaz in 2: 12, and the Hebrew reader would naturally connect them. Boaz is invited to become partner in the Lord's blessing of Ruth.

10–13. He responds with admiration for her *loyalty*, or 'gracious fidelity', and with appreciation for the fact that she has chosen him. *kinsman even closer:* by the civil law, the closest male relative according to an order which is no longer clear to us had the right and responsibility of acting as *go'el*. It is not made clear who this nearer kinsman is or in what relationship he stands; Jewish traditions have suggested that he was a brother of Elimelech. How Naomi could be ignorant of the existence of this nearer kinsman is a question that cannot be answered satisfactorily. We may see here the skill of the narrator who thus heightens the suspense: will Boaz lose Ruth after all?

14–18. Ruth stays through the night, protected by Boaz, and leaves before daylight with a handsome gift. Events have occurred swiftly, and suddenly the whole matter is to be completed that very day. ✻

RUTH AND BOAZ MARRY

Now Boaz had gone up to the city gate, and was **4** sitting there; and, after a time, the next-of-kin of whom he had spoken passed by. 'Here,' he cried, calling him by name, 'come and sit down.' He came and sat down. Then **2**

Boaz stopped ten elders of the town, and asked them to
3 sit there, and they did so. Then he said to the next-of-kin,
'You will remember the strip of field that belonged to
our brother Elimelech. Naomi has returned from the
4 Moabite country and is selling it. I promised to open the
matter with you, to ask you to acquire it in the presence of
those who sit here, in the presence of the elders of my
people. If you are going to do your duty as next-of-kin,
then do so, but if not, someone must do it. So tell me,
and then I shall know; for I come after you as next-of-
5 kin.' He answered, 'I will act as next-of-kin.' Then Boaz
said, 'On the day when you acquire the field from
Naomi, you also acquire Ruth[a] the Moabitess, the dead
man's wife, so as to perpetuate the name of the dead man
6 with his patrimony.' Thereupon the next-of-kin said, 'I
cannot act myself, for I should risk losing my own
patrimony. You must therefore do my duty as next-of-
kin. I cannot act.'

7   Now in those old days, when property was redeemed
or exchanged, it was the custom for a man to pull off his
sandal and give it to the other party. This was the form of
8 attestation in Israel. So the next-of-kin said to Boaz,
9 'Acquire it for yourself', and pulled off his sandal. Then
Boaz declared to the elders and all the people, 'You are
witnesses today that I have acquired from Naomi all that
belonged to Elimelech and all that belonged to Mahlon
10 and Chilion; and, further, that I have myself acquired
Ruth the Moabitess, wife of Mahlon, to be my wife, to
perpetuate the name of the deceased with his patrimony,
so that his name may not be missing among his kindred

[a] *So Vulg.; Heb.* from Ruth.

and at the gate of his native place. You are witnesses this
day.' Then the elders and all who were at the gate said, 11
'We are witnesses. May the LORD make this woman,
who has come to your home, like Rachel and Leah, the
two who built up the house of Israel. May you do great
things in Ephrathah and keep a name alive in Bethlehem.
May your house be like the house of Perez, whom Tamar 12
bore to Judah, through the offspring the LORD will give
you by this girl.'

---

* The fifth and next-to-last scene takes place rapidly and, like
the others before it, is constructed on the basis of a conversation.

1. *city gate:* a broad area at the opening of the gate, which
afforded enough space for people to congregate; here sat the
elders who dispensed legal opinions in lawsuits (Amos 5: 15,
'enthrone justice in the courts [Hebrew, gate]'), and who
heard wrong-doing denounced by plaintiffs or prophets
(Amos 5: 10, 'you that hate a man who brings the wrongdoer
to court [Hebrew, gate]'). Boaz sat waiting to meet the *go'el*,
next-of-kin, who took precedence over him in the case. The
anonymity of the man is preserved in the Hebrew by calling
him 'Mr So-and-So'.

2. Boaz next collects *ten elders* to hear the case and to act as
witnesses. Many years later ten became the number of men
necessary to constitute a synagogue in Judaism.

3. Suddenly a *strip of field*, hitherto unmentioned, enters the
story.

4. The law relating to this transaction is written in Lev.
25: 25, 'When one of you is reduced to poverty and sells part
of his patrimony, his next-of-kin who has the duty of redemp-
tion shall come and redeem what his kinsman has sold.' But
had Naomi sold the land earlier? We do not know. The book
of Ruth probably affords a glimpse of the custom at an early

period, after which it may have undergone some alteration; perhaps the *go'el* had first chance to buy before it was offered to someone else (Jer. 32: 7–8 is usually cited as an example).

5. This is the most difficult passage in the book to interpret because the text is uncertain and the custom is insufficiently known. The Hebrew speaks of acquiring the field from Naomi *and from* Ruth; the versions speak of acquiring the field *and* Ruth. Furthermore, the law applying to the situation, Deut. 25: 5–10, does not agree in all details with the case.

Ruth probably reflects a case older than the law in Deuteronomy; otherwise the issue would have been presented in conformity with the law, or at least with reference to it at the points of difference. Ruth is no doubt not a property to be acquired just like any other. In the ancient Hebrew society a wife was something 'acquired' by a man, but she had rights which other types of acquisitions obviously did not. The point is that the *go'el*, next-of-kin, would in acquiring the property also have to take Ruth as wife, get children by her, and give the acquired property to that offspring.

6. *I cannot act myself*: he decided that he could not afford to risk losing some of his own inheritance in the bargain. Even though in Israel polygamy was permitted, most men probably could not afford more than one wife anyway.

7–8. '*in those old days* in Israel', which is the full expression in Hebrew, seems to place the story in a past which is remote from the present author; this expression is a primary piece of evidence used to support the claim that Ruth was written late. But three considerations weaken the argument: (1) the reference to *old days* might reflect a difference of much less than 600 years; (2) verse 7 might be a later editorial addition; and (3) the allegation that the custom was an obsolete relic from the dim past seems empty because Deut. 25: 5–10 with the entire law on the subject was certainly well known and perhaps even in force at any date chosen for a 'late authorship' of Ruth. The phrase is simply a story-teller's elaboration of the setting for the custom, added at some time during the history of the transmission of the tradition, and paraphrasing the law in Deuteronomy. According to Deut. 25: 9, if the next-of-kin refuses to act, the woman pulls the sandal off his foot, and then spits in his face.

9–12. The final phase of this scene is the little ceremony whereby Boaz proudly and solemnly announces his acquisition of the property of Elimelech, Mahlon, and Chilion, and his acquisition of *Ruth the Moabitess* as wife. The names of Mahlon and Elimelech should now be perpetuated in the children of Ruth and Boaz. The goal of Boaz' blessing in 2: 12 and Naomi's praise of God in 2: 20 has been attained.

11. The elders respond with a chorus of attestation and blessing, wishing many children for the couple, like *Rachel* and *Leah*, who, with their two slave girls, were the mothers of the twelve sons of Jacob and the twelve tribes of Israel (cp. Gen. 35: 23–6).

12. The last blessing makes a direct reference to the only other instance of the levirate marriage in the traditions, the marriage of Tamar and Judah in Gen. 38. Tamar and Ruth are incidentally two of the total of four women mentioned in the genealogy of Jesus in Matt. 1: 1–16.

Many scholars have difficulty with this blessing on Boaz, because it is Mahlon whose name is to be preserved in the levirate marriage. The law (Deut. 25: 6) however ascribed only the first-born son to the deceased husband. The blessing falls upon both the memory and name of Mahlon, and upon Boaz and his descendants. *

A CHILD IS BORN

So Boaz took Ruth and made her his wife. When they 13 came together, the LORD caused her to conceive and she bore Boaz a son. Then the women said to Naomi, 14 'Blessed be the LORD today, for he has not left you

without a next-of-kin. May the dead man's name^a be kept
15 alive in Israel. The child^b will give you new life and cherish
you in your old age; for your daughter-in-law who loves
you, who has proved better to you than seven sons, has
16 borne him.' Naomi took the child and laid him in her lap
17 and became his nurse. Her neighbours gave him a name:
'Naomi has a son,' they said; 'we will call him Obed.'
He was the father of Jesse, the father of David.

18 This is the genealogy of Perez: Perez was the father of
19, 20 Hezron, Hezron of Ram, Ram of Amminadab, Ammina-
21 dab of Nahshon, Nahshon of Salmon,^c Salmon of Boaz,
22 Boaz of Obed, Obed of Jesse, and Jesse of David.

✻ The sixth and final scene of the story is in 4: 13–17, with
the birth of a son to Ruth and Boaz. The story closes in idyllic
beauty and peace. The misery and the agony of fear and uncertainty are in the past for Ruth and Naomi; the LORD has
blessed them, and filled their lives. Ruth's single-minded
fidelity, with no intention or expectation of gain or compensation, is richly rewarded beyond her hopes. Orpah and Moab
are far behind, and forgotten; the LORD (Yahweh) has blessed
the living and the dead.

14. In the end it is Naomi who is recognized, adding to the
evidence cited by some scholars to the effect that the story is
principally about Naomi and not Ruth.

15. But Ruth is also remembered, and tenderly so, in the
recognition of Naomi.

16. Scholars see in this verse an adoption-process, whereby
the child becomes Naomi's child. It is clear that the neighbouring women rejoice that Naomi has a son (verse 17);
perhaps the old law of levirate marriage made the mother give

[a] *Lit.* May his name.   [b] *Lit.* He.
[c] *So some MSS.; others* Salmah.

up her child to the widowed mother-in-law in such cases. But verse 16 speaks of her as a nurse, and the actions correspond to the nurse's role. Little Obed (verse 17) is called Naomi's son, being actually her grandson; it is better not to assume a legal adoption here.

17. The story has proceeded quietly and effectively until this passage at the very end, when suddenly there is as it were an explosion on the horizon which alters the whole account and puts everything into a new dimension. Ruth's little son turns out to become the grandfather of King *David*.

Until this point, the story was a narrative about very human, everyday problems and anxieties which were resolved by matching solution to need: husband for the young widow, food for the hungry, security for the vulnerable, and posterity for those who had no future. But with David the blessing changes.

18-22. The genealogy at the end of the book, added after the book was written, is based on 1 Chron. 2: 5, 9-15 or on the source used by Chronicles. But the point has remarkably changed here too; it is not Mahlon or Elimelech who is counted in the list, but rather Boaz. The genealogy is history's broader verdict on the meaning of the story.

The genealogy of Perez: a title related to the reference to Perez in 4: 12; the genealogical information is assembled beginning with him. Perez was a prominent family in Judah. ✳

✳   ✳   ✳   ✳   ✳   ✳   ✳   ✳   ✳   ✳   ✳   ✳   ✳

THE MESSAGE OF RUTH

The book of Ruth is a gentle, pastoral tale of a girl whose life is illuminated by divine providence. It lacks the dramatic quality of urgency and fatefulness seen in the account of another heroine, Esther, who has to decide what to do 'in such a time as this'. A quiet human being, living simply in

undistinguished circumstances and in a comparatively obscure place – as most people may feel, at least sometimes, about themselves – is lifted out of the rest in order that we may see God's providence at work.

That providence is portrayed as mightily effective. Fears are calmed, immediate daily needs are satisfied, and suddenly a whole life-time of fulfilment is achieved and the life has new meaning. Providence is also characterized by grace and surprise; when they returned to Bethlehem Ruth and Naomi could never have dreamed of what eventually happened to them in the marriage to Boaz and the birth of a son. Boaz' generosity is a symbol of the LORD's generosity. The book of Ruth does not generalize, or preach or say that providence always acts thus or may do so under specific circumstances; many widows lived out miserable lives in Palestine. But the LORD does bless and establish lives.

The book bears a message about Ruth, her loyalty, and her nationality. Without much ado, and with simple and sure strokes, there is painted a word-portrait of a woman who is truly admirable, a worthy mother in Israel. The author also never lets the reader forget that she was a Moabitess; the book certainly bears a challenge to the law in Deut. 23: 3 which stipulated that an Ammonite or Moabite could not 'become a member of the assembly of the LORD' for ten generations. Ruth has been compared with Jonah, and claimed to be an appeal against the narrow discrimination introduced by Ezra in the late fifth century or early fourth century B.C., whereby mixed marriages were dissolved and the foreign wives were sent away (Ezra 10: 17, 44). This may have been what the book was saying to Israel in those days; but it carried ultimately a larger purpose.

Most important in the annals of history is the fact that Ruth was the great-grandmother of David, and this was surely a major reason for remembering the story. Some scholars have turned this feature into an argument for claiming that the story survived because it preserved the recollection of David's

Moabite origin; remarkably, David went to the king of Moab in order to seek refuge from Saul's anger against his parents (1 Sam. 22: 3–4). But in the book of Ruth the reader's attention is fastened upon David, and on the significance of his relationship to Ruth, rather than on Moab. Unobtrusively, and with the impact of an awareness that dawns, then grows, and finally sheds light over everything, David is mentioned only in the last word in the book before the genealogy! The great king, founder of the dynasty, the ideal figure in late tradition (2 Chron. 28: 1), and titular father of the Messiah ('Son of David', Mark 12: 35), proves to be Ruth's ultimate fulfilment. She becomes a mother of David, and a mother in the genealogy of Jesus (Matt. 1: 5).

God's providence is therein further disclosed, and tied together with his mighty acts in the history of salvation. Ruth never knew that her descendants would be king, and Messiah; she died content in the satisfactions granted to her during her lifetime. But God acted upon her fidelity and used her as an honoured participant in the history of salvation for his people. Providence and the story of salvation are distinct, and the link between them is mysterious and often beyond our knowledge. Nevertheless, they were joined in the life and experience of this Moabite woman, as a symbol of God's will and deed.

ESTHER

WHAT THE BOOK IS ABOUT

No book in the Old Testament has occasioned more antipathy for some readers, and more enjoyment for others, than the book of Esther. In Judaism it has been a favourite among the people throughout the centuries, placed in some manuscripts immediately after the Pentateuch – Genesis, Exodus, Leviticus, Numbers, Deuteronomy – and existing in more manuscript copies than any other books of the Old Testament. In Christendom the book has generally been treated in one of two ways: either it is read as an allegory or as a prophetic (in the sense of foretelling) statement regarding Christ and the Virgin Mary, or it is regarded with bewilderment and with scorn for its lack of theological material and reference, and for its sanctioning of harsh, barbarous deeds against non-Jews.

This great diversity can be understood when one looks at the plain meaning of the book. It is not a recitation of the mighty acts of God; it is a story about the survival of the Jews. To be sure, the book obviously did not originate outside Israel and its faith, and it was intended for no other public than Israel. But God is not mentioned by name in Esther, and in fact may not even be referred to in the Hebrew text. Rather, the objective of the book of Esther would seem to be to encourage the reader to remain confident that Jews and Judaism will prevail over their enemies.

Events recounted in Esther also describe the historical setting and circumstances for the introduction of the festival of Purim (see pp. 36–7). This festival, although it was not, like the other great festivals, traced back to Moses, became extremely popular among the Jewish people. Esther tells the story behind Purim.

THE STORY IN THE BOOK

In this well-told story the Jews in the Persian Empire escape a plan which, if carried out, would have exterminated them. A young and beautiful Jewish orphan girl named Esther, under the guardianship of Mordecai, her father's nephew, becomes queen of the Persians and Medes. Her predecessor Vashti has lost the crown because she refused an order by King Ahasuerus to display her beauty at one of his banquets. But Mordecai incurs the hatred of Haman, the king's principal adviser, and Haman sets out to have all the Jews slain as a consequence.

Mordecai convinces a hesitant Queen Esther that she ought to undertake the effort to save her people. In a well-known passage (4: 14) he reminds her that she will also die if the Jews are liquidated, even though for the moment no one knows that she is Jewish, and he causes her to contemplate her own reason for living as resting in this very opportunity to save the Jews.

Dramatic tension mounts throughout the first half of the book, accelerating in chs. 3–5; the plot against the Jews develops, and Esther's cryptic plans are not reassuring while Haman is puffed up with pride and with passion to destroy his adversary Mordecai. With ch. 6 the tale unwinds, as Haman is first humiliated in a few brilliantly composed paragraphs, and then hanged; after this the Jews are given authority to counterattack against their enemies, and taking the initiative they execute terrible vengeance. The day after that on which the enemies' attack upon the Jews was to occur, and on which the Jews turned the tables, is established as the festival of Purim, to be remembered and honoured forever.

The dramatic turns in the story are full of irony (see the commentary) as Haman witnesses one mishap after another in his plans, finally losing his life on the gallows which he has prepared for Mordecai. His hatred for Mordecai because the latter will not bow down to him, a trivial matter in itself compared with Haman's great power, leads him to conspire to have a whole people killed; but this brings about his own undoing.

Some scholars are convinced that the story is a result of the combination of some separate accounts: one about Vashti and her downfall, for instance, another about the good fortune and great deed of Esther, and still another about the struggle between Haman the Jews' archenemy and 'Mordecai the Jew'. It is evident that Mordecai has special significance in the book – he is the authority behind Esther, he is by title 'the Jew', and he is the person lauded and remembered in the closing paragraph; Mordecai also figures predominantly in the subsequent tradition – in the earliest reference to Purim in 2 Macc. 15: 36, the fourteenth day of Adar (the twelfth month, about March) is called 'Mordecai's Day', and in Jewish tradition the celebrants at Purim were allowed to drink until they could no longer distinguish between 'Blessed be Mordecai' and 'Cursed be Haman'. However, such attempts to perceive separate narrative elements have not been universally accepted; it is better to identify distinct threads of plot in the story and to leave open the question of their original separation. These threads are skilfully woven together, and there surely was never any combining of three written sources to form the present book of Esther.

THE ADDITIONS TO ESTHER, AND TEXTUAL PROBLEMS

The problems regarding the text of Esther are unique in Old Testament literature. The degree of uniformity found for this book in the Hebrew manuscripts is unusually great; probably the late date of the book's origin and its early popularity encouraged the handing down in the Hebrew of essentially one text-form. But there is nevertheless evidence of variant forms of the material, and it is in the early translations that we find this. There is no other Old Testament book which has been so amplified in the translations. Two separate Targums

(Aramaic versions) add a very large amount of material, about which most readers know little or nothing; a convenient presentation of this material is included in the rather dated Esther commentary by L. B. Paton (see p. 263).

The Greek manuscripts pose critical problems which are not totally understood even today. Large additions are made to the Hebrew text (see 'The Rest of the Chapters of the Book of Esther' in *The Shorter Books of the Apocrypha* in this series) which not only add theological content but also lend a different context to the book. But the Greek manuscripts differ radically among themselves; one text type, which has in the past been designated as the Lucianic revision of the Septuagint, is much briefer than, and often different from, other Greek witnesses to the text. It is in these Greek variants that it may be possible to detect Hebrew traditions strikingly different from those which were preserved in the standard text.

COMPARISON WITH JUDITH

The book of Esther has been compared with Daniel, and indeed close scrutiny reveals similarities; but this is more evident when Daniel is compared with the Greek text of Esther and the 'Rest of Esther'. The nearest parallel with the whole book of Esther is the book of Judith. Not finally adopted into the Hebrew canon but retained in the Greek manuscripts and included in the Roman Catholic and Greek Orthodox canons, Judith is like Esther in describing how a dedicated Jewess saved her people. Judith is however much more theologically self-conscious than Esther, referring to God's involvement in her life and motives, and placing great weight upon keeping the law and maintaining Jewish purity. The 'Rest of Esther' added a considerable body of material which makes the Greek version of Esther also more like the book of Judith than is the Hebrew book of Esther. For further information, see the commentary on Esther below, and consult p. 131 and the 'Rest of Esther' in *The Shorter Books of the Apocrypha*.

ESTHER'S RELATIONSHIP TO PURIM

A primary factor in the transmission of Esther over the centuries has been its relationship to Purim, providing as it does the historical background and basis for this popular Jewish holiday. The word first appears in Esther 3: 7 where we read about the casting of lots, called *Pur* (cp. 9: 24); in 9: 26–8 the festival of Purim is described as something that the Jews determined to celebrate annually in commemoration of their great release and victory.

Purim is a thoroughly secular celebration in Jewish tradition, and over the years it developed a kind of carnival atmosphere, with people wearing masks, giving each other presents, and acting out the baiting of the evil Haman. Popular and noisy, it has also been a fundamentally serious reminder of Jewish perils in the past, a remembrance of a glorious deliverance, and a subtle way to renew convictions that the Jewish people were not to be exterminated.

Its origin is a subject of great debate. It has been called the one major Jewish holiday of a wholly secular nature; but major holidays in the ancient world were not exclusively secular, and rather were naturally rooted in religious convictions and practices as well. Because the name of the festival is a foreign word, it is widely supposed that Purim originated outside Israel and was adopted by the Jews, with Esther subsequently attached to it. Purim has been claimed to come from a Persian Festival of the Dead, on the basis of word similarity between the name of that festival, *farvardigan*, and a Greek rendering of the word Purim, *phrourai*. Some scholars have sought to connect it with the Persian New Year festival, and many similar motifs or elements have been identified in the Persian holiday. Attempts have also been made to trace it to Babylonian rites and festivals, or to Jewish celebrations in the days of the Maccabees (about 170–140 B.C.).

A recent theory seems to point to the most promising and satisfying explanation yet. This stresses the themes held in common between Purim and the Persian New Year festival, without it being asserted that the Jewish celebration was entirely parallel with, and dependent on, the Persian high day and also suggests that there may have been some altercation, or even violent hostility, against the Jews on one New Year's occasion in Persia, which resulted in a story which indeed attached itself to the holiday. According to this theory, the story of Esther arose among Jews in connection with Purim: this festival was associated with the casting of lots, and was widely celebrated as a holiday or as part of a larger festival, in Mesopotamia and in Persia. It was borrowed by the Meso-potamian Jewish communities in the Persian empire, losing its non-Jewish religious content and meaning, and acquiring instead the story of the great deliverance from some threat or attack upon the Jews which was repulsed or thwarted. The historicity of a Mordecai or an Esther cannot be proved; but the fact that there are no parallel Persian records of the event is no indication that everything was fabricated by the author or by tradition. We have to remember that our knowledge of Jewish life under Persian rule is very limited indeed. Most probably some event occurred in the empire which touched off both the celebration of Purim by the Jews and the stories about Mordecai and Esther which, in the re-telling, received ever greater elaboration and embellishment for centuries after.

The celebration of Purim was no doubt subject to modifica-tion as time passed. In Palestine at the turn of the Christian era it was joyfully celebrated on the fourteenth and fifteenth of Adar, accompanied by the exchange of gifts and charitable donations to the poor. The fourteenth was called Mordecai's Day, and the preceding day, observed with fasting, was called Nicanor's Day, after the Syrian general who threatened Jewish survival and independence by attacking on the Sabbath and who was defeated and killed in a notable battle by Judas Maccabaeus in 160 B.C. (cp. 2 Macc. 15: 1–37). His body was mutilated and put on display in Jerusalem; this event is remarkably similar to Esther's request for the display of the corpses of Haman's ten sons (Esther 9: 12–14), and the incidents must have been remembered together.

INTERPRETATIONS OF THE BOOK AND ITS MEANING

Some tantalizing evidence which has supported theories of the non-Jewish origin of Purim has to do with the personal names in the book. These names are strikingly similar to those of ancient Babylonian and Elamite gods: Mordecai – Marduk, great god of the Babylonian pantheon; Esther – Ishtar, principal female deity in the Babylonian fertility and death cults; Haman – Humman, an Elamite god; Vashti – Mashti, an Elamite goddess. Accordingly numerous scholars have postulated that Esther was a narrative which turned legends about the battles between gods and about the victory of the Babylonian gods over the Elamite gods into historical human events, thereby historicizing the legends. This might be termed the mythological interpretation of Esther.

Closely connected with this approach is the position which views Esther as a reflection of action taking place in the Babylonian cult, either in fertility rites and celebrations or in the creation myths which accompanied observance of the New Year's festivities. These mythological and cultic explanations for the story in Esther have been presented in several forms, but all have difficulty in clarifying satisfactorily how the forms and myths were adopted by the Jews, and for what purpose.

Many scholars in the Christian tradition have over the centuries tried to explain Esther as a kind of prophecy, foreshadowing the events and revelation in the New Testament. Esther has been held to be a type or pattern of the Virgin Mary, and the gigantic gallows built by Haman is supposed to foreshadow the cross of Jesus Christ (the Hebrew word for 'gallows' most often means 'tree').

More probably correct than all these speculations is that class of simpler interpretations which characterize the Jewish attitude towards the book of Esther, and which describe it as a historical novel, or a festal legend which took shape around, and was read both in celebration and in explanation of, the feast of Purim. The book rests on some historical names and events from the Jewish exile which attached to Purim; tales grew up around these names and events, and these early stories were further amplified as time went on. Echoes of Babylonian and Elamite deities, and of cultic myths, remind the reader of the Mesopotamian and Persian background against which the narrative materials came into existence. But the meaning of the book and its various parts, like the intention for it, lay in the narration of an experience of survival and victory for the Jews; by the declaration of this event through the story, the book at the same time functioned as the traditional reading, or legend, for Purim.

Recently the presence of elements of wisdom thought and expression have been detected in Esther. The absence of historical references in the book, the attention to secular events without theological identification or comment, the emergence of Mordecai as a wise man and counsellor to the king, and the triumph of the righteous Mordecai over the wicked Haman are among the aspects attributed to the influence of Hebrew wisdom upon Esther. The presence of such motifs and features is of course obvious; however, they are not sufficiently peculiar or numerous for the book to be attributed to the deliberate influence of a wisdom writer. These elements rather show evidence of the penetration of Jewish culture and religion by wisdom thinking, and the utilization of some such motifs and features by the author.

THE ORIGIN OF THE BOOK

Nothing is known about the author of the book of Esther, or about those responsible for its origin in the early stages of the story-telling, except that they were persons rather well acquainted with Persian customs, with the Jewish traditions around Purim, and with wisdom characteristics which were common in the ancient Near East.

Stories which may have come from the days of Xerxes were carried orally through the years in Persia. The present written form of the book may be traceable to the early part of the second century B.C. in Palestine; this dating is based on studies of the book of Esther's vocabulary and literary style, as well as on the lack of earlier references to the book. It was certainly not written later than that date, and it may have attained its final form somewhat earlier. The Greek translation of Esther and additions to the Hebrew text seem to reflect, as well as to address, the situation around the middle of the second century B.C., and to bring to Esther the apocalyptic point of view which was widely current in those days, namely the belief that the end of the age was about to come (cp. Dan. 7–12).

Many scholars believe that 9: 20 – 10: 3 is material which was added to the original complete story. The vocabulary differs somewhat from that in the rest of the book, there is a summary of some main lines of the story (9: 24–5), and the section introduces the festival of Purim which is not mentioned earlier. The small paragraph 9: 29–32 poses additional problems (see the commentary) and may have been added even later than the material beside it.

ESTHER AS A JEWISH BOOK

The popularity of Esther in Judaism is a natural result of the history, intention, and message of the book. In the Middle Ages it was copied profusely, and its manuscripts were richly decorated. It was joyfully heard and remembered as Purim was celebrated each year, and pleasurable as well as dramatic elements were added to the story by the tradition. It was 'The Scroll' (cp. p. 1), above the other four, in Jewish references. To understand this popularity we need only to look carefully at the contents of the book. The Jewish reader does not fail to identify with Mordecai; he is 'the Jew' in the book. He prevails because he is Jewish (6: 13); and his victory is the victory of the Jewish people. Yearnings, pleasures, and fears of centuries are touched by the story of Esther and Mordecai; the book directly addresses the problems of life and existence for those Jews who were scattered over the world – in the dispersion or Diaspora as it is often described – without a national security.

THE PLACE OF ESTHER IN THE BIBLE

The Jewishness of Esther affected its reception by Jews and Christians. The reverence accorded it in Jewish circles contrasts sharply with Christian views. No Christian commentary was written on it for seven centuries, and it failed to appear in many lists of biblical books in the early church, especially in the eastern Mediterranean area. No doubt for many the reason for some of this disaffection may be represented in the opinion of Martin Luther, who complained that he found Esther to be alien to him, to contain much heathenish bad conduct, and to *Judaize too much*. Many Christians have experienced difficulty in sympathizing with Esther.

On the other hand the earliest indications are that Esther was accepted into the Old Testament canon only with many reservations. No scrap of it has yet been discovered at Qumran, among the multitude of Dead Sea scroll fragments from that place, although every other Old Testament book is represented. Interestingly, Purim was also not celebrated at Qumran. Esther is not mentioned in the list of important persons in the recitation of history found in Ecclus. 44–9, which dates to 180 B.C. Rabbis down to the third century A.D. are on record expressing the view that the book of Esther was not a holy book or at least that it was different from the holy books. Esther's willingness to become the queen of a pagan ruler, and her readiness to be subservient to him – points to which the Greek translators show some sensitivity – might well have been unacceptable for stricter Jews who were

41

strongly resistant to foreign pressures. This would be true of the Qumran community and of others.

Perhaps the relation of the book of Esther to Purim was at first an impediment to accepting it; but perhaps also that relationship decided in the end that it would be included among the holy books, and into the Bible. Its lack of reference to God in any way, and failure to call the faith of Israel to mind, no doubt also shaped some opinions.

✢   ✢   ✢   ✢   ✢   ✢   ✢   ✢   ✢   ✢   ✢   ✢   ✢

Esther chosen as queen by the Persian king

THE ROYAL BANQUETS

1 THE EVENTS HERE RELATED happened in the days of Ahasuerus, the Ahasuerus who ruled from India to 2 Ethiopia,[a] a hundred and twenty-seven provinces. At this 3 time he sat on his royal throne in Susa the capital city. In the third year of his reign he gave a banquet for all his officers and his courtiers; and when his army of Persians and Medes, with his nobles and provincial governors, 4 were in attendance, he displayed the wealth of his kingdom and the pomp and splendour of his majesty for many 5 days, a hundred and eighty in all. When these days were over, the king gave a banquet for all the people present in Susa the capital city, both high and low; it was held in the garden court of the royal pavilion and lasted seven days. 6 There were white curtains and violet hangings fastened to silver rings with bands of fine linen and purple;[b] there

[a] *Heb.* Cush.   [b] bands...purple: *or* white and purple cords.

were alabaster pillars and couches of gold and silver set on a mosaic pavement of malachite and alabaster, of mother-of-pearl and turquoise. Wine was served in golden cups 7 of various patterns: the king's wine flowed freely as befitted a king, and the law of the drinking was that there 8 should be no compulsion, for the king had laid it down that all the stewards of his palace should respect each man's wishes. In addition, Queen Vashti gave a banquet for the 9 women in the royal apartments of King Ahasuerus.

* The story begins with an elaborate explanation of why and how Esther came to be queen of the Persians and Medes. The unlikelihood of such a circumstance is resolved in the first and second chapters by showing how the position suddenly became vacant and also how a person of Esther's background might get to this position in the reign of the great Xerxes. In the course of this explanation the reader is also drawn into the scene of the lavish oriental court and before the presence of the mighty and arbitrary monarch.

Relating an account of three separate banquets might seem to be an unnecessary effort by the author, but it in fact accomplishes three purposes. It calls to attention the vast scale in which the king exhibited his riches and power in the first banquet, it provides the setting for the surprising dethronement of the beautiful Queen Vashti in the second banquet, and it offers a hint of the royal authority and energy exercised by the queen herself in the third. Thus the reader is prepared for a situation in which the king later lets Haman issue an order for the destruction of a whole people, and Queen Esther in a subsequent banquet brings about the undoing of Haman, chief adviser to the king, and the rescue of her people.

Some speculation has been given to the prominence of banquets in the book, especially comparing these banquets in ch. 1 with those offered by Esther in 5: 5 and 6: 14 wherein

Esther reveals Haman's plot. The comparison however should be much broader than that. The prominence of banqueting and feasting throughout the book is remarkable; the English reader needs to know that the same Hebrew word is translated here as 'banquet' but also as 'feasting' in 8: 17 and in ch. 9. 'Feasting and joy' in fact becomes a common term, used four times in 9: 17–22. Finally, when the occasions for fasting and lamenting are considered, the reader is left wondering whether the author's skill was not also applied to use the contrast of feasting and fasting, joy and lament, in developing a dramatic movement in the book and in creating an emotional crescendo for those who celebrated Purim while the book was being read.

I. Ahasuerus must be Xerxes I, great king of the Persians for 20 years (486–465 B.C.), although the Septuagint assumed that he was Artaxerxes and so translated the name. Xerxes followed his father Darius on the throne, and is generally recognized for being the Persian leader in the historic defeats at the hands of the Greeks at Thermopylae and Salamis. A foundation tablet uncovered at Persepolis does indeed confirm that he controlled territory from India to Ethiopia; however, the number of provinces is a problem because Dan. 6: 2 mentions only 120 for the time of Darius, and because identification of these provinces has not been made. The Persian Empire was organized by Darius into larger areas called satrapies. *the Ahasuerus who:* it is argued today that the name Ahasuerus may have been a title meaning 'the chief of rulers' and have been applied to other persons also known to the author, thereby necessitating further identification of the king.

2. Commentators point out that the scene in mind here is not just that of *the capital city*, but rather the acropolis or citadel which was located upon an elevation above and apart from the rest of the city.

3–4. The first banquet mentioned is described in fantastic terms, with the whole army present, and lasting for 180 days. Commentators have wrestled with the problem of such a large multitude at a banquet, some trying to avoid the problem by

44

reading 'power' or 'elite' instead of *army*, others simply assuming that so many were not present to be fed. Perhaps all such attempts miss the point of the introduction in painting the monarch with grand, monumental strokes. Feasting for *a hundred and eighty* days also seems fantastic, and is paralleled by a 120-day celebration in Judith 1: 16. However, an Assyrian record from the early ninth century B.C. tells of 69,574 guests present for a 10-day palace dedication. The statistics in 2 Chron. 7: 5 about Solomon offering 22,000 oxen and 120,000 sheep in sacrifice at the dedication of the temple, or in 1 Kings 4: 22 about his daily provision including 30 oxen and 100 sheep, must be pondered in the light of these and other references to memorable feasts. That the ancient author did not mean to offer a ridiculously exaggerated portrait is clear; even if the statistics seem unbelievable, the author did not mean to set us in the world of fairy tales.

5. The second banquet was a somewhat more modest affair, given for *all the people* (literally, 'who were found in Susa, the capital') but for just *seven days*.

5–7. The details given of the site and the scene encourage those who interpret the book from a strictly historical viewpoint. Conclusions in scholarship today are not inconsistent with such banquets taking place during the reign of Xerxes. However, Susa existed for many centuries after the Persian Empire, and no doubt an author could have been familiar with, and could even have gleaned, many details from visiting the ruins of subsequent palaces; of course the curtains would not have remained! Targumic additions to Esther tell about such a quantity of cups that no man drank twice from the same cup, and about such provisions that each man received wine that was as many years old as he was.

8. *no compulsion:* the meaning of the phrase has eluded interpreters; it may suggest that the usual rules of etiquette, custom, and order were suspended, for example, the traditional rule requiring a man to drain at one draught the cup from which he began to drink; or else it may mean that a man could drink

whenever and however much he chose. It has been observed that the details of the banquet concentrate on the drinking; nothing is said about food. The Hebrew word for 'banquet' means 'a drinking', or 'a symposium', but even more important is the ancient tradition carried by Greek writers that the Persians were notable drinkers. As years went by and Purim was celebrated by the Jews, imbibing was also practised heartily; one wonders how much they were influenced by the book of Esther itself.

9. In comparison Vashti's little banquet seems quite modest. But reference to it does introduce her with dignity and set the stage for the importance of her position. Herodotus, the Greek traveller and historian, says that the name of Xerxes' queen was Amestris. Whether there was ever such a Vashti, or for that matter an Esther, cannot be proved from extra-biblical sources. *

VASHTI LOSES HER CROWN

10 On the seventh day, when he was merry with wine, the king ordered Mehuman, Biztha, Harbona, Bigtha, Abagtha, Zethar, and Carcas, the seven eunuchs who

11 were in attendance on the king's person, to bring Queen Vashti before him wearing her royal crown, in order to display her beauty to the people and the officers; for she

12 was indeed a beautiful woman. But Queen Vashti refused to come in answer to the royal command conveyed by the eunuchs. This greatly incensed the king, and he grew hot with anger.

13 Then the king conferred with his wise men versed in misdemeanours;[a] for it was his royal custom to consult

14 all who were versed in law and religion, those closest to him being Carshena, Shethar, Admatha, Tarshish, Meres, Marsena, and Memucan, the seven princes of Persia and

[a] *Or* times.

Media who had access to the king and held first place in the kingdom. He asked them, 'What does the law require 15 to be done with Queen Vashti for disobeying the command of King Ahasuerus brought to her by the eunuchs?' Then Memucan made answer before the king and the 16 princes: 'Queen Vashti has done wrong, and not to the king alone, but also to all the officers and to all the peoples in all the provinces of King Ahasuerus. Every 17 woman will come to know what the queen has done, and this will make them treat their husbands with contempt; they will say, "King Ahasuerus ordered Queen Vashti to be brought before him and she did not come." The great 18 ladies of Persia and Media, who have heard of the queen's conduct, will tell all the king's officers about this day, and there will be endless disrespect and insolence! If it please 19 your majesty, let a royal decree go out from you and let it be inscribed in the laws of the Persians and Medes, never to be revoked, that Vashti shall not again appear before King Ahasuerus; and let the king give her place as queen to another woman who is more worthy of it than she. Thus when this royal edict is heard through the 20 length and breadth of the kingdom, all women will give honour to their husbands, high and low alike.' Memucan's 21 advice pleased the king and the princes, and the king did as he had proposed. Letters were sent to all the royal 22 provinces, to every province in its own script and to every people in their own language, in order that each man might be master in his own house and control all his own womenfolk.[a]

[a] and control...womenfolk: *prob. rdg.; Heb.* and speak in his own language.

✻ In the first section of the book the stage is set and a principal character, the king, is introduced. It is the function of this second section to explain the vacancy in the role of another principal actor in the story, the queen, and to show how it could ever be that the Jewish girl Esther might be offered the opportunity to become queen of the Persians and the Medes.

The incident which provokes the wrath of Ahasuerus is quickly recounted, and the bulk of this section is given to the deliberation between the king and Memucan, one of the seven wise men and princes, about the social consequences if Vashti's refusal to obey should become an example for the other women of the empire. It is impossible to know just how this section was originally meant to be understood, but we may imagine that it produced scorn for the king in the earliest Jewish audiences. Even though sympathy for Vashti was lost in Jewish traditions by speculating on the wickedness which she had committed, the king had made an ill-fated request and consequently was challenged by the prospect of a massive revolt by the women of the empire. A feminine revolution in a man's world has over the ages been the subject of concern, drama, and unfortunately even humour; how seriously it was meant to be taken here we can only guess.

10. The king's command was not made in cold blood, as we might say, but rather while under the influence of much *wine*. The *eunuchs* played an important role in the administrative offices of ancient empires, sometimes even in affairs of state as well as the customary responsibility for harem supervision. For the names of the eunuchs, see verse 14.

11. Early Jewish traditions took the reference to *crown*, itself an unusual word in Hebrew, to mean that Vashti was to appear wearing only the crown, or queenly turban, in other words naked. The Greek historian Herodotus records a somewhat similar experience in which a Lydian king was so proud of his wife's beauty that he arranged for her to be seen naked by a principal servant. Early rabbis counted Vashti, Sarah,

Rahab, and Abigail as the four most beautiful women in the world. Others put Esther in the list instead of Vashti.

12. Vashti's refusal to 'display her beauty' publicly at the king's command makes her a memorable, if nevertheless minor, figure in the biblical panorama. An eighteenth-century commentator has been quoted to say that she 'is the only decent character in the book'. Her staunch independence sets off an ensuing discussion about the effects of women's liberation which the twentieth century can well understand.

14. Considerable attention has been devoted to explaining the names offered here. They are transmitted by manuscripts and versions in very different forms. Little has been concluded from this study, although one must pause at a scholar's recent observation that the list in verse 14 seems to repeat the list in verse 10, except that it repeats it backwards. Certainly Carcas–*Carshena* and Zethar–*Shethar* at one end, and Mehuman–*Memucan* at the other, suggest some relationship even to the casual reader.

16–21. Memucan's advice to the king offers another instance to some commentators of historical implausibility, and has even been understood as a humorous note in the story. Women in the Persian Empire seem to have enjoyed a greater degree of freedom, especially as regarded table customs, than those in other nations; perhaps this was a gentle jibe at the Persian liberalism. Still another mode of understanding these verses is to focus again on the grand scale of the adviser's suggestion, namely, that the whole empire must be protected from any unfortunate precedent. In any case, the king is counselled to be harsh with Vashti and put her away for ever.

This section provides the basis upon which Esther may eventually become the queen, without fear of Vashti's reinstatement. It furthermore puts before the reader an awareness that the queen is vulnerable when she disobeys or displeases the king, and we become conscious of the danger present for those who lived with an absolute and somewhat unpredictable monarch. These feelings are aroused later as

Haman schemes for the Jews' destruction, and Esther risks her life to intervene.

19. Persian law and the strictness with which it was enforced became legendary. However, there is not found in Persian sources the reference to the irrevocability of decrees which Esther and Daniel (cp. Dan. 6: 8) make so prominent a feature.

22. The Persian Empire developed an excellent communications system, and was especially successful in permitting the survival of regional customs and organizing territorial administrations. *control all his own womenfolk:* a passage which has caused some problems. The Hebrew clearly says, 'and speak according to the language of his people' (cp. footnote); but what does that mean in this context? One interpretation is that the man should be able to say, or command, whatever he wishes. ✻

ESTHER ENTERS THE COMPETITION TO BE VASHTI'S SUCCESSOR

2 Later, when the anger of King Ahasuerus had died down, he remembered Vashti and what she had done and
2 what had been decreed against her. So the king's attendants said, 'Let beautiful young virgins be sought out for
3 your majesty; and let your majesty appoint commissioners in all the provinces of your kingdom to bring all these beautiful young virgins into the women's quarters in Susa the capital city. Let them be committed to the care of Hegai, the king's eunuch in charge of the women, and
4 let cosmetics be provided for them; and let the one who is most acceptable to the king become queen in place of Vashti.' This idea pleased the king and he acted on it.
5 Now there was in Susa the capital city a Jew named Mordecai son of Jair, son of Shimei, son of Kish, a

Benjamite; he had been carried into exile from Jerusalem 6 among those whom Nebuchadnezzar king of Babylon had carried away with Jeconiah king of Judah. He had a 7 foster-child Hadassah, that is Esther, his uncle's daughter, who had neither father nor mother. She was a beautiful and charming girl, and after the death of her father and mother Mordecai had adopted her as his own daughter. When the king's order and his edict were published, and 8 many girls were brought to Susa the capital city to be committed to the care of Hegai, Esther too was taken to the king's palace to be entrusted to Hegai, who had charge of the women. She attracted his notice and received his 9 special favour: he readily provided her with her cosmetics and her allowance of food, and also with seven picked maids from the king's palace, and he gave her and her maids privileges in the women's quarters.

Esther had not disclosed her race or her family, because 10 Mordecai had forbidden her to do so. Every day Morde- 11 cai passed along by the forecourt of the women's quarters to learn how Esther was faring and what was happening to her.

* The groundwork was laid in ch. 1, and in ch. 2 the Hebrew protagonists, Mordecai and Esther, are introduced. The Greek additions in 'The Rest of the Chapters of the Book of Esther' (see commentary on *The Shorter Books of the Apocrypha*, pp. 138–9) envelope the whole story with the recitation of a dream of Mordecai and an explanation of its fulfilment.

2–4. The competition arranged for the purpose of finding the most acceptable queen for the king is often compared with the story in *A Thousand and One Nights*, in which the king takes a new bride each night and executes her in the morning, only to be entranced and won by the beautiful Scheherazade who fascinates him with her stories while captivating him with her charms. Other parallels for royal searches for a virgin to be queen can also be found.

5. After Ahasuerus, the next principal character to come on the scene is Mordecai, who for many reasons has the most important role in the story. He guides Esther's fortunes, gives her advice, is the adversary of Haman, becomes identified with the fate of the Jews (6: 13), provides the records and notifies his people (9: 20–1), and emerges as the ascending and honoured figure of the narrative (10: 1–3). He is, in the story, 'the Jew' (see 5: 13).

In a book notoriously lacking in references to Israel's history, the author's effort to bind Mordecai to the past by offering genealogical information is noteworthy. *Kish, a Benjamite* is obviously the father of Saul, Israel's first king; according to many scholars *Shimei* refers to the man who cursed David during Absalom's rebellion (2 Sam. 16: 5), but it is intriguing to wonder whether the name might not rather refer to the brother of Zerubbabel (1 Chron. 3: 19) who led the Jews back to Palestine after the exile, which would remind the Jewish hearer of Mordecai's noble family connections after the exile. The name *Mordecai* is Babylonian, and not Hebrew at all, based on the name of the great god Marduk. Perhaps he also had a Hebrew name as did Daniel and his three friends (Dan. 1).

6. The chronology implied in this verse is a stumbling block. If Mordecai was indeed among the exiles in 597 B.C., he would have been about 120 years old in the days of Xerxes (486–465 B.C.). Commentators have suggested that it was his ancestor who left Jerusalem with the exiles. More probably there was confusion in later years about the exact chronology, as the story about Mordecai was handed down, and the name may even have been confused with the Mordecai mentioned in Ezra 2: 2 as returning with Zerubbabel; clearly the author had no idea of how many years after Nebuchadnezzar (605–

562 B.C.) Xerxes had reigned. *Jeconiah:* or Jehoiachin, taken into exile in 597 B.C. (cp. 2 Kings 24: 8–17).

7. Esther is presented under her Hebrew name, *Hadassah*, which means 'myrtle'. The name *Esther* may be Persian, derived from a word meaning 'star'; on its supposed mythological significance, cp. p. 38. She is described as the daughter of Mordecai's uncle; if she was indeed his cousin she must at least have been much younger, and the Latin versions call her his niece. Mordecai's role after the death of her parents was that of foster-father, trustee, or caretaker, and the Hebrew says literally that after her parents' death 'Mordecai took her to himself as a daughter'. Some scholars have furthermore proposed that Mordecai was a eunuch (cp. 1: 10) because he approached the harem daily and with no apparent difficulty (2: 11), he seems to have had a position at court (2: 21), and there is no mention of his wife. As Mordecai's orphaned cousin, according to Hebrew custom, Esther was a prime candidate to be taken as his own wife; but then of course she could never have become Ahasuerus' queen. *beautiful and charming:* literally, beautiful of figure and good-looking.

8–10. Attempts to explain the presence or absence of scheming by Mordecai and Esther in order to enter the competition are beside the point; she was collected with the others because she was a beautiful virgin. The important feature is Mordecai's instruction to keep her *race* and *family* a secret. Thus fears of anti-Jewish bias appear in the book long before Haman's plot; strictly speaking by Persian rule it was not enough to be Persian in order to be queen, for she was supposed to come from one of seven principal families, and by that standard she would have been immediately known and disqualified.

11. Mordecai moves as the benign eminence throughout the story, and here hovers over Esther. *

ESTHER BECOMES QUEEN

12 The full period of preparation prescribed for the women was twelve months, six months with oil and myrrh and six months with perfumes and cosmetics. When the period was complete, each girl's turn came to

13 go to King Ahasuerus, and she was allowed to take with her whatever she asked, when she went from the women's

14 quarters to the king's palace. She went into the palace in the evening and returned in the morning to another part of the women's quarters, to be under the care of Shaashgaz, the king's eunuch in charge of the concubines. She did not again go to the king unless he expressed a wish for her; then she was summoned by name.

15 When the turn came for Esther, daughter of Abihail the uncle of Mordecai her adoptive father, to go to the king, she asked for nothing to take with her except what was advised by Hegai, the king's eunuch in charge of the

16 women; and Esther charmed all who saw her. When she was taken to King Ahasuerus in the royal palace, in the seventh year of his reign, in the tenth month, that is the

17 month Tebeth, the king loved her more than any of his other women and treated her with greater favour and kindness than the rest of the virgins. He put a royal crown

18 on her head and made her queen in place of Vashti. Then the king gave a great banquet for all his officers and courtiers, a banquet in honour of Esther. He also proclaimed a holiday[a] throughout the provinces and distributed gifts worthy of a king.

[a] *Or* an amnesty.

Mordecai was in attendance at court;[a] on his instruc- 19,20
tions Esther had not disclosed her family or her race, she
had done what Mordecai told her, as she did when she
was his ward.

✻ With this portion it may be said that the introduction to
the book is concluded; the explanations and presuppositions
have been put forth and the dramatic action can com-
mence.

There are varied judgements on Esther's morality at this
point. Submitting to the pagan preparations and to the arms
of the king, as well as concealing her Jewish identity, are un-
questionably different from the strictness of Ezra or the stern,
self-conscious piety and purity of Judith. Perhaps all that can
and should be said is that many and various are the ways and
rewards of God's children; it is essential to remember that the
tradition, while enjoying the story of Esther, did not regard
her or Mordecai as ethical or religious examples, and such
diverse communities as Qumran and the Christian fathers gave
little attention to the book.

15. Esther's pliability, or, as we may think, her cunning and
willingness to subject her own desires to the advice of Hegai,
are illustrated here. The Hebrew for *charmed all who saw her* is
literally 'she gained favour in the eyes of all who saw her'.
The reader will keep in mind that at this point Esther's efforts
are not spent to gain anything noble for her people, but to
win the contest. And win she does!

16–17. Someone has calculated that by this time more than
1400 comely candidates had passed through the royal quarters,
a truly astounding and formidable competition. *Tebeth:* about
January, the Babylonian month-name.

18. The first part of the book, chs. 1–2, closes as it opened,
with a *great banquet*; but this time it is, literally, with 'Esther's
banquet', a finely and artfully wrought piece of story-telling.

[a] *So Sept.; Heb. adds* when the virgins were brought in a second time.

What begins with a Persian king presiding elegantly over an imperial celebration ends with a banquet for a Jewish queen and a *holiday*, or amnesty, for the empire. Esther has now acquired her position and is ready for her famous role. The book of Esther is most commonly compared with Judith, but a striking contrast in the narrative structure and content is evident in that Judith is not introduced until almost the half-way point in that book; and in Judith 8 and 9 the narrator's preparation for her role is a description of her piety, her fighting spirit, and her prayerful dedication.

19. One of the most difficult passages in all the book, or anywhere in the Old Testament, is this verse. The Hebrew plainly says, 'when the virgins were gathered together a second time', or something similar (cp. footnote). There is no satisfactory or generally accepted interpretation for these words; the Septuagint simply omitted the passage. A good assumption is that it refers to what went on in verse 14 when the virgins returned 'to another part of the women's quarters', where the Hebrew word for 'two' would be translated as 'another'. Then it means that Mordecai was on duty in the court as the ladies returned to their quarters, when the events recounted in verses 21–3 took place.

20. As in verses 10–11, Mordecai guides Esther – another element in sharp contrast to Judith – while she continues to hide her racial identity. *

A PLOT UNCOVERED BY MORDECAI

21 One day when Mordecai was in attendance at court, Bigthan and Teresh, two of the king's eunuchs, keepers of the threshold, who were disaffected, were plot-
22 ting to lay hands on King Ahasuerus. This became known to Mordecai, who told Queen Esther; and she
23 told the king, mentioning Mordecai by name. The affair was investigated and the report confirmed; the two men

were hanged on the gallows. All this was recorded in the
royal chronicle in the presence of the king.

* With the artist's gift for understatement and for timing, the
author quietly injects here an element which is indispensable
to the later development of the story, and which for the
moment is unobtrusive; yet he leaves a hint of its future importance, with the words 'investigated', 'confirmed', and
'recorded'.

21. The *king's eunuchs* (cp. 1: 10) had special control over
some entrance, perhaps that of the king's personal chambers.
It may not be accidental to the story that Xerxes was in fact
assassinated in 465 B.C. in just such a circumstance.

23. *chronicle:* 'the book of daily events' represented the
annals of the empire, the record of important occurrences;
this is in Hebrew the same phrase as that used for the title of
the book of Chronicles, and for other documents, referred
to by the historians, e.g. 'the annals of the kings of Judah'
(or 'the Book of the Chronicles of the Kings of Judah' as
other translations put it) (2 Kings 15: 6). *

Haman's plot against the Jews

HAMAN'S CONFLICT WITH MORDECAI, AND HIS PLOT

AFTER THIS, King Ahasuerus promoted Haman son of **3**
Hammedatha the Agagite, advancing him and giving
him precedence above all his fellow-officers. So the king's 2
attendants at court all bowed down to Haman and did
obeisance, for so the king had commanded; but Mordecai
did not bow down to him or do obeisance. Then the 3
attendants at court said to Mordecai, 'Why do you flout
his majesty's command?' Day by day they challenged 4

him, but he refused to listen to them; so they informed Haman, in order to discover if Mordecai's refusal would be tolerated, for he had told them that he was a Jew.
5 When Haman saw that Mordecai was not bowing down
6 to him or doing obeisance, he was infuriated. On learning who Mordecai's people were, he scorned to lay hands on him alone, and looked for a way to destroy all the Jews throughout the whole kingdom of Ahasuerus, Mordecai and all his race.

7 In the twelfth year of King Ahasuerus, in the first month, Nisan, they cast lots, Pur as it is called, in the presence of Haman, taking day by day and month by month, and the lot fell on the thirteenth day of the
8 twelfth month,[a] the month Adar. Then Haman said to King Ahasuerus, 'There is a certain people, dispersed among the many peoples in all the provinces of your kingdom, who keep themselves apart. Their laws are different from those of every other people; they do not keep your majesty's laws. It does not befit your majesty
9 to tolerate them. If it please your majesty, let an order be made in writing for their destruction; and I will pay ten thousand talents of silver to your majesty's officials, to be
10 deposited in the royal treasury.' So the king took the signet-ring from his hand and gave it to Haman son of
11 Hammedatha the Agagite, the enemy of the Jews; and he said to him, 'The money and the people are yours; deal with them as you wish.'

12 On the thirteenth day of the first month the king's secretaries were summoned and, in accordance with Haman's instructions, a writ was issued to the king's

[a] and the lot. . .twelfth month: *prob. rdg.*, *cp. verse 13*; Heb. the twelfth.

satraps and the governor of every province, and to the
officers over each separate people: for each province in its
own script and for each people in their own language. It
was drawn up in the name of King Ahasuerus and sealed
with the king's signet. Thus letters were sent by courier 13
to all the king's provinces with orders to destroy, slay, and
exterminate all Jews, young and old, women and children,
in one day, the thirteenth day of the twelfth month, the
month Adar, and to plunder their possessions. A copy of 14
the writ was to be issued as a decree in every province and
to be published to all the peoples, so that they might be
ready for that day. The couriers were dispatched post- 15
haste at the king's command, and the decree was issued in
Susa the capital city. The king and Haman sat down to
drink; but the city of Susa was thrown into confusion.

* The drama now unfolds more rapidly, and before this
chapter is done the whole Jewish people is threatened with
extermination. Esther is not mentioned in the chapter, and the
adversaries are Mordecai, who takes on the dimension of
representing the Jewish people and personally causing the
terrible danger they all must now face, and Haman, who is
newly introduced into the story.

1. *Haman son of Hammedatha the Agagite* is the full title used
in ch. 3 (twice), and then not again until after his death (chs.
8 and 9). Scholars have proposed that the names *Haman* and
Hammedatha are from Persian words, or even that they are
related to the Elamite god Humman or Humban; there are no
final answers established for these questions. *Agagite* is generally agreed to refer to Agag, king of the Amalekites, whom
Saul son of Kish defeated (1 Sam. 15: 7–9) but whose life Saul
spared. The Amalekites were an ancient enemy of Israel, from
the days of the wilderness (Exod. 17: 8–13). Thus the conflict

which brews between Mordecai and Haman is a renewal of
the old and unconsummated battle between Saul and Agag;
in this re-play, the new 'Agagite' is not spared by the new
'Saul'. Who Haman actually was and where he came from
is not essential to the story. For the author he is simply the
arch-adversary, enemy of Mordecai and 'enemy of the Jews'
(3:10).

2–4. Why Mordecai refused to bow before Haman has
often been pondered. The Greek additions explain it on the
basis of his strict fidelity to God. In ch. 2 he advised Esther to
hide her Jewishness; now he asserts his boldly (verse 4). Why
his Jewishness prevented him from doing obeisance is also not
clear. But it spoils the story to argue about such inconsisten-
cies; the tale moves on now with the provocation of haughty
Haman based squarely on Mordecai's Jewishness. This is the
issue; decisions may be made on occasion to conceal this
identity (1: 10, 20), but it cannot be denied.

5–6. The physical problem in the book is reached quickly;
the whole nation is threatened, because it is Jewish. The rest of
the book spells out the escape, and the consequences.

7. The casting of *lots* takes place 5 years after Esther becomes queen. For purposes of penetrating the secrets of the
future it was common practice in the ancient Near East to use
lots; these objects may have been stones or pebbles, something
akin to modern dice, or arrows, or sticks and pieces of wood.
Sometimes they were drawn out of a container, a bag; here
they were thrown down. On the road to Jerusalem, Nebuchadnezzar is portrayed by the prophet Ezekiel to be casting lots
with arrows, as well as utilizing other means of divination, in
order to receive guidance about which way he should go
(Ezek. 21: 21). *Pur:* see note on 9: 24. *thirteenth day* is a textual
addition, based in part on such passages as 3: 13 and 8: 12.
The Septuagint plainly says 'fourteenth day'; in the Hebrew
it does not necessarily say what day of the month it was at all,
and the text can be translated 'twelfth [month], that is, the
month Adar'.

Casting lots was an appropriate thing to do in the first month of the year because then the fates of men were fixed by the gods, according to Babylonian records. It is not clear whether lots were cast concerning each day of the year, to find out what was the right day for some intended action, or whether they were cast day after day until Adar, eleven months of wearisome casting; the former alternative is much more likely.

8. Jewish experience in the Diaspora, scattered over the world, is aptly described: dispersed, keeping apart, having unique laws, in a word keeping alive Jewish existence and identity. Although there is no reason to believe that Jews did not *keep your majesty's laws*, Mordecai who stood for all Jews had refused to honour Haman as Ahasuerus had commanded (verse 2).

9. The penalty for living like a Jew is destruction! The person guilty of the misdemeanour, Mordecai, is not mentioned by Haman, and all the innocents are to suffer – a picture typical of pogroms and persecutions of many peoples over the ages. We cannot fail to understand why Esther became so popular among Jews; in a most direct and explicit way it touched the heart of their experiences in the Diaspora.

How and why the money should be paid is not clear. Did Haman offer it from his own pocket, or was it to be booty from the Jews? Was it a bribe to the king? Mordecai's explanation in 4: 7 would suggest that it was a bribe, or, shall we say, an inducement. It has been estimated that the amount equalled two-thirds of the total annual revenue of the empire. Whatever the explanation, the incident further illustrates the evil and determination in Haman's character.

10. The *signet-ring*, used to impress the seal of the king on a document and functioning in a manner similar to a signature in our day, conveyed to Haman the king's authority to prepare documents. The author neatly draws the line of conflict more clearly by adding to Haman the title which he must bear, *enemy of the Jews*.

11. The king declines to accept Haman's offer of money, and says, literally, 'the money is given to you'. Haman now has his heart's desire, at no cost to himself.

12–15. The order goes out that in eleven months the slaughter of the Jews will occur. The efficient Persian postal system dispatches the news to all parts of the empire, and the satraps, governors, and officers or princes have time to make preparations for the thirteenth of Adar. The heaping up of verbs – *destroy, slay, and exterminate* – and the cataloguing of victims – *young and old, women and children* – may be examples of legal precision and thoroughness, but they also serve to build up the feeling of doom and awfulness as the story is read.

The king and Haman sat down to drink, or to feast as the phrase implies here and in 7: 1, while the city is in confusion. The irony intended here may be accompanied by a subtler chain of implication; the banqueting is mentioned in this order: (1) the king's imperial festival (1: 3); (2) the king's garden-court banquet (1: 5); (3) Vashti's dinner (1: 9); (4) Esther's great banquet (2: 18); and (5) Haman and the king feast together (3: 15). The varying form and significance of the banquet motif follow the narrative thread in the story. ✻

MORDECAI ENLISTS ESTHER'S HELP

4 When Mordecai learnt all that had been done, he rent his clothes, put on sackcloth and ashes, and went through 2 the city crying loudly and bitterly. He came within sight of the palace gate, because no one clothed with sackcloth 3 was allowed to pass through the gate. In every province reached by the royal command and decree there was great mourning among the Jews, with fasting and weeping and beating of the breast. Most of them made their beds of 4 sackcloth and ashes. When Queen Esther's maids and eunuchs came and told her, she was distraught, and sent

garments for Mordecai, so that they might take off the
sackcloth and clothe him with them; but he would not
accept them. Then Esther summoned Hathach, one of the 5
king's eunuchs who had been appointed to wait upon her,
and ordered him to find out from Mordecai what the
trouble was and what it meant. Hathach went to Morde- 6
cai in the city square in front of the palace gate, and 7
Mordecai told him all that had happened to him and how
much money Haman had offered to pay into the royal
treasury for the destruction of the Jews. He also gave him 8
a copy of the writ for their destruction issued in Susa, so
that he might show it to Esther and tell her about it,
bidding her go to the king to plead for his favour and
entreat him for her people. Hathach went and told Esther 9
what Mordecai had said, and she sent him back with this 10
message: 'All the king's courtiers and the people of the 11
provinces are aware that if any person, man or woman,
enters the king's presence in the inner court unbidden,
there is one law only: that person shall be put to death,
unless the king stretches out to him the golden sceptre;
then and then only shall he live. It is now thirty days since
I myself was called to go to the king.' But when they told 12
Mordecai what Esther had said, he bade them go back to 13
her and say, 'Do not imagine that you alone of all the
Jews will escape because you are in the royal palace. If you 14
remain silent at such a time as this, relief and deliverance
for the Jews will appear from another quarter, but you
and your father's family will perish. Who knows whether
it is not for such a time as this that you have come to
royal estate?' Esther gave them this answer to take back 15
to Mordecai: 'Go and assemble all the Jews to be found 16

in Susa and fast for me; take neither food nor drink for
three days, night or day, and I and my maids will fast as
you do. After that I will go to the king, although it is
17 against the law; and if I perish, I perish.' So Mordecai
went away and did exactly as Esther had bidden him.

✻ After a pause, Esther resumes her role in the account. This
chapter, incidentally, is the only one in the book (excepting
10: 1–3) which does not refer to banqueting or feasting; and
here we end in fasting! For many readers the highest and most
important point in the book occurs in this chapter, especially
in verse 14 with Mordecai's admonition to Esther. This is
however a very severe way of looking at Esther; certainly in
the design of the book the story is scarcely half finished, the
moment of real tension is still to come, and the fun has not yet
begun.

1–3. The word quickly got out, in the court where Mordecai was and in the provinces. Why a plot is published eleven
months before it is to occur, allowing for mourning but also
for escape, has puzzled some commentators. But even assuming that the author's intention was to provide time for events
in chs. 4–8 to happen, where and how were the Jews going to
flee from the Persian authority in any case?

4–7. Esther learns of Mordecai's grief, seeks to comfort him,
and finally undertakes to find out the cause. The grief and
lamentation exhibited by him seem to be as much a protest as
a bewailing.

8. With a *copy* available on the spot, it would appear that
the order had been well publicized; or perhaps Mordecai as an
official had access to it. He now turns to Esther, the queen for
five years, and requests her assistance.

9–11. Esther's reply is disappointing. After five years the
king seems to have lost his ardour for her; she has not been
summoned for *thirty days*. But her answer is also an excuse;
she cannot safely and confidently assume to intervene.

64

12–14. Mordecai responds with a rebuke and a challenge. Under these conditions no Jew is safe, even those in high position whose race has not been disclosed – a warning to Jews, and members of persecuted peoples, in every time. The rebuke is based on common sense. But his challenge is based on faith; *relief and deliverance* will come *from another quarter*, literally, 'another place'. Many commentators suggest that there is here an indirect reference to God, the nearest the book comes to mentioning him. In later Jewish writings the word 'place' is sometimes used as a substitute for the word 'God', to avoid direct mention of him ('place' meaning 'holy place', 'temple'). But the phrase may have other meanings: it may simply imply 'If you do not act as the agent of deliverance, another as yet undisclosed will appear.' Mordecai's faith and convictions are in the eventual rescue of the Jewish people; whether that confidence rested in his faith in God is not stated, although it may certainly be taken for granted. The challenge to Esther is that which in a moment of crisis confronts every man who has some resources to apply to the solution. Realization of one's destiny and end in life necessitates coming to terms with the possibility that all must be risked in the moment in question.

15–16. Esther's response is a dramatic turn in the story. Without guarantees of survival she casts her lot with her people. Her preparations are similar to, and yet in contrast with, those of Judith in Judith 9. Both engage in ritual subjection – fasting for Esther, humiliation for Judith – but Judith dedicates herself in prayer as well. The Greek additions to Esther supply what the Hebrew does not, and Esther 14 (see 'Rest of Esther' in *The Shorter Books of the Apocrypha*, pp. 152–4) is closely parallel with Judith 9, even exceeding it in fervour and in explanation of Esther's personal feelings.

17. A slight, but important, touch in the narrative comes with the inversion of roles; heretofore the adviser and guide, Mordecai leaves to follow Esther's orders. Did the author

deliberately place together the compliance of someone powerful and dominant (Mordecai) and, as a consequence of the
dedication, of someone whose time had come (Esther)? ✶

ESTHER LAYS HER PLANS

5 On the third day Esther put on her royal robes and
stood in the inner court of the king's palace, facing the
palace itself; the king was seated on his royal throne in
2 the palace, facing the entrance. When the king caught
sight of Queen Esther standing in the court, she won his
favour and he stretched out to her the golden sceptre
which he was holding. Thereupon Esther approached and
3 touched the head of the sceptre. Then the king said to her,
'What is it, Queen Esther? Whatever you ask of me, up
4 to half my kingdom, shall be given to you.' 'If it please
your majesty,' said Esther, 'will you come today, sire,
and Haman with you, to a banquet which I have made
5 ready for you?' The king gave orders that Haman should
be fetched quickly, so that Esther's wish might be fulfilled; and the king and Haman went to the banquet
6 which she had prepared. Over the wine the king said to
Esther, 'Whatever you ask of me shall be given to you.
Whatever you request of me, up to half my kingdom, it
7 shall be done.' Esther said in answer, 'What I ask and
8 request of you is this. If I have won your majesty's
favour, and if it please you, sire, to give me what I ask
and to grant my request, will your majesty and Haman
come tomorrow[a] to the banquet which I shall prepare for
you both? Tomorrow I will do as your majesty has said.'

[a] *So Sept.; Heb. om.*

66

✻ The threat to the Jews has been presented, the enemy
Haman is identified, and the whole basis upon which hope is
founded has been carefully laid out. Esther is ready to gamble
everything for her nation. Ch. 5 therefore stands as an inter-
lude, subtly raising the dramatic tension to its utmost.

The reader is presented first with Esther's plan; but the plan
surprises us, and skilfully stretches our curiosity and interest.
How can yet another banquet solve the problem?

1. We are led into the throne room of the king, to share the
suspense with Esther.

2. The queen waits tremulously; in Esther 15, in the Greek
text of the 'Rest of Esther', the reader is treated to a highly
descriptive picture of the delicate moment, attention resting on
the stern and forbidding bearing of the king on the one hand
and on the tender loveliness of Esther on the other. In the
Greek, he accepts her with touching ardour and concern,
moved by God to receive her.

3. Offering *half* the *kingdom* may be seen as an expression of
oriental lavishness and as a manner of speaking; it is no mere
exaggeration by the author. King Herod offered nothing less
than that to the daughter of Herodias when she danced for
him (Mark 6: 23), and she chose the head of John the
Baptist.

4. Esther's request seems innocuous, and remarkably
inadequate for dealing with such a grave predicament. But it
is pointless to wonder why she asked for a banquet instead of
directly pleading her case; banquets are a theme in the book,
and the story could not do without this intriguing turn in the
events. This is in fact the first turn of the screw applied to the
unwitting Haman. We watch Esther, and the author, carefully weave a web around him. The banquet without his
presence is unthinkable; she invites the enemy of the Jews, not
to honour him but to destroy his plot before the very eyes of
the king.

5–8. The banquet passes uneventfully, but three important
things have happened. The king repeats his pledge to grant

Esther's wish, the pledge is made this time in the presence of Haman, and Haman is raised one step further, from which he must fall. ✳

HAMAN PLOTS ON IN HIGH HOPES

9 So Haman went away that day in good spirits and well pleased with himself. But when he saw Mordecai in attendance at court and how he did not rise nor defer to
10 him, he was filled with rage; but he kept control of himself and went home. Then he sent for his friends and his
11 wife Zeresh and held forth to them about the splendour of his wealth and his many sons, and how the king had promoted him and advanced him above the other officers
12 and courtiers. 'That is not all,' said Haman; 'Queen Esther invited no one but myself to accompany the king to the banquet which she had prepared; 'and she has
13 invited me again tomorrow with the king. Yet all this means nothing to me so long as I see that Jew Mordecai
14 in attendance at court.' Then his wife Zeresh and all his friends said to him, 'Let a gallows seventy-five feet*a* high be set up, and recommend to the king in the morning to have Mordecai hanged upon it. Then go with the king to the banquet in good spirits.' Haman thought this an excellent plan, and he set up the gallows.

✳ Like a pot of water over intense heat, Haman's fortunes quickly reach their peak; but when achieved, they are discovered to be ready to consume him.

9. In seeing Haman in *good spirits*, rejoicing and happy at heart, one is reminded that Mordecai like the other Jews in

[a] *Lit.* fifty cubits.

Susa is fasting (4: 16). Haman's rage at seeing the unrepentant Mordecai only adds to his villainy in the scene. Meanwhile Mordecai's behaviour effectively draws a firm line between the adversaries; the Jew and the enemy will not both survive this contest.

10. Haman's stifling of his wrath is a prelude to the reader's enjoyment of his downfall; the haughty man, with difficulty in control of himself, will soon lose everything. Nevertheless he has his last day, full of boasting and evil, arrogant plans.

11–13. He satisfies his thirst for power over others by submitting his wife and friends to his self-praise (verse 11), and his craving for recognition by reminding everyone that only he has been invited to the queen's banquet with the king (verse 12). He has everything except obeisance from Mordecai the Jew. *all this means nothing to me* is a kind of faint prediction; so will it eventually be for Haman.

14. But the last is the best. That he may achieve complete happiness, his wife and friends recommend building *a gallows* for Mordecai; then he can attend the banquet rejoicing. He erects a monumental structure, to match his ego. Now he is ready to be happy. ✻

Haman's downfall and Mordecai's triumph

HAMAN IS HUMILIATED

THAT NIGHT sleep eluded the king, so he ordered the **6** chronicle of daily events to be brought; and it was read to him. Therein was recorded that Mordecai had **2** given information about Bigthana and Teresh, the two royal eunuchs among the keepers of the threshold who had plotted to lay hands on King Ahasuerus. Whereupon **3**

the king said, 'What honour or dignity has been conferred on Mordecai for this?' The king's courtiers who were in attendance told him that nothing had been done for
4 Mordecai. The king asked, 'Who is that in the court?' Now Haman had just entered the outer court of the palace to recommend to the king that Mordecai should be hanged on the gallows which he had prepared for him.
5 The king's servants answered, 'It is Haman standing
6 there'; and the king bade him enter. He came in, and the king said to him, 'What should be done for the man whom the king wishes to honour?' Haman said to himself, 'Whom would the king wish to honour more than
7 me?' And he said to the king, 'For the man whom the
8 king wishes to honour, let there be brought royal robes which the king himself wears, and a horse which the king
9 rides, with a royal crown upon its head. And let the robes and the horse be delivered to one of the king's most honourable officers, and let him attire the man whom the king wishes to honour and lead him mounted on the horse through the city square, calling out as he goes: "See what is done for the man whom the king wishes to
10 honour."' Then the king said to Haman, 'Fetch the robes and the horse at once, as you have said, and do all this for Mordecai the Jew who is in attendance at court. Leave
11 nothing undone of all that you have said.' So Haman took the robes and the horse, attired Mordecai, and led him mounted through the city square, calling out as he went: 'See what is done for the man whom the king wishes to honour.'

12 Then Mordecai returned to court and Haman hurried
13 off home mourning, with head uncovered. He told his

wife Zeresh and all his friends everything that had happened to him. And this was the reply of his friends[a] and his wife Zeresh: 'If Mordecai, in face of whom your fortunes begin to fall, belongs to the Jewish race, you will not get the better of him; he will see your utter downfall.'

While they were still talking with Haman, the king's 14
eunuchs arrived and hurried him away to the banquet which Esther had prepared.

☆ Haman's plot, and the threat to the Jews, are all developed in the first half of the book. The moment of tension concerning the king's willingness to receive and hear Esther is past. Now begins that part of the book which is a delight to the Jew who identifies with Mordecai. This chapter elegantly combines several themes and images to present in a few words the complete picture of a man's well-deserved humiliation.

1–2. The tiny fragment placed modestly at the end of ch. 2 suddenly springs to the centre of attention. Mordecai's good deed, so meticulously verified and recorded, is by an accident of fate (the versions credit God with the king's sleeplessness) brought before Ahasuerus. Asking for the annals of the empire to be read at such a time is not a bad idea for a monarch with vast administrative operations around him, and is not necessarily an artifice of the author.

3. It was normal for a king to reward richly someone who had done him some such great service. The royal neglect earlier made possible the book of Esther; if the king had known sooner, Haman might have had more difficulty in getting permission to wipe out the Jews.

4. Haman enters fatefully at just this moment, and full of plans to kill Mordecai publicly and memorably. The irony increases swiftly now.

6. Haman's unbridled arrogance is his great pitfall. Events

[a] *So Sept.; Heb.* his wise men.

proceed logically, effortlessly, and inevitably. The king's question reminds us of Nathan's words to David about an evil rich man, David promptly passing judgement without realizing that he was the guilty one (2 Sam. 12: 1–7).

7–8. Irony is added to irony as Haman prescribes in his conceit and with himself in mind the reward which will be given to his hated adversary.

The traditional contrast so widely found in Hebrew wisdom literature between the wise and the foolish is reminiscent of the contrasts which emerge and shift throughout Esther, especially here. The contrast is between Haman and Mordecai, and shifts according to this pattern: dominant–subordinate in ch. 3, moving to the hunter–hunted (chs. 4–5), becoming inverted in ch. 6 to become the unlucky–lucky, the foolish–wise, the miserable–honourable (6: 11–12), and finally the damned (7: 10) and the blessed (10: 3).

The *crown* on the horse's head is well known from Persian relief inscriptions.

9. Haman plunges on in his humiliation; the menial task which he had in mind for some other chief officer, in honouring him, suddenly becomes his own as he must honour Mordecai.

10–11. Haman is the picture of misery. The reader may have difficulty imagining the king honouring someone like Mordecai who is shortly to be destroyed along with all his people, at the expense of Haman, the king's chief adviser. Of course the king's word had been given, and must be carried out in some way. But to quibble with the text is to miss what happens to Haman and Mordecai. *Mordecai the Jew*, introduced as a term in 5: 13, becomes virtually a title through the remainder of the book. But it is more than a title; Mordecai represents, and in the drama is, the Jew through all the years of Jewish experience in the Diaspora and exile, and Haman is the embodiment of the enemy. The book of Esther is plainly a patriotic history, and originally was not intended to be more than that; it therefore came into the tradition without apology as a nationalistic document, profoundly expressing the Jewish concern for survival. It was not written to be a 'book of the acts of God', like Genesis or Kings.

Any speculation about what words or feelings passed between Mordecai and Haman, as some have tried, is fruitless. The story moves speedily, and without contemplative digressions, to its objective.

12–13. The most ominous note in the woeful account of the unfortunate Haman is the word he received upon returning home in mortification and disgrace. It is at the same moment the fighting slogan of a Jewish author, who has confidence in the outcome and destiny of his people. Haman cannot prevail, because Mordecai is a Jew. *If:* this is not to express any doubt about Mordecai being a Jew, but to underline the point. It stresses the assurance of God's protection of his people. The same point is made in Judith 5: 5–21 in a speech by an Ammonite who stresses the impossibility of defeating the faithful people.

14. The narrative hurries on now, with Haman thoroughly humiliated and with his doom forecast and impending. ✻

HAMAN IS HANGED

So the king and Haman went to dine with Queen **7** Esther. Again on that second day, over the wine, the king 2 said, 'Whatever you ask of me will be given to you, Queen Esther. Whatever you request of me, up to half my kingdom, it shall be done.' Queen Esther answered, 3 'If I have found favour with your majesty, and if it please your majesty, my request and petition is that my own life and the lives of my people may be spared. For we have 4 been sold, I and my people, to be destroyed, slain, and exterminated. If it had been a matter of selling us, men and women alike, into slavery, I should have kept silence;

for then our plight would not be such as to injure the
5 king's interests.' Then King Ahasuerus said to Queen
Esther, 'Who is he, and where is he, who has presumed
6 to do such a thing as this?' 'An adversary and an enemy,'
said Esther, 'this wicked Haman.' At that Haman was
dumbfounded in the presence of the king and the queen.
7 The king rose from the banquet in a rage and went to the
garden of the pavilion, while Haman remained where he
was, to plead for his life with Queen Esther; for he saw
8 that in the king's mind his fate was determined. When the
king returned from the garden to the banqueting hall,
Haman had flung himself across the couch on which
Esther was reclining. The king exclaimed, 'Will he even
assault the queen here in my presence?' No sooner had
the words left the king's mouth than Haman hid his face
9 in despair.[a] Then Harbona, one of the eunuchs in attendance on the king, said, 'At Haman's house stands the
gallows, seventy-five feet[b] high, which he himself has
prepared for Mordecai, who once served the king well.'
10 'Hang Haman on it', said the king. So they hanged him
on the gallows that he himself had prepared for Mordecai.
After that the king's rage abated.

✻ The almost playful way in which Haman's humiliation is
effected has ended, and the narrative strikes to the crux of the
whole matter.

1–2. Once again a banquet provides the setting. On the
second day the king repeats his promise, made twice before,
to grant Esther her wish.

3–4. Esther gets directly to the issue; in the account she of

[a] Haman...despair: *prob. rdg.; Heb.* they covered Haman's face.
[b] *Lit.* fifty cubits.

course has had no opportunity to learn of Haman's humiliation, and her accusations and petitions are made boldly in the
face of what she must still assume to be a most formidable
opponent. The queen places herself in the balance with her
people; she reveals for the first time that she belongs to those
who have been condemned.

4. The queen makes an ingratiating statement, so it might
appear, to claim that she would have remained silent if her
people had only been sold into slavery, instead of into death.
But one must not leap to hasty conclusions, just because she
would in that case not have had to risk anything for herself.
A considerable body of Jewish experience, ancient and contemporary, supports this profession of willingness to suffer in
silence, and to cry out only in the greatest extremity. *for then
our plight would not. . .injure the king's interests:* an extremely
difficult passage to translate; yet with all the various suggestions, most of them approximate to the reading given here.
The point is that as slaves the Jews would continue to serve the
king, but if they were killed, he would suffer serious loss.

5. Since the king well knew that Haman proposed the destruction of the Jews, perhaps he is being represented as unaware
only of the exact nature of what Esther is describing. The
rapidity of short phrases implies some excitement on the part
of Ahasuerus.

6. Esther's answer is likewise excited, and almost staccato
in form: '*adversary*', '*enemy*', '*this wicked Haman*'.

7. It is ironic, but perhaps inevitable, that Haman does not
follow the outraged king into the garden, and therefore that
he turns to plead for his life with one whom he had previously
contrived to condemn to death.

8. In his alarm and desperation, Haman approaches the
queen who is lying on her banquet couch, according to the
custom at feasting. *flung himself* is too strong in translation;
literally, the text says that he fell, or was falling. Whatever his
accident or wild act of carelessness, the king catches him in the
moment, as the most unexpected and accidental irony in the

book, and Haman is doomed. *hid his face:* the Hebrew form 'they covered Haman's face' (cp. footnote) may signify a seal of judgement and death upon him, although the custom of covering the face of the condemned was otherwise unknown among the Persians.

9. Haman is driven one step lower as the king receives news of the gallows prepared for Mordecai, who *served the king well.* The verdict and its method are decided: Haman shall hang on the gallows.

10. The final irony in the career of Haman is his last moment. In dying he symbolizes the blunderer, losing his life on the very instrument which was to complete all his happiness (5: 14). *

MORDECAI IS HONOURED, AND JEWISH DEFENCE IS AUTHORIZED

8 On that day King Ahasuerus gave Queen Esther the house of Haman, enemy of the Jews; and Mordecai came into the king's presence, for Esther had told him how he 2 was related to her. Then the king took off his signet-ring, which he had taken back from Haman, and gave it to Mordecai. And Esther put Mordecai in charge of Haman's house.

3 Once again Esther spoke before the king, falling at his feet in tears and pleading with him to avert the calamity planned by Haman the Agagite and to frustrate his plot 4 against the Jews. The king stretched out the golden sceptre 5 to Esther, and she rose and stood before the king, and said, 'May it please your majesty: if I have found favour with you, and if the proposal seems right to your majesty and I have won your approval, let a writ be issued to recall the letters which Haman son of Hammedatha the Agagite wrote in pursuance of his plan to destroy the Jews

in all the royal provinces. For how can I bear to see the 6
calamity which is coming upon my race? Or how can I
bear to see the destruction of my family?' Then King 7
Ahasuerus said to Queen Esther and to Mordecai the Jew,
'I have given Haman's house to Esther, and he has been
hanged on the gallows, because he threatened the lives of
the Jews. Now you shall issue a writ concerning the Jews 8
in my name, in whatever terms you think fit, and seal it
with the royal signet; for an order written in the name of
the king and sealed with the royal signet cannot be
revoked.'

And so, on the twenty-third day of the third month, 9
the month Sivan, the king's secretaries were summoned;
and a writ was issued to the Jews, exactly as Mordecai
directed, and to the satraps, the governors, and the officers
in the provinces from India to Ethiopia, a hundred and
twenty-seven provinces, for each province in its own
script and for each people in their own language, and also
for the Jews in their own script and language. The writ 10
was drawn up in the name of King Ahasuerus and sealed
with the royal signet, and letters were sent by mounted
couriers riding on horses from the royal stables. By these 11
letters the king granted permission to the Jews in every
city to unite and defend themselves, and to destroy, slay,
and exterminate the whole strength of any people or
province which might attack them, women and children
too, and to plunder their possessions, throughout all the 12
provinces of King Ahasuerus, in one day, the thirteenth
day of the twelfth month, the month Adar. A copy of the 13
writ was to be issued as a decree in every province and
published to all peoples, and the Jews were to be ready for

14 that day, the day of vengeance on their enemies. So the couriers, mounted on their royal horses, were dispatched post-haste at the king's urgent command; and the decree was issued also in Susa the capital city.

15   Mordecai left the king's presence in royal robes of violet and white, wearing a great golden crown and a cloak of fine linen and purple, and all the city of Susa shouted for
16 joy. For the Jews there was light and joy, gladness and
17 honour. In every province and every city reached by the royal command and decree, there was joy and gladness for the Jews, feasting and holiday. And many of the peoples of the land professed themselves Jews, because fear of the Jews had seized them.

* The tension in the personal drama between Mordecai and Haman is over, and the abatement of the king's rage (7: 10) corresponds to the subsiding of the individual struggle. But the problems are far from resolved. The decree against the Jewish people is still in effect, and their enemies, the little Hamans, are everywhere. The last three chapters of the book deal with these problems.

1–2. The first step in reparation and adjustment is to give to Esther Haman's *house*, which is to say, probably, his property which included most of what he had. The Persian government confiscated the property of criminals who were condemned to death. The relationship of Esther and Mordecai is revealed to the king, and Haman's position, symbolized by the *signet-ring* (cp. 3: 10), is given to Mordecai. Even the property of his old adversary is put under Mordecai's control; death does not terminate Haman's role as *enemy of the Jews*.

3. Unlike her seemingly calm posture in her previous approach with an entreaty for the king (5: 1), Esther falls down, weeping, and pleads for her people.

4–6. Esther's request seems modest enough – *recall the*

78

letters. It will be remembered that destruction of her *race* and *family* would still of course mean her own death (cp. 4: 13–14). Ahasuerus doubtless needed no one to remind him of that fact.

8. The king agrees to send another decree in writing, to resolve the problem, for the first decree was irrevocable by Persian law (cp. 1: 19).

9. The precision in noting the date of the dispatching of the letter from Esther and Mordecai is curious, and remains unexplained. It has been observed that this day is seventy days after Haman's letter in 3: 13, counting thirty days to each month; perhaps the figure seventy signifies the completion of the episode, or of the actions, within this interval of time. The name *Sivan* (about June), like Adar (3: 7), and Tebeth (2: 16), is a Babylonian term for the month, and not the old Hebrew name.

11. The tables are turned, and the Jews are urged by the Persian king to unite and defend themselves. The same terrible vocabulary once aimed at them by Haman (3: 13) is now used to direct their retaliation against anyone who is hostile. The text really suggests more than self-defence, against any who *might attack them*; it justifies a Jewish attack on their enemies, those who are hostile to them. The issuing of such a letter would create enormous problems for any emperor or ruler.

13. At the end of the verse, the text literally translated reads, 'and for the Jews to be ready for that day, to take revenge upon their enemies'. Some readers find the book becoming unpleasant in this part. The law of vengeance that pervaded the societies of the ancient Near East was indeed instinctive and cruel, no matter how important to the stability of social structures; it penetrated the hearts and lives of people who could otherwise be highly sensitive and generous. It was a cultural feature that made its way through Israel's religion, and appears in revered portions of the Old Testament; yet nobler grace and higher vision were present also, for example in the Suffering Servant songs of the Isaiah of the exile (cp.

Isa. 53). The book of Esther gives free vent to natural human urges and impulses, not all of which are to be condoned.

15. Mordecai's apparel befits his position as the king's right-hand man, and therefore resembles the elegance of the king's own clothing. *shouted for joy:* literally, 'cried shrilly (as a horse whinnies), and rejoiced'.

16–17. The toll of words of celebration rings like a bell, at the end of this section: *light, joy, gladness, honour, joy, gladness, feasting* and *holiday*.

17. *professed themselves Jews:* the earliest reference to such a conversion experience. Many non-Hebrews in the past had affiliated with Israel, including such notables as Ruth the Moabitess and Uriah the Hittite (2 Sam. 11), but nowhere is there a movement like this. The Hebrew verb form can imply, 'call oneself a Jew', and it has been assumed by scholars that this was an occasion when the 'converts' only pretended to be Jewish. There is no Persian record of the event. Other scholars take the phrase to be evidence of a late date for the origin of the book of Esther, down to the Greek period (cp. 9: 27) when proselytizing was widespread. ✳

SLAUGHTER OF THE JEWS' ENEMIES

9 On the thirteenth day of the twelfth month, the month Adar, the time came for the king's command and his edict to be carried out. The very day on which the enemies of the Jews had hoped to gain the upper hand over them was to become the day when the Jews should
2 gain the upper hand over those who hated them. On that day the Jews united in their cities in all the provinces of King Ahasuerus to fall upon those who had planned their ruin. No one could resist them, because fear of them had
3 seized all peoples. All the officers of the provinces, the satraps and the governors, and all the royal officials, aided

the Jews, because fear of Mordecai had seized them.
Mordecai had become a great personage in the royal 4
palace; his fame had spread throughout all the provinces
as the power of the man grew steadily greater. So the 5
Jews put their enemies to the sword, with great slaughter
and destruction; they worked their will on those who
hated them. In Susa, the capital city, the Jews killed five 6
hundred men and destroyed them; and they killed also 7
Parshandatha, Dalphon and Aspatha, Poratha, Adalia and 8
Aridatha, Parmashta, Arisai, Aridai and Vaizatha, the ten 9, 10
sons of Haman son of Hammedatha, the enemy of the
Jews; but they did not touch the plunder.

That day when the number of those killed in Susa the 11
capital city came to the notice of the king, he said to 12
Queen Esther, 'In Susa, the capital city, the Jews have
killed and destroyed five hundred men and the ten sons
of Haman. What have they done in the rest of the king's
provinces? Whatever you ask further will be given to
you; whatever more you seek shall be done.' Esther 13
answered him, 'If it please your majesty, let tomorrow be
granted to the Jews in Susa to do according to the edict
for today; and let the bodies of Haman's ten sons be hung
up on the gallows.' The king gave orders for this to be 14
done; the edict was issued in Susa and Haman's ten sons
were hung up on the gallows. The Jews in Susa united 15
again on the fourteenth day of the month Adar and killed
three hundred men in Susa; but they did not touch the
plunder.

The rest of the Jews in the king's provinces had united 16
to defend themselves; they took vengeance on[a] their

[a] *Prob. rdg.; Heb.* got respite from.

enemies by killing seventy-five thousand of those who
17 hated them; but they did not touch the plunder. This was
on the thirteenth day of the month Adar, and they rested
on the fourteenth day and made that a day of feasting and
18 joy. The Jews in Susa had united on the thirteenth and
fourteenth days of the month, and rested on the fifteenth
19 day and made that a day of feasting and joy. This is why
isolated Jews who live in remote villages keep the fourteenth day of the month Adar in joy and feasting, as a
holiday on which they send presents of food to one
another.

* The mood in the book has been set by the preceding two
verses, 8: 16–17, and the spirit of the rest remains on the level
of 'feasting and joy'. However earnest may be the description
of the slaughters in 9: 5–16, the emotional flavour is affected
by the mood created. The reader whose ethical sensibilities
are offended by the killings must remember the fictional
character of the book; there is no record of such slaughters,
and it is most unlikely that they ever happened. We must not
forget that the book of Esther was written for people whose
well-being is imperilled and who feel threatened by enemies
around them; it is a story of similar people who acted aggressively and who survived, confident that enemies of the Jews
cannot prevail; anyone who defends severe preventive measures for self-defence will at least understand the principle
behind this account in Esther.

1. *command* and *edict:* the reference is to the first letter, sent
with Haman's instructions, concerning the annihilation of the
Jews. This order, given by a king whose word could not be
rescinded, commanded the local authorities to destroy the
Jews; the second letter of 8: 9 did not contravene that command, but rather only added an authorization for the Jews to
defend themselves and to strike back. The story is based upon

the assumption that both of these commands are to be obeyed; a truce seems out of the question. Therefore, if one is looking for someone to blame for atrocities, one must certainly add Ahasuerus and the Persian system of law to the list!

2. The root word for *united* is related to the Hebrew word for 'congregation', 'assembly'. This concept is stressed in this chapter, occurring four times in verses 2, 15, 16, and 18, as well as in 8: 11; it provides a reminder to the reader that he belongs to the community to which these things happened. The Greek version does not mention this significant feature.

3. As remarkable as the co-operation of the whole Persian upper administrative apparatus in the Jewish endeavours, is the claim that the officials co-operated because the *fear of Mordecai* 'fell' upon them.

4. Mordecai's position is made clear in this, as well as in the preceding verse; he, like the people he represents, is the terror of all.

5. One scholar has described the Jewish onslaught as 'a case of do unto others as they would have done unto you'.

6-9. The names of the sons of *Haman, the enemy of the Jews*, are written in a peculiar, distinctive way in Hebrew manuscripts – in lists and not in linear fashion as in the N.E.B. – and call formal attention to this act of blotting out the national enemy as well as pointing to a special way of reading these verses in public.

10. *but they did not touch the plunder*: the Septuagint contradicts the Hebrew and says that they took plunder, although it agrees with the Hebrew in verses 15 and 16 by stating that on subsequent slaughters the next day they did not plunder. The restraint displayed, in not following the explicit instructions of Ahasuerus given in 8: 11 to 'plunder their possessions', removes from the Jewish retaliation any pecuniary motive. It was a fight for survival, not for monetary gain.

13. Esther's last wish, except for her participation in the establishment of Purim (9: 29-32), is that the dead bodies of Haman's sons be hanged. Public display of the dead was a

particularly violent means of humiliation. Thus Esther exacts merciless revenge on the enemies, and acquires in the eyes of many a reputation for cold, ruthless vindictiveness.

15. There are still enemies in Susa, and they are attacked the next day. There is no explanation for the extension of time for the slaughter; presumably the enemies of the Jews would also have continued beyond the appointed day, had they seized the initiative.

16. The killing in the provinces had reached huge proportions; enemies of the Jews must have been numerous. The reading in the Hebrew text (cp. footnote) makes good sense: they 'got respite from' instead of *they took vengeance on*.

17. *feasting and joy* is a phrase typifying this last segment of the book of Esther (cp. verses 18, 19, and 22); the plot has been broken, the enemies are vanquished, and the Jews have triumphed. When this part of the book was read, there was rejoicing with Esther and Mordecai by the people who had endured centuries of exile, harassment, and hate.

18–19. These verses explain a peculiar situation in which the Jews found themselves; some Jews evidently celebrated the festival of Purim, and the Jewish victory, on the fifteenth of Adar, while the general custom was to recognize it on the fourteenth of the month.

19. What is described in this verse is clearly a tradition which has been of long standing, and proves that the book was written long after there had arisen a feast of Purim, which itself was connected to previous events in the life of Esther. The picture described here is that of a comfortably established custom. The book must surely be an effective re-telling of an old story which tradition has determined to be the occasion for the celebration of Purim. ✱

THE ESTABLISHMENT OF PURIM

20 Then Mordecai set these things on record and sent letters to all the Jews in all the provinces of King Ahasuerus,

far and near, binding them to keep the fourteenth and 21
fifteenth days of the month Adar, year by year, as the days 22
on which the Jews obtained relief from their enemies and as
the month which was changed for them from sorrow into
joy, from a time of mourning to a holiday. They were
to keep them as days of feasting and joy, days for send-
ing presents of food to one another and gifts to the poor.

So the Jews undertook to continue the practice that 23
they had begun in accordance with Mordecai's letter. This 24
they did because Haman son of Hammedatha the Agagite,
the enemy of all the Jews, had plotted to destroy the Jews
and had cast lots, Pur as it is called, with intent to crush
and destroy them. But when the matter came before the 25
king, he issued written orders that the wicked plot which
Haman had devised against the Jews should recoil on his
own head, and that he and his sons should be hanged on
the gallows. Therefore, these days were named Purim 26
after the word Pur. Accordingly, because of all that was
written in this letter, because of all they had seen and
experienced in this affair, the Jews resolved and undertook, 27
on behalf of themselves, their descendants, and all who
should join them, that they would without fail keep these
two days as a yearly festival in the prescribed manner and
at the appointed time; that these days should be remem- 28
bered and kept, generation after generation, in every
family, province, and city, that the days of Purim should
always be observed among the Jews, and that the memory
of them should never cease among their descendants.

Queen Esther daughter of Abihail gave full authority 29
in writing to[a] Mordecai the Jew, to confirm this second

[a] *Prob. rdg.; Heb.* and.

30 letter about Purim. Letters wishing peace and security
were sent to all the Jews in the hundred and twenty-seven
31 provinces of King Ahasuerus, making the observance of
these days of Purim at their appointed time binding on
them, as Mordecai the Jew[a] had prescribed. In the same
way they had prescribed regulations for fasts and lamen-
32 tations for themselves and their descendants. The command of Esther confirmed these regulations for Purim,
and the record is preserved in writing.

* This section almost at the end of the book seems strangely
set apart from the rest of the story, a summary drawing together and directing the whole narrative to the purpose of
remembering and celebrating the festival of Purim. Heretofore
the book is a finely spun tale, tightening and complicating,
then relaxing and solving the dramatic involvements. The
previous paragraph, 9: 16–19, also establishes the fourteenth
and fifteenth days of Adar as occasions for commemoration
and celebration. But 9: 20–32 repeats basic lines of the narrative, and introduces the reader to the feast of Purim. It thereby
historically knits the foregoing tale to the festival, and fur-
nishes an explanation for the origin of the name, Purim. It
therefore functions as a supplement which fixes the book in
the festal calendar of Judaism.

20–1. Both days, *the fourteenth and fifteenth* of Adar, as
though by a compromise, are set by Mordecai for the celebration of the Jewish victory. On the fourteenth the provincial
successes are remembered, and on both the fourteenth and the
fifteenth the double slaughters in Susa (9: 5 and 15). The
Jewish historian Josephus, writing after A.D. 70, records that
the feast of Purim was kept on both days in Palestine.

22. *gifts to the poor:* a feature not mentioned earlier in 9: 19.
24–5. From the standpoint of the wholeness of the book,

[a] *Prob. rdg.; Heb. adds* and Queen Esther.

this brief résumé of the plotting and failing of Haman is quite unnecessary; the reader, or hearer, has better information about the story than these verses could ever convey. They are a repetition and an application, in the manner of an after-thought or addition. *enemy of all the Jews:* the familiar phrase describing Haman is extended and more explicit, *all* the Jews. *cast lots:* the slight mention of this small episode, in 3: 7, was insignificant in the main story; in the intention of this supplement, however, it becomes an essential element to call to mind. *Pur:* this word, translated into Hebrew as it is in the text, is not Hebrew. It is rather based upon an Akkadian word meaning 'lot' or 'destiny', and was used by the Babylonians when lots were cast in order to obtain clues to the future. The word may have been commonly known and used by the Jews in the Mesopotamian communities of the Persian Empire, where the festival of Purim originated.

27. *all who should join them:* this phrase may refer to prose-lytes, who were converted to Judaism, and not just to sympathizers (cp. 8: 17). The fact that an increasing number of converts recorded were won to Judaism, beginning in the second century B.C., does not determine that this section of Esther was added at that time; but it does make the book seem very applicable to that situation.

29–32. This paragraph has been suspected of being added later to the book. In any event it exhibits signs of being an appendage: an issue (the *second letter*) which is extraneous to the story, repetition of a matter fully explained and developed earlier (prescribing the festival's observance), and a sobering admonition (regulations for fasts and lamentations). These characteristics are similar to those of the added portions in Ecclesiastes (see on Eccles. 12: 9–14, pp. 154–5).

29. *second letter:* can only refer to the letter about to be sent and mentioned in the following verse.

31. The Hebrew adds 'and Queen Esther' after *Mordecai the Jew* (cp. footnote). The text probably included it in the original; the fact of its presence in the Hebrew text outweighs

the argument that she is not mentioned in 9: 20 where Mordecai sends out the message. *fasts and lamentations:* literally, 'fasts
and crying out'; this has been an issue omitted from the
celebration at the end of the book, but is very much a part of
it in ch. 4. The thirteenth of Adar was also a day of fasting, in
ancient and modern Jewish tradition, in preparation for
Purim. *

THE EPILOGUE

10 King Ahasuerus imposed forced labour on the land and
2 the coasts and islands. All the king's acts of authority and
power, and the dignities which he conferred on Mordecai,
are written in the annals of the kings of Media and Persia.
3 For Mordecai the Jew was second only to King Ahasuerus; he was a great man among the Jews and was popular
with the mass of his countrymen, for he sought the good
of his people and promoted the welfare of all their
descendants.[a]

* The last paragraph brings the book to a close quietly and
with composure. Ahasuerus is governing with a strong hand,
and Mordecai the Jew is solid, powerful, and good for his
people. Esther is not mentioned; she has played her role
faithfully and well. Mordecai, the Jew, has survived and is
thriving.
   1. Why the author brings up this subject at this point is
anyone's guess; there are no precedents or connections for it.
forced labour: the same term applied to the servitude laid on
Israel by the Egyptians (Exod. 1: 11; cp. also the note on
Lam. 1: 1, p. 217).
   2. *All the king's acts...are written:* this is a common phrase
strongly reminiscent of other Hebrew history; cp. 2 Kings 15:
36, 'The other acts and events of Jotham's reign are recorded

[a] *Or* and was in friendly relations with all his race.

in the annals of the kings of Judah.' *annals:* the source is unknown. It is conjectured that these were the official records of the Persian Empire, or that they were a popular historical summary of tales from the Persian court.

3. After a rather tempestuous career in the book, Mordecai ends up as a model for human, and Jewish, behaviour: second to the king, great among the Jews, pleasing to the mass of his countrymen, seeking good for his people, and speaking *shalom* (welfare, peace) to all his descendants. *

✻   ✻   ✻   ✻   ✻   ✻   ✻   ✻   ✻   ✻   ✻   ✻   ✻

THE MESSAGE OF ESTHER

It is noteworthy that many Christians have had to struggle in order to justify the presence of the book of Esther in their Bible. Obviously the problem is not the same in Judaism. This variance indicates where the message of the book is to be found, but also where Christians have suffered from theological stiffness.

To be sure little theology is evident in Esther. An ethical consciousness appears in the abstention from taking spoil and booty during the slaying (9: 10, 15, 16). Historical awareness glimmers faintly through references to Agag and Amalek. But these concerns are largely absent; the book has a different purpose. Its message is nationalistic.

Esther does not describe what should happen, but what does happen. Jews have been confined to ghettoes, discriminated against, and terrified and tortured by inquisitions, and all this for no other reason than for being Jewish. The book of Esther cries out against this evil, from centuries before ever there was a Christian faith and 'Christian' persecutors. This book satisfied and helped generations who felt the hatred of their neighbours. Esther indeed 'Judaizes' very much; Luther saw that clearly, but could not appreciate it because he himself shared deeply in the prejudice.

But the book offers more. It speaks of a people who are moved, guided, and protected. Things work out satisfactorily for Israel, because it is Israel. Speaking with convictions born of a long history and centuries of faith, the author rejoiced in his Jewishness; he addressed times of threat and peril with a word of hope, which was built on confidence and faith in a very ancient promise. 'If Mordecai, in face of whom your fortunes begin to fall, belongs to the Jewish race, you will not get the better of him; he will see your utter downfall' (6: 13).

ECCLESIASTES

✱　✱　✱　✱　✱　✱　✱　✱　✱　✱　✱　✱　✱

PROBLEMS WITH THE BOOK

'It has become almost a proverb that every interpreter of this book thinks that all previous interpreters have been wrong.' So wrote an eminent scholar in a commentary more than ninety years ago, and matters have hardly changed since his day. The book of Ecclesiastes poses such severe problems to its readers that they have differed radically in their opinions of it.

Unfortunately, there is more unanimity in the generally negative spirit with which Ecclesiastes is read and received. 'The most heretical book of the third century B.C.', someone has called it; the author 'had faith, but he lacked love and hope', says another. It is claimed that God in Ecclesiastes is not Providence, but blind fate; that not God, but rather man, is the centre of things.

This small book certainly is unlike the rest of the Old Testament. It poses harder questions, raises graver doubts, and arrives at more despairing conclusions than any other book. Its message is unique in Old Testament literature; it asks its readers to search their hearts and convictions, and shares with them its own unbeliefs.

A BOOK OF WISDOM

In order to understand the message one must take into account what kind of book it is, and the thought-world from which it comes. Ecclesiastes belongs to the wisdom literature of the Old Testament and of the ancient Near East; this vast body of material, most of it unknown until the twentieth century, represented a cultural feature which existed in the civilizations of the Nile and Mesopotamian valleys throughout the period of Israel's history, and for fully 1000 years before.

The ancient wise men, the transmitters and authors of this literature, played an important and complex role in their societies. They were engaged in the activity of gathering, composing, and preserving the folklore and the sayings of their people. In addition the task of some of them probably included responsibility for communicating the learning of the day, through the schools in which the primary exercise was writing and the basic content was the material of the wisdom literature. In this undertaking the wise man was often associated with the royal court: Daniel (Dan. 1) and Joseph (Gen. 37ff.) are two examples of such wise men. Solomon himself came to be seen as the epitome of the wise man (1 Kings 4: 29-34), whose 'wisdom surpassed that of all the men of the east and of all Egypt', and who 'uttered three thousand proverbs' and 'a thousand and five' songs.

There was another side to the activity of wise men outside the royal court. Old and wise men in the villages, skilled artisans, and local teachers all played their part; the content of the wisdom literature as well as the influence of wisdom in the culture were dependent upon them also. Wisdom activity could be an uncritical science, in contrast to the historical interests of religious leaders and teachers and to the message and style of the prophets, or the legal and historical concerns of the priests. But if wisdom lacked the religious fervour of the prophets, or the preoccupation for laws, ritual, and tradition of the priests, it preserved and transmitted cherished knowledge and treasured folklore. It included popular and folk proverbs and stories, lists of names and bits of information, insights accumulated through centuries of social experience, and advice for behaviour in social situations ranging from common domestic relationships to court etiquette.

In the Old Testament the term 'wisdom' does not describe an organized movement or a class in society; it is a label for a type of thinking and activity which permeated the culture and was especially practised by some people whom we designate as 'wise men'. These men, analysing the world of man and of nature, shared with their counterparts in other nations the observations and the wisdom which they obtained. Wisdom was universal in interest and style.

The style tended to be synthetic and cumulative, adding together pieces of information, advice, and tradition without paying strict attention to classification. This characteristic is illustrated in Proverbs, for example, as well as in Ecclesiastes. Wisdom also used a framework of contrasts in formulating proverbs: rich and poor, wise and foolish, righteous and wicked. The principle of contrasts applied also when proverbs were collected to express two opposite sides of a question: 'Bad temper provokes a quarrel, but patience heals discords' (Prov. 15: 18).

Yet there existed another, quite different function and style in the wisdom tradition. There were wise men, schooled and trained in the learning of their people, who subjected this knowledge and folklore to searching cross-examination, and who applied what they knew to the complex questions of justice, human destiny, life and death, the meaning of pain and suffering, and the goal of human life. In both the Egyptian and Babylonian civilizations, this speculative force in wisdom produced impressive documents, one of which, known as 'A Dialogue About Human Misery', has been called the 'Babylonian Ecclesiastes'. Job and Ecclesiastes are the foremost examples of speculative wisdom in the Old Testament.

This speculative wisdom was of a rigorous, inquiring sort, putting challenges to accepted doctrines and beliefs because the claims these made did not conform to the wise man's evidence or conclusions. It scrutinized the answers from the past which were adopted too easily, and produced for the religious tradition a testimony to new affirmations and new viewpoints on life's ultimate problems.

Ecclesiastes goes further than Job in its analysis of the human situation, and asserts more plainly its own drastic solution. Its assertions were perhaps never very popular, and after the appearance in Judaism of the belief in a general resurrection of the dead and the advent of Christianity with even greater emphasis upon the resurrection and a life hereafter, it seemed to have less to say about the human predicament, and its way of describing that predicament may have seemed less congenial. But the revival of sympathy for Ecclesiastes in recent years may indicate a change of feeling about its viewpoint and its message. We shall note this as we look at the book (cp. also 'The Message of Ecclesiastes', pp. 155–8).

WHAT IS THE STRUCTURE OF ECCLESIASTES?

All the discussion concerning the interpretation of the book of Ecclesiastes has been accompanied by a long-standing search for the best hypothesis regarding its structure. No biblical book has received more suggestions about the arrangement of its material; a notable commentary of the last century, by C. D. Ginsburg, compiled an enormous assortment of suggestions, and more have continued to come forth since that day. The nature of Ecclesiastes, with its many repetitions, its development of argumentation followed by seemingly aimless digression, and its fascinating ebb and flow of advice, has intrigued scholars who try to relate a theory of the book's structure to an interpretation of its message.

In the N.E.B. the format necessarily commits the reader to a certain concept of organization. The book is divided into three sections with corresponding titles:

1: 1 – 6: 12   *The emptiness of all endeavour*;
7: 1 – 11: 6   *Wisdom and folly compared*;
11: 7 – 12: 14   *Advice to a young man*.

Many commentators have been reluctant to go even that far in identifying literary structure.

The material indeed poses great difficulty for the one who would connect structure with content; but some observations can be ventured on the basis of data which are apparent. The thought of the book moves in one large circle, encompassing the whole of the original book, from 1: 2 to 12: 8, and beginning and ending with the sentence, 'Emptiness, emptiness, says the Speaker, all is empty.' So also Ecclesiastes falls into sections which describe smaller circles, discernible through the indications of the author's negative analysis of life and his positive notes and admonitions. The positive words, reaching their apex in 9: 7–10, are exemplified in 2: 24, 'There is nothing better for a man to do than to eat and drink and enjoy himself in return for his labours. And yet I saw that this comes from the hand of God.' Such thoughts are found in: 2: 24–5; 3: 12–15; 3: 22; 5: 18–20; 8: 15; 9: 7–10. The three great issues that provoke the author's pessimism – inequity, ignorance of life's meaning and of the future, and death – are summarized in 3: 11–22 and in 8: 9 – 9: 6. A small but noticeable feature is that the Hebrew expression which introduces 4: 1 (and 4: 7) is also used to begin 9: 11 (literally it may be rendered: 'So again I saw'). Therefore it would seem that three major sections begin at 1: 2, 4: 1, and 9: 11, with the second and third sections recycling the ideas which are stated in the first. This threefold structure may be seen to be like that of the dialogue in Job 3–27.

Although it is ill-advised to attempt to apply a structure which is too narrow and detailed upon the book, the following commentary does elaborate the text with sections according to this design, as well as with the titles given in the N.E.B. text. Ecclesiastes' author was not captured by a tight scheme for developing what he had to say, and he felt free to meander among the treasures of his tradition in wisdom. But his materials do indicate that his thoughts returned in a pattern, first small, and then like concentric circles in a large and all-embracing arc back to his starting-point.

THE MESSAGE MATCHES THE STRUCTURE

Parallel with the structure go the main lines of the message of the book. In 1: 1 – 3: 22 the fundamental sources of emptiness are treated, after an extensive description of the search for meaning in life. The positive solution is introduced in 2: 24-5 and reaffirmed in 3: 12-15; but the problems remain alongside the positive advice, and the section closes with both positive and negative sides of the dilemma joined in 3: 22.

In 4: 1 the journey begins again, this time through what are digressions and intrusions (or so it might seem if we insist on strict attention to the matter at hand). The positive word appears in 5: 18-20, and at 8: 9 the focus narrows back to the principal concerns of the author. The section closes with the full declaration of the positive solution for man, in 9: 7-10.

The author is not given to easy answers and carefree conclusions. The world that he sees requires more sober treatment, and so he turns around for a third cycle; however, this time he does not repeat the positive word, and is content to admonish his reader in ch. 11, before he closes with a magnificent and evocative poem on death, and with his final refrain.

THE COMPOSITION OF ECCLESIASTES

Ecclesiastes is the word commonly used as the name for both the book and the author of the book. It is the Greek and Latin translation of the Hebrew, 'Koheleth', which is given as 'Speaker' in the N.E.B. and which can be translated as 'spokesman in the assembly', 'convener of an assembly', or even 'teacher'; the word is actually a feminine form based on a Hebrew root meaning 'to assemble', 'to congregate'. Throughout this commentary Ecclesiastes will be used to signify the book, and Koheleth will designate the author.

The author of Ecclesiastes remains anonymous, called simply by his self-assumed title, 'Koheleth'; we know nothing about him, although some commentators have tried to deduce from the book that he was an old man and some have produced nearly a whole personality from no evidence at all.

Ecclesiastes is written entirely in the first person, except for the opening sentence (1: 1), the closing epilogue (12: 9–14), and the note, 'says the Speaker', in 1: 2; 7: 27, and 12: 8. Koheleth refers to himself in 1: 12 as 'king over Israel', and is called 'son of David, king in Jerusalem' in 1: 1 (although the Aramaic meaning of 'counsellor' has been proposed for the word for 'king'). This identification, together with references in the book to his own unsurpassed wisdom and wealth, would suggest that he wished to be thought of as Solomon, and so for centuries indeed he was except by a few scholars who, like Luther, saw that Solomon in fact could not have been responsible for the book.

As one scholar has put it, if a history of the Hebrew language can be written at all, Ecclesiastes cannot have come from Solomon. Its language bears striking differences from the rest of biblical Hebrew, using many words which are not found elsewhere in the Bible but which were common in later Hebrew. Two Persian words, for 'parks' in 2: 5 and 'sentence' in 8: 11, show that at the earliest it must belong to the period of Persian influence. It was probably not written before 300 B.C., and could not have originated after 200 B.C. because it is alluded to in Ecclesiasticus, a book written around 180 B.C. Attempts are occasionally made to connect some section, or allusion, in Ecclesiastes with an historical event, and thus date the book; no such attempt has proved to be convincing.

An exact place for the book's composition cannot be ascertained. Linguistic elements have been thought to point to the Mediterranean coasts of Phoenicia, 'the coastal plain in southern Phoenicia' as someone has put it, as a most likely spot. Phoenician parallels in expressions and forms of the language have been shown; whether this is enough to prove where the author lived when he wrote is however a matter which cannot be determined now. Some scholars have defended a theory that the book was first written in Aramaic, and only later translated into Hebrew; but this theory has not been accepted.

Whether Koheleth himself wrote the whole book has been a source of intense debate in the past. The sharply varying ideas in the book have caused many scholars to suppose that editors generously added their own glosses to the text, according to their own theological positions or biases. One theory even postulated as many as nine different sources for the book. However, such speculations usually reckon without the propensity of the wise man to collect varying, and some-times opposite, bits of wisdom side by side; they ignore his way of moving easily amid pieces of mental furniture which are very different and not logically or schematically arranged. When the whole book can demonstrate such circular thinking, and show such clear signs that the author had the mental habits of a collector, it becomes very precarious to insist that a given passage must have been inserted by someone else because the author would not have written it, would not have placed it where it is, or could not have accepted and believed it as his own thought.

It is in the concluding section, 12: 9–14, where there is most suspicion of later hands adding material. The book ends at 12: 8, verses 9–10 are in clear contrast because they are written in the third person, verse 12 is a warning in the second person, and verses 13–14 provide a conclusion quite foreign to the primary thrusts of Ecclesiastes. This section may have been added by as many as three persons, verses 9–10, 11–12, and 13–14 each coming from a new annotator.

OUTSIDE INFLUENCE UPON ECCLESIASTES

Much has been said about alleged influence upon the book and its author by sources from outside Israel. Signs of Greek philosophy and Greek expressions are said to abound in the book, and the detection of Egyptian influence, especially through the powerful Jewish community in Alexandria, has been claimed. Ecclesiastes is said to give special evidence of familiarity with the busy world of international trade, and to reflect an author who was involved in broad intellectual and cultural movements, and who therefore would be likely to have lived in Alexandria, or in a Phoenician seaport.

The book does not however suggest an atmosphere of foreign elements. Its language is Hebrew; its alleged Greek expressions are not convincingly demonstrable. While it speaks of ideas which bear some superficial similarity or even close agreement with certain ideas in Greek philosophies, upon closer examination the links appear to exist in congenial or parallel concerns and not in dependence.

The outside influence upon Koheleth lay indeed at a much more profound level, in the cross-cultural similarities and harmonies within the wisdom traditions and among the wise men. For example, in the Old Babylonian version of the Gilgamesh epic (cp. *The Making of the Old Testament* in this series, p. 7), on tablets written long before Israel existed as a nation in Palestine and composed even earlier, we read these words which are so like Koheleth's own positive advice:

> Gilgamesh, whither rovest thou?
> The life thou pursuest thou shalt not find.
> When the gods created mankind,
> Death for mankind they set aside,
> Life in their own hands retaining.
> Thou, Gilgamesh, let full be thy belly,
> Make thou merry by day and by night.
> Of each day make thou a feast of rejoicing,
> Day and night dance thou and play!
> Let thy garments be sparkling fresh,
> Thy head be washed; bathe thou in water.
> Pay heed to the little one that holds on to thy hand,
> Let thy spouse delight in thy bosom!
> For this is the task of (mankind)!

(translation by E. A. Speiser, in *Ancient Near Eastern Texts*, ed. J. B. Pritchard, p. 90).

It is not likely that Koheleth was dependent upon this Gilgamesh tradition. Such an example does not of course preclude any amount of possible Greek or Egyptian influence; but it does illustrate the broad scope of common traditions and the impressive spread of ideas over the ancient Near East, not only geographically but also chronologically. The diffusion of information and materials in those days makes it impossible for us to speak of dependence or influence unless the evidence is clearer and more plentiful.

THE PLACE OF THE BOOK

Ecclesiastes always seemed to be somewhat unusual, and its acceptance into the collection of books that was finally called the Old Testament did not take place without objection. The book was a renegade from the traditional faith of Israel. It makes no reference to Israel's history, and 'Israel' as a word is mentioned only once, in 1 : 12 in the phrase 'king over Israel'. The personal name for God, Yahweh, is never used. The position taken by Ecclesiastes seems thoroughly rooted in present existence; time is thought of not as historical sequence, but rather in static categories of past–present–future. Furthermore, the past is behind man, full of emptiness and disappointment, and the future is beyond, dark and uncertain. The crucial vocabulary in Ecclesiastes is a mixture of orthodox wisdom terminology and an unusual stress on present satisfaction and pleasure: 'emptiness', 'gain', 'labour', 'lot' (or 'portion, share'), 'eat', 'drink', 'enjoy', 'folly', 'sin', 'evil', 'good', 'knowledge', and 'wisdom'. The author clearly stood with one foot on each side of the edge of the mainstream of the faith of Israel.

In this situation, Ecclesiastes, although often quoted in the rabbinic literature and probably alluded to in the New Testament, was interpreted as an allegory of Israel's history, or of the religious life, by the Midrash – early Jewish commentary on the scriptures – and by the early church fathers. It was customarily read on the third day of the Feast of Tabernacles, the Jewish autumn festival, perhaps just to supply a sobering note for the holiday! It has been variously described as a gloomy, suicidal treatise, a cheery, worldly alternative to the gloomy life of monasticism, and an appropriate preparation for Christ; one scholar even called it the most shattering messianic prophecy in the Old Testament.

It was perhaps rescued for the Bible by the appeal to Solomon as its author. But we may be pardoned for believing that many of the old rabbis, who accepted Ecclesiastes, felt a strange power surge through their being as they read its word, and concluded that such a book should indeed be regarded as holy (see pp. 3–4).

✳   ✳   ✳   ✳   ✳   ✳   ✳   ✳   ✳   ✳   ✳   ✳   ✳

The emptiness of all endeavour

THERE IS NOTHING NEW UNDER THE SUN

THE WORDS OF THE SPEAKER,*a* the son of David, 1 king in Jerusalem.

Emptiness, emptiness, says the Speaker, emptiness, all 2 is empty. What does man gain from all his labour and his 3 toil here under the sun? Generations come and genera- 4 tions go, while the earth endures for ever.

The sun rises and the sun goes down; back it returns to 5 its place*b* and rises there again. The wind blows south, the 6 wind blows north, round and round it goes and returns full circle. All streams run into the sea, yet the sea never 7 overflows; back to the place from which the streams ran they return to run again.

[a] the Speaker: *Heb.* Koheleth, *Sept.* Ecclesiastes.
[b] back...place: *prob. rdg.; Heb.* to its place panting.

8 All things are wearisome;[a] no man can speak of them all. Is not the eye surfeited with seeing, and the ear sated 9 with hearing? What has happened will happen again, and what has been done will be done again, and there is 10 nothing new under the sun. Is there anything of which one can say, 'Look, this is new'? No, it has already exis- 11 ted, long ago before our time. The men of old are not remembered, and those who follow will not be remembered by those who follow them.

* In setting forth arguments and ideas about life and its meaning, the author of Ecclesiastes introduces his book with one of the principal insights which he has received from observing the world around him: the world of God's creation, in its inscrutable rhythms and enduring forces, overwhelms mankind into insignificance. The conclusion of the book, in 12: I–8, portrays that certain and inevitable end of man in death which stamps all his efforts as absurd and empty. And when man sees that the world goes on around him, and after him, as it always has, the end to human aspiration which is brought about by death becomes all the more bitter and mocking. So the pain and anger of his frustration is present at the outset in the book.

Human living and experience indeed seem empty and in-significant when pictured against the background of the unfathomable repetition and impenetrable depth of the uni-verse. For the author does not weigh man against the measure of human history; it is with the elements – wind and water – and the sun in the heavens that human endeavour is matched. The vastness of this image appears also in Isa. 40: 15, 'Why, to him [God] nations are but drops from a bucket, no more than moisture on the scales.'

1. In this foreword the author is called *Speaker*; the Hebrew

[a] *Prob. rdg.; Heb.* weary.

term, 'Koheleth', implies someone connected with the congregation of the faithful, like 'teacher', or 'convenor', or 'spokesman in the assembly'. The commonly used title, 'preacher', is misleading and not very helpful in rendering the term. The author is identified with Solomon, who was *son of David, king in Jerusalem*; several other books written or finally collected at the end of the Old Testament period (Proverbs, the Song of Songs, the Wisdom of Solomon, the Psalms of Solomon) were also transmitted under the name of Solomon who was reputed to be both wise and the composer of many proverbs and songs (cp. 1 Kings 4: 32).

2. The theme of the book, with which it closes in 12: 8, is struck here at the beginning. Everything in human experience is *empty*, or as the Hebrew also means, 'wind', 'vanity', 'nothingness', 'vapour'; everything is 'fleeting and perishable'.

3. Directly following the theme of the book comes the question which is posed as a consequence of the theme: in other words, 'Where is that use, that enduring value, or that meaning of our lives which is sufficient and satisfying?' The Hebrew word for *gain, yithron*, found only in Ecclesiastes, is also translated as 'profit' or 'advantage' in this book; it conveys the notion of 'that which is left over, that which remains or exceeds', and throughout the commentary will be referred to as 'gain/*yithron*'.

under the sun is a phrase frequently used in the book of Ecclesiastes, and found elsewhere in Phoenician sources. Its meaning would seem to be simply, 'in the world'; but the verse suggests also that the sun relentlessly makes *labour* and *toil* hard, as relentlessly exposes everything to view, showing how 'empty' it is, and just as relentlessly measures the passage of ceaseless days and nights.

4–7. All around are signs of movement and change, and yet the world outlasts this movement; there is something in creation that is able to mock those who would change it, because it dwarfs them by the irresistible patterns in nature.

it returns to its place: the N.E.B. footnote preserves the Hebrew picture of the sun moving rapidly, with a breathless-ness that the reader is invited to imagine, as it rushes back beneath the earth to the east in order to perform its task each day. This concept of the sun's movements is well known from ancient Egypt, where in addition it was believed that the sun travelled eastward in a large ship at night and fought the underworld dragon in order to reach the eastern horizon of the world before dawn.

Sun, wind and water (*sea, streams*) – what more durable images could be found?

8–9. The passage might be better translated as a declaration, not a question: 'All words are weariness; no man can express it. The eye is not sated with seeing, and the ear is not filled with hearing.'

nothing new: a theology in sharp contrast with prophetic expectations ('a new thing', Jer. 31: 22; 'a new covenant', Jer. 31: 31) or the apocalyptic theology of revelation and the end ('new heavens and a new earth', Isa. 65: 17); this thinking is burdened with the despair of old emptiness and ancient disillusions. It represents that in human experience which recognizes that history 'repeats itself', and that the present and the future are tied to the past and conditioned – some would say determined and delimited – by it.

11. The text does not specify *men of old*, but speaks of 'former things' or 'old things'. A noteworthy conclusion is that for the viewpoint in which nothing (should we add, 'no one'?) is new, where there are no fresh dreams and fresh values, the old is also forgotten. *

GREAT DISAPPOINTMENTS

12 I, the Speaker, ruled as king over Israel in Jerusalem;
13 and in wisdom I applied my mind to study and explore all that is done under heaven. It is a sorry business that
14 God has given men to busy themselves with. I have seen

all the deeds that are done here under the sun; they are all
emptiness and chasing the wind. What is crooked cannot 15
become straight; what is not there cannot be counted. I 16
said to myself, 'I have amassed great wisdom, more than
all my predecessors on the throne in Jerusalem; I have
become familiar with wisdom and knowledge.' So I 17
applied my mind to understand wisdom and knowledge,
madness and folly, and I came to see that this too is
chasing the wind. For in much wisdom is much vexation, 18
and the more a man knows, the more he has to suffer.

I said to myself, 'Come, I will plunge into pleasures and 2
enjoy myself'; but this too was emptiness. Of laughter I 2
said, 'It is madness!' And of pleasure, 'What is the good
of that?' So I sought to stimulate myself with wine, in the 3
hope of finding out what was good for men to do under
heaven throughout the brief span of their lives. But my
mind was guided by wisdom, not blinded by*a* folly.

I undertook great works; I built myself houses and 4
planted vineyards; I made myself gardens and parks and 5
planted all kinds of fruit-trees in them; I made myself 6
pools of water to irrigate a grove of growing trees; I 7
bought slaves, male and female, and I had my home-born
slaves as well; I had possessions, more cattle and flocks
than any of my predecessors in Jerusalem; I amassed silver 8
and gold also, the treasure of kings and provinces; I
acquired singers, men and women, and all that man
delights in.*b* I was great, greater than all my predecessors 9
in Jerusalem; and my wisdom stood me in good stead.
Whatever my eyes coveted, I refused them nothing, nor 10

[a] not blinded by: *prob. rdg.; Heb.* to grasp.
[b] *Prob. rdg.; Heb. adds two unintelligible words.*

did I deny myself any pleasure. Yes indeed, I got pleasure from all my labour, and for all my labour this was my
11 reward. Then I turned and reviewed all my handiwork, all my labour and toil, and I saw that everything was emptiness and chasing the wind, of no profit under the sun.

* The argument proceeds to express the author's great disillusion with wisdom and with pleasure. Recalling the things for which Solomon was most famous, the author contemplates the value of formidable human achievement in knowledge and of massive acquisitions of pleasurable objects and experiences. He concludes that all this is emptiness, a 'chasing the wind', a wasting of time and an aimlessness of life.

It is most noteworthy that at the outset Koheleth, a wisdom thinker and writer, boldly and bluntly dismisses wisdom and the accumulation of knowledge as a solution for his problem; enduring value and adequate meaning for life are not to be found in the pursuit of wisdom, where one might expect him to find comfort and the necessary satisfaction for his own life (cp. later, 8: 6–8).

12. With reference to himself, Koheleth repeats the information in 1: 1, leaving the reader to conclude that he wished to identify his work with the name of Solomon.

13. *under heaven:* the meaning is that of the phrase used more often in Ecclesiastes, 'under the sun' (cp. 1: 3); many manuscripts and versions in fact read 'sun' and not 'heaven'. The word for *business* is found only in Ecclesiastes, and means 'task' or 'travail'; *sorry* might also be translated as 'evil' or 'unfortunate'.

14. *emptiness and chasing the wind:* this phrase of two terms is repeated frequently, in the style of a refrain, although only in the first half of the book. *chasing* might be also translated as 'striving' or 'seeking'; related to another Hebrew verb root, it was often interpreted as meaning 'to feed on, to graze upon' (cp. Hos. 12: 1 footnote, Ephraim 'feeds on wind').

15. These little adages may have been well-known proverbs in Koheleth's day.

17. True to the ideals of the wise man in Israel, he sought to know both good and bad, both *wisdom* and *folly*. But other wise men have also not discovered in their knowledge and understanding the key to fulfilled living.

18. The practical test uses discomfort and pain as indices. The reader might already ask whether the test is adequate, and whether Koheleth is not too narrowly seeking answers that come from a comfortable life of pleasure and contented ease.

2: 1. The answer to the question suggested by the previous verse is immediately given by Koheleth; he has tried *pleasures* (or, 'joy') and enjoyment (literally, 'seeing good'), and is equally unsatisfied with what they provide.

3. *brief span:* more literally, 'a numbered span', indicating the limit which is placed on human life. *not blinded by:* the Hebrew text rather suggests an effort to grasp or to lay hold upon folly, by means of wine, in order to learn whether joy in life is to be found in this way. The author takes pains to make it clear that his attempt *was guided by wisdom,* and that he did not turn to wine in despair or out of foolishness.

4–8. Acquisition of the things traditionally associated with royal luxury was the next step in the search for satisfying enjoyment. In verse 8 the word *delights* means 'exquisite, or dainty, delight'. In the Hebrew of the verse two words are added; they are not found anywhere else and their meaning is uncertain, although scholars have suggested that they mean 'concubines' or 'harem beauties'. We might render the phrase as 'girls, and yet more girls'.

9. All this was undertaken consciously, with the application of wisdom and not in foolish libertarianism or as a slave to sensual lust. The author stresses here, as in verse 3, that he honestly tried, out of the sober and defensible motivation of his *wisdom,* to find satisfaction in pleasure. In other words, the reason why pleasure failed him was not that he undertook the

investigation as a fool might; literally, 'also my wisdom remained with me'.

11. The end of pleasure-seeking was also *emptiness*; nothing in it was of enduring value, sufficient to give meaning to life. ✳

WHAT IS THE USE OF WISDOM?

12 I set myself to look at wisdom and at madness and
13 folly.*ᵃ* Then I perceived that wisdom is more profitable
14 than folly, as light is more profitable than darkness: the wise man has eyes in his head, but the fool walks in the dark. Yet I saw also that one and the same fate overtakes
15 them both. So I said to myself, 'I too shall suffer the fate of the fool. To what purpose have I been wise? What*ᵇ* is the profit of it? Even this', I said to myself, 'is empti-
16 ness. The wise man is remembered no longer than the fool, for, as the passing days multiply,*ᶜ* all will be for-
17 gotten. Alas, wise man and fool die the same death!' So I came to hate life, since everything that was done here under the sun was a trouble to me; for all is emptiness
18 and chasing the wind. So I came to hate all my labour and toil here under the sun, since I should have to leave its fruits to my successor. What sort of a man will he be who succeeds me, who inherits what others have acquired?*ᵈ*
19 Who knows whether he will be a wise man or a fool? Yet he will be master of all the fruits of my labour and skill here under the sun. This too is emptiness.
20   Then I turned and gave myself up to despair, reflecting
21 upon all my labour and toil here under the sun. For

[a] *The rest of verse 12 transposed to follow verse 18.*
[b] *Prob. rdg.; Heb.* Then.
[c] for…multiply: *prob. rdg.; Heb.* because already.
[d] What sort…acquired: *see note on verse 12.*

anyone who toils with wisdom, knowledge, and skill must leave it all to a man who has spent no labour on it. This too is emptiness and utterly wrong. What reward 22 has a man for all his labour, his scheming, and his toil here under the sun? All his life long his business is pain and 23 vexation to him; even at night his mind knows no rest. This too is emptiness. There is nothing better for a man 24 to do than*a* to eat and drink and enjoy himself in return for his labours. And yet I saw that this comes from the hand of God. For without him who can enjoy his food, 25 or who can be anxious? God gives wisdom and know- 26 ledge and joy to the man who pleases him, while to the sinner is given the trouble of gathering and amassing wealth only to hand it over to someone else who pleases God. This too is emptiness and chasing the wind.

* If the collection of wisdom (1: 12–18) and pleasurable objects and experiences (2: 1–11) are emptiness, even when guided by wisdom, then what is the value of wisdom itself? Koheleth, the wise man, presses on in his train of thought to inquire whether wisdom is of any use at all, or whether it is just as well to be a fool as to be wise.

12. *I set myself:* this verse begins with exactly the same words as verse 11; 'Then I addressed myself to' would be a more precise translation.

The second half of the verse is transposed by the N.E.B. to the end of verse 18, because that verse treats the subject of the one who 'comes after', that is, a successor. The clause has always been difficult for interpreters; literally, it reads, 'What (of) the man who comes after the king? that which already they have done?', or some such translation, and it fits neither its traditional place nor the preceding verse where some

[*a*] than: *so some Sept. MSS.; Heb. om.*

scholars have also tried to attach it. The meaning of these words remains uncertain.

13. All the accumulated insight of the ages had taught the ancient wise men that some things were better than others, for example, that wisdom was preferable to folly. Again literally, the text says, 'Then I saw that there is more "gain/*yithron*" (cp. 1: 3) in wisdom than in folly, as there is more in light than in darkness.' This fact is all too obvious; the evidence of the world of nature makes it clear.

14. The problem which inevitably comes to the fore when the value and meaning of life are considered is that of the end of man. In this verse Koheleth for the first time specifically mentions the issue which rests at the heart of his despondency: the wise man and the fool meet the same fate, namely, they both must die. *fate:* the word is seldom used outside Ecclesiastes (cp. Ruth 2: 3); it suggests that which meets man by accident or chance, and lacks the independent and predestined quality of 'fate' in Greek philosophy as well as in our popular thinking.

15. Koheleth uses a particularly forceful way of speaking, a characteristic in the book but especially found in this chapter, here and in each preceding verse from verse 11, in saying 'Then I said, even I, in my heart' (N.E.B. *So I said to myself*).

16. It would be rewarding and reassuring if the final end of the wise man were visibly different from that of the fool. But death comes alike to both, and nullifies the wise man's aspiration to excel at the last moment of life; for both wise and foolish are forgotten.

17–18. Under the final verdict of death and oblivion, one's deeds lose importance (verse 17; cp. *trouble*, translated as 'sorry' in 1: 13). Even what one gathers and accomplishes must be left to a *successor* (literally, 'him who comes after me'; cp. on verse 12).

19. The reader may regret that Koheleth seems to take no pleasure or satisfaction in succeeding generations, as seems to be the case generally in ancient Israel. Perhaps he had no

children, and therefore his own name would be extinguished with him. But also, he realizes that wisdom cannot be automatically handed down from generation to generation. The presence of death in human existence cancels the certain hope of transmitting wisdom and establishing constant human progress; one generation's wisdom may be destroyed by the folly of the next one.

20–1. Death creates a situation in mankind's affairs which causes gross unfairness, and brings *despair* to the fair-minded person.

24. For the first time in the book, Koheleth brings out the answer which he has found, which he repeats from time to time and with little variation. The elements in this answer are discussed under 5: 18–20 and 9: 7–10. We must however observe here that he introduces a new note in his reflections: *this comes from the hand of God.* Up to this point he has occupied himself with the problems of acquiring and retaining and suffering loss; but simple daily enjoyment comes from God's hand, and the secret to fulfilment is in accepting, instead of in getting, worrying about, and clinging to, things.

26. *God gives:* wisdom, knowledge and joy alike are not gained, but rather given. The argument in this verse seems to contradict what Koheleth has been saying in verses 18–21; the reader must ask about the new criterion of pleasing God, which has not appeared earlier, and about a process of rewarding such persons which Koheleth nowhere else appears to appreciate or mention. Some scholars accordingly have decided that this verse is an editorial insertion; but it may also be taken as the author's employment of popular theology which stressed God's fairness and distributive justice to those he loves, a theology which always seems so appealing but which Koheleth like other Old Testament authors found to be flatly refuted by the facts of life.

So Koheleth dismisses this cheerful hope of reward by reciting his refrain, without argument here: *This too is emptiness and chasing the wind.* ✳

THERE IS A TIME FOR EVERYTHING, BUT FOR
MANKIND NO COMPREHENSION OF GOD'S WORK

3 For everything its season, and for every activity under heaven its time:

2   a time to be born and a time to die;
    a time to plant and a time to uproot;

3   a time to kill and a time to heal;
    a time to pull down and a time to build up;

4   a time to weep and a time to laugh;
    a time for mourning and a time for dancing;

5   a time to scatter stones and a time to gather them;
    a time to embrace and a time to refrain from
      embracing;

6   a time to seek and a time to lose;
    a time to keep and a time to throw away;

7   a time to tear and a time to mend;
    a time for silence and a time for speech;

8   a time to love and a time to hate;
    a time for war and a time for peace.

9   What profit does one who works get from all his
10 labour? I have seen the business that God has given men
11 to keep them busy. He has made everything to suit its time; moreover he has given men a sense of time past and future, but no comprehension of God's work from beginning to end.

✻ Just as the author began his book by regarding the vastness of the circular movement in nature, and the enormous sameness in great natural forces, so here he turns to the infinite variety of occasions and moments in life, in the presence of which man must contemplate the meaning of his life and the significance of events in it. Reference is made again in 8: 5–6 to knowing times and ways of dealing with events.

The passage may have been built around a separate poem about the 'times'; whether Koheleth wrote the poem cannot be determined, but it appears not to have been written at the same moment that its context was composed.

1. *activity:* in 8: 6 the term is translated as 'enterprise'. The word *time* bears the implication of 'occasion', or 'event', or 'time when...'.

9. The poem is abruptly terminated by Koheleth's question: *What profit* (or 'gain/*yithron*'; cp. 1: 3) is there for one's hard work?

10–11. Inclusion of the poem in verses 2–8 might seem to be pointless because of what immediately follows in verses 9–10, but verse 11 clarifies the observation in verse 10 and explains what the author sees in the poem. *to suit* is traditionally translated as 'beautiful', but the N.E.B. has caught the point: everything 'fits', or is 'right' for its own occasion, man is able to observe. Also, man has been given *a sense of time past and future*, that is, a vision of the wholeness of time and an instinct to wonder about the meaning of life in its totality. In other words God has invested man with tantalizing powers of insight, and has implanted the questions which lead to that which is ultimate.

but no comprehension....: literally, 'except that man does not find out the work which God has done from beginning to end'. This thought pierces to the centre of the frustrations of wise men in all ages, expressing the glory and the mystery of being a man. Although he can contemplate not only himself, but also the very beginning and end of God's work, he is unable to unlock its secrets. Given the shadow of the Ultimate and empowered to ask about it, he cannot get the answer. ✳

THERE IS AN ANSWER FOR MAN

12 I know that there is nothing good for man*a* except to be happy and live the best life he can while he
13 is alive. Moreover, that a man should eat and drink and enjoy himself, in return for all his labours, is a
14 gift of God. I know that whatever God does lasts for ever; to add to it or subtract from it is impossible. And he has done it all in such a way that men must feel awe in his
15 presence. Whatever is has been already,*b* and whatever is to come has been already, and God summons each event
16 back in its turn. Moreover I saw here under the sun that, where justice ought to be, there was wickedness, and where righteousness ought to be, there was wickedness.
17 I said to myself, 'God will judge the just man and the wicked equally; every activity and*c* every purpose has its
18 proper time.' I said to myself, 'In dealing with men it is God's purpose*d* to test them and to see what they truly
19 are.*e* For man is a creature of chance and the beasts are creatures of chance, and one mischance awaits them all: death comes to both alike. They all draw the same breath. Men have no advantage over beasts; for everything is
20 emptiness. All go to the same place: all came from the
21 dust, and to the dust all return. Who knows whether the spirit*f* of man goes upward or whether the spirit*f* of the
22 beast goes downward to the earth?' So I saw that there is

[a] for man: *prob. rdg., cp. 2: 24; Heb.* in them.
[b] *Or* Whatever has been already is.
[c] *Prob. rdg.; Heb.* and upon.
[d] it is God's purpose: *prob. rdg.; Heb. obscure.*
[e] *Prob. rdg.; Heb. adds* they to them.
[f] *Or* breath.

nothing better than that a man should enjoy his work, since that is his lot. For who can bring him through to see what will happen next?

✻ Kept from penetrating the counsels of the Almighty, mankind can still find satisfaction. Repeating ideas from 2: 24, Koheleth discovers much to say about a positive attitude towards life. However, the positive statements are qualified by several factors which he resolutely and persistently calls to mind: the irresistible cycle in events (3: 15), wickedness (3: 16), the death which annuls bright hopes of vindication and advantage (3: 19), and man's limited understanding (3: 22).

12–13. All the elements set forth in 2: 24 are reiterated here. For further discussion, see 5: 18–20 and 9: 7–10.

14. The word *for ever* here is the same as in verse 11, translated there as 'time past and future'. God's work, like nature's ponderous cycles and life's fine variety, dwarfs man; it endures *for ever*, whereas man has only the thought of 'for ever' implanted in his mind (verse 11).

feel awe: Koheleth's point of view may be compared with that of one of the psalmists. The Hebrew word here translated as *feel awe* is given as 'revered' in Ps. 130; here one feels awe because of God's eternal and unchangeable works, there we read, 'But in thee is forgiveness, and therefore thou art revered' (Ps. 130: 4).

15. Reference is made to the point of 1: 4–7; there is nothing new or different. *and God summons each event back in its turn:* this passage is difficult to interpret; it can be translated, 'and God seeks (or, requires) that which has been pursued', and expounded to mean that God causes to return to him everything that his creatures have sought for themselves.

16. Injustice and *wickedness* intrude where *justice* and *righteousness* should be; this disturbs Koheleth and threatens his confidence in God's work.

17. *judge...equally:* better translated, 'judge between'. The

author's certainty of God's judgement and its equity is later in the book revealed to be deeply shaken and a source of little solace to him.

18. *what they truly are:* the Hebrew text of the whole verse is difficult, and has provoked varying attempts to solve its meaning; most scholars agree that these words must say something like 'to show them that they are beasts'. The argument thus both disparages the importance or superiority of man and leads directly to the next point to be raised.

19. Better translated, 'for the fate (cp. 2: 14) of mankind and the fate of the beasts is the same fate, for the death of one is like the death of the other. They all draw the same breath; man has no advantage [or gain, cp. 1: 3; the form of the Hebrew word here is not *yithron*, but is related to it] over the beasts.' Death, the great leveller of God's creatures, shatters man's hope of lasting distinction. He who alone in nature has visions of immortality and eternity must die like the beasts, and at the last has no gain over them.

20. The author anticipates his conclusion in 12: 7 in saying that man goes to the dust at death. The creation story in Gen. 2: 7 may be in mind, or the curse after the fall of man in Gen. 3: 19 ('Dust you are, to dust you shall return'). It is noteworthy that in the old Babylonian concept of the place of the dead all was dark and dusty.

21. *upward* and *downward* are not signs of a world-view which imagined that man's eternal home in heaven is above the ground; in the ancient Hebrew concept the soul, or we might say 'personality', of a person went to Sheol after death. Sheol (cp. 9: 10) was the city of the dead, located beneath the earth, where all dead men resided. The soul, or personality (in Hebrew *nephesh*), died; it was the *spirit* (Hebrew, *ruaḥ*, the word also for 'breath' and for 'wind') which did not die. Perhaps the common Hebrew view in that day was that man's spirit left to remain with God at the time of death (so also in 12: 7), although here Koheleth appears ready even to doubt that.

22. Once more, as in 3: 12–13 and 2: 24, the answer to the question of meaning in life for man is found in the simple satisfaction of accomplishing the work which is given to man to do. *lot* is an important concept, and is discussed under 5: 18–20. The verse closes with the dilemma that challenges human happiness and a satisfying domination of life and fate: we do not know *what will happen next*! *

ACHIEVEMENT IS EMPTY

* Doomed to repeat the past and faced with an unknowable future, man is thus trapped between absurdity and uncertainty. In that situation death rings the final knell upon the disappearance of human claims to control of life and destiny.

Koheleth, with some aimlessness of argument and digression into the quotation of popular literature or tradition – literary features which are encountered more frequently as the book goes on – has managed to pack the principal points of his argument into the first three chapters of Ecclesiastes. His complaints are that life is empty and without enduring gain or value, that human experience is burdened with ignorance and uncertainty, and that death renders absurd all human expectations of enduring satisfaction. On the other hand, he finds that in which he can be content with his life and lot, and in which he can be sure of some meaning for his life, even if that does not mean that he can dream grand designs of assured permanency.

Even the qualified or limited character of this solution for fulfilment in his life is made plain early in the book, although it is more clearly asserted at the end.

What follows in chs. 4–6 is a recapitulation of the major topics already dealt with in the book, except that in this section of material more attention is given to the emptiness of the life of him who has achieved. The typical digressions are present here also, and there is no smooth or logical development of thought. *

117

EXAMPLES OF EMPTINESS

4 Again, I considered all the acts of oppression here under
the sun; I saw the tears of the oppressed, and I saw that
there was no one to comfort them. Strength was on the
side of their oppressors, and there was no one to avenge
2 them. I counted the dead happy because they were dead,
3 happier than the living who are still in life. More fortunate than either I reckoned[a] the man yet unborn, who
had not witnessed the wicked deeds done here under the
4 sun. I considered all toil and all achievement and saw that
it comes from rivalry between man and man. This too is
5. emptiness and chasing the wind. The fool folds his arms
6 and wastes away. Better one hand full and peace of mind,
than both fists full and toil that is chasing the wind.

7, 8   Here again, I saw emptiness under the sun: a lonely
man without a friend, without son or brother, toiling
endlessly yet never satisfied with his wealth – 'For whom',
he asks, 'am I toiling and denying myself the good things
9 of life?' This too is emptiness, a sorry business. Two are
better than one; they receive a good reward for their toil,
10 because, if one falls, the other[b] can help his companion up
again; but alas for the man who falls alone with no
11 partner to help him up. And, if two lie side by side, they
keep each other warm; but how can one keep warm by
12 himself? If a man is alone, an assailant may overpower
him, but two can resist; and a cord of three strands is not
quickly snapped.

13   Better a young man poor and wise than a king old and

[a] I reckoned: *so Vulg.; Heb. om.*
[b] if one falls, the other: *prob. rdg.; Heb. obscure.*

foolish who will listen to advice no longer. A man who 14
leaves prison may well come to be king, though born a
pauper in his future kingdom. But I have studied all life 15
here under the sun, and I saw his place taken by yet
another young man, and no limit set to the number of the 16
subjects whose master he became. And he in turn will be
no hero to those who come after him. This too is emptiness and chasing the wind.

✻ In this section Koheleth draws together some miscellaneous
and very different examples of emptiness. The arguments are
loosely put, with little logical coherency, and in a somewhat
rambling manner.

1. The author has a habit of beginning a new thought or
section with a phrase like 'Then I turned' (2: 11) (in 2: 20 a
different word, translated the same way). Here, behind the
words *Again, I considered* is an important phrase, 'Then I
returned and I saw', which is repeated exactly in 4: 7 and
approximately in 9: 11. The phrase marks a definite shift in
the book; after presenting the fundamental issues and solution,
the author turns back to re-examine the subject again.

What might have been construed as a desire to keep neatly
the distinctions between justice and wickedness in 3: 16–17
appears now to be genuine social consciousness. But Koheleth's
is not the prophetic task; he has rather embarked on the mis-
sion to seek meaning and lasting substance of value in life, and
for him the presence of social problems must also constitute
a threat to the hope of finding his answer. The tables of justice
seem to be tilted in favour of the oppressors, and experience
affords no easy solutions and certain correction. *comfort* and
avenge are different translations for the same Hebrew word.

2–3. Koheleth's despair sinks ever deeper as he comes to
regret life and to count non-existence as preferable to existence. Such thinking is utterly new in the literature of ancient
Israel, and foreign to the rest of the Old Testament.

4. Even human aspiration and endeavour is disparaged as originating from *rivalry*, or envy, of one's neighbour.

5–6. Two common proverbs, or aphorisms perhaps invented by Koheleth, argue the emptiness of human achievement and ambition. *wastes away:* literally, 'eats his own flesh'. What the first proverb contributes to the argument is not clear; perhaps it is a statement uttered simply to be refuted by the next statement in verse 6.

7–12. Another effort to portray emptiness is launched in pointing to the loneliness of the solitary man who gains wealth but who must then ask, 'for whom am I working?', and to the vulnerability or weakness of the person who is all alone. The potential good in social or collective strength, in the co-operation of human beings, which Koheleth as a wise man cannot disregard or ignore, is nevertheless not applied to the problem and it would seem affords no solution to the fundamental emptiness.

13–16. In a rambling, loosely-constructed collection of expressions, the author comments upon the emptiness which is experienced in very high positions. Scholars have futilely sought to identify some historical situation behind these words. Koheleth seems to be concentrating on the hopes which arise when youth challenges old age for dominion; while the *young man* may be better than the old, and even the ex-convict might become king, another young man will eventually come along and replace the former, and so on it goes with no one caring about those who were replaced and are gone. *

ADVICE AMID EMPTINESS

5 1*a* Go carefully when you visit the house of God. Better draw near in obedience than offer the sacrifice of fools,
2*b* who sin without a thought. Do not rush into speech, let there be no hasty utterance in God's presence. God is in

[a] *4: 17 in Heb.* [b] *5: 1 in Heb.*

heaven, you are on earth; so let your words be few. The 3
sensible man has much business on his hands; the fool
talks and it is so much chatter. When you make a vow to 4
God, do not be slow to pay it, for he has no use for fools;
pay whatever you vow. Better not vow at all than vow 5
and fail to pay. Do not let your tongue lead you into sin, 6
and then say before the angel of God that it was a mistake; or God will be angry at your words, and all your
achievements will be brought to nothing.*[a]* You must fear 7
God.

If you witness in some province the oppression of the 8
poor and the denial of right and justice, do not be surprised at what goes on, for every official has a higher one
set over him, and the highest*[b]* keeps watch over them all.
The best thing for a country is a king whose*[c]* own lands 9
are well tilled.

*⁎ Beginning with this section the book makes fewer refer-
ences to emptiness, the arguments become more extended, and
the author introduces large collections of proverbs into his
material.*

*There are two parts in this small section, the first treating
the need for sober deliberation before a person speaks and the
heavy responsibility that one has in making vows, the second
dealing with the problem of the administration of justice.
Neither part adds anything to the argument of the book;
perhaps it was simply written in here as another of Koheleth's
ruminations. This is the only passage in the book that has
anything at all to do with worship.*

[a] *Prob. rdg.; Heb. adds* for in a multitude of dreams and empty things
and many words.
[b] for every. . .the highest: *or* though every. . .over him, the Highest. . .
[c] whose: *prob. rdg.; Heb.* for.

1. *obedience:* the concept is, 'to hearken to, to listen obediently'. *who sin without a thought:* literally, 'for they do not know how to do evil', or 'that they are doing evil', or 'so that they do evil'.

2. *God is in heaven, you are on earth:* a passage which someone has called the keynote of Ecclesiastes. The good advice to speak guardedly and little, like advice to be silent, is however broken by the one who gives it, for Koheleth himself is speaking much.

3. *The sensible man has much business on his hands:* a phrase usually translated like 'for a dream comes with much trouble' (cp. 2: 26), or 'much business' (cp. 4: 8).

4–5. Making vows is a particularly tempting occasion for saying too much. Koheleth's advice is very similar to Deut. 23: 22–3, and brings to mind the hasty vow of Jephthah (Judg. 11: 31, 34).

6. *angel:* this word has been interpreted in another of its meanings, namely, 'messenger' of the temple who was dispatched to collect the vow after it had been publicly made.

The words in the N.E.B. footnote, together with verse 7 in the N.E.B., in the Hebrew can mean, 'for in spite of many dreams, and emptiness, and many words, verily, fear God!'

8–9. Corruption in judicial and administrative systems is observed, but accepted as normal because of a hierarchical pattern in the placing over some persons of others who themselves are presumably corrupt. The *best thing* (or 'gain/*yithron*'; cp. 1: 3) is a ruler who is himself careful and capable. ✳

GOOD ADVICE FOR THE LOVER OF WEALTH

10 The man who loves money can never have enough, and the man who is in love with great wealth enjoys no
11 return from it. This too is emptiness. When riches multiply, so do those who live off them; and what advan-
12 tage has the owner, except to look at them? Sweet is the

sleep of the labourer whether he eats little or much; but the rich man owns too much and cannot sleep. There is a 13 singular evil here under the sun which I have seen: a man hoards wealth to his own hurt, and then that wealth is 14 lost through an unlucky venture, and the owner's son left with nothing. As he came from the womb of mother 15 earth, so must he return, naked as he came; all his toil produces nothing which he can take away with him. This 16 too is a singular evil: exactly as he came, so shall he go, and what profit does he get when his labour is all for the wind? What is more, all his days are overshadowed; 17 gnawing anxiety*a* and great vexation are his lot, sickness*b* and resentment. What I have seen is this: that it is good 18 and proper for a man to eat and drink and enjoy himself in return for his labours here under the sun, throughout the brief span of life which God has allotted him. More- 19 over, it is a gift of God that every man to whom he has granted wealth and riches and the power to enjoy them should accept his lot and rejoice in his labour. He will not 20 dwell overmuch upon the passing years; for God fills his*c* time with joy of heart.

✳ After digressing from his primary concern, Koheleth returns in this section to the central issue of the book: the emptiness of an acquisitive life, of getting and conniving to keep for ever, can be filled by simple and honest enjoyment of the things which God has given, in the spirit of receiving and not of claiming and acquiring.

10. The emptiness of possessing and loving wealth is

[a] gnawing anxiety: *so Sept.; Heb.* he eats.
[b] sickness: *prob. rdg.; Heb.* and his sickness.
[c] his: *prob. rdg.; Heb. om.*

summarized in this one sentence: there is neither satisfaction nor permanent claim to it.

11–12. Koheleth etches out a caricature of the person obsessed with getting things and increasing property. Whether this portrait describes every wealthy person is not the point. He is intent upon painting a picture which reveals the hollowness, anxiety, and final emptiness of such a life.

13–14. *singular:* the word connotes 'sickliness' or 'painfulness'. Not only can it happen that the wealthy man damages his own life and character by dedicating himself to accumulating possessions, but it also happens that the estate is lost through misfortune, and the whole enterprise is thus undone.

15–16. So in this way the uncertainty and unpredictability of wealth is represented; man cannot control his life or his future with it, and cannot guarantee fulfilment or satisfaction. There is then no *profit* ('gain/*yithron*'; cp. 1: 3) from all his effort.

17. *all his days...anxiety:* the Hebrew can be rendered, 'also during all his days he eats in darkness'.

18–20. Once again Koheleth speaks of what is or can be good for man who has no hope of permanent and inevitable 'gain/*yithron*' in life. Elaborating on the elements mentioned before in 2: 24; 3: 12–13, and 3: 22, these verses declare more fully than ever the essential affirmation of the author and contain his basic and characteristic terminology.

18. *good* and *proper* are significant adjectives which are used to express Koheleth's standards; they are modest words, suitable for one who can evaluate firmly but also who can be content with simple things.

eat, drink, enjoy himself in all his works: an uncomplicated way to react to life's experiences, focusing on the essentials necessary to sustain life and accepting as sufficient the enjoyment of whatever one is given to do. When a person can resign himself to such 'good and proper' satisfaction, the limits imposed by the *brief span of life* are also more tolerable for they too are understood to be what *God has allotted* (given).

Since one cannot usefully quarrel with God, it is better to receive quietly and enjoy what is given. Ecclesiastes propounds the point of view that striving and getting is an empty way of life, and contradicts the facts and experiences of human existence; this point of view has been often compared with that of the Stoic philosophers in the Greek culture of that day. Ecclesiastes also adopts a modest stance towards life's pleasures, similar to the so-called 'higher' Epicureanism of the day which decried excesses and extravagances of any kind and which instead advocated a simple life of refined and moderate tastes. So the motto of *eat and drink and enjoy himself* was not meant by Koheleth to be a licence for sensual gluttony and abandonment of rational and spiritual restraints; it was rather a Spartan philosophy of resignation to the limits and boundaries of life which are imposed by God, and an openness to what God offers through life.

allotted: in Hebrew the verse closes with 'for this is his (i.e. man's) lot'. The word for 'lot' is important in gaining insight into Koheleth's thinking; it means in general 'an apportionment, a share', and can designate that portion of the booty of war, for example, which falls to one of the victorious warriors. It signifies that to which one has a claim by chance or by some other process of division over which one does not exercise control. It is therefore a good word to describe that which an individual receives in his life-time, from the standpoint of Koheleth; 'portion' is translated in the N.E.B. in Lam. 3: 24 as 'all that I have', in Ps. 73: 26 as 'possession', and as 'holding' in passages related to the distribution of land to the twelve tribes of Israel in the conquest of Canaan. One's 'lot' is one's portion in life, that which a merciful Creator has destined for one and one's share. The word is important in Koheleth's statements in 3: 22 and 9: 9.

19. Even the ability to accept what God offers to each of us as our *lot*, as well as *wealth and riches and the power to enjoy them*, is *a gift of God*. Koheleth's is a total concept of grace, in which nothing that man does endures or makes his life worth while,

and in which what is the 'good and proper' for man is entirely God's gift, even to the extent of recognizing and enjoying the gifts which he confers.

20. Like verse 18 this passage declares that brevity of life-span and swiftness of passing years need not preoccupy a person if he will only concentrate on that with which God endows him. ✳

THE EMPTINESS OF WEALTH

6 Here is an evil under the sun which I have seen, and it
2 weighs heavy upon men. Consider the man to whom God grants wealth, riches, and substance,*a* and who lacks nothing that he has set his heart on: if God has not given him the power to enjoy these things, but a stranger enjoys
3 them instead, that is emptiness and a grave disorder. A man may have a hundred children and live a long life; but however many his days may be, if he does not get satisfaction from the good things of life and in the end receives no burial, then I maintain that the still-born child
4 is in better case than he. Its coming is an empty thing, it departs into darkness, and in darkness its name is hidden;
5 it has never seen the sun or known anything,*b* yet its state
6 is better than his. What if a man should live a thousand years twice over, and never prosper? Do not both go to one place?

7 The end of all man's toil is but to fill his belly,*c* yet his
8 appetite is never satisfied. What advantage then in facing life has the wise man over the fool, or the poor man for
9 all his experience? It is better to be satisfied with what is before your eyes than give rein to desire; this too is
10 emptiness and chasing the wind. Whatever has already

[a] *Or* honour.   [b] *Or* it.   [c] *Lit.* mouth.

existed has been given a name, its nature is known; a man
cannot contend with what is stronger than he. The more 11
words one uses the greater is the emptiness of it all; and
where is the advantage to a man? For who can know 12
what is good for a man in this life, this brief span of empty
existence through which he passes like a shadow? Who
can tell a man what is to happen next here under the sun?

✶ Next Koheleth goes back to portraying the empty quality
of the person who has accumulated great substance. The passage ends with a rehearsal of the fact that man, entrenched
around with signs of emptiness and disorder, must also suffer
ignorance of his future or even of what is good for him.

2. Yet another claim of emptiness is established on the
grounds that the things that a man acquires may on occasion
not be enjoyed by him. This has already been a steady concern
and emphasis (cp. 2: 18–19; 5: 11, and 5: 13–14) and continues
to be through the book.

3. *children* and *long life* were among the traditional blessings
with which Israel believed God benefited man. Koheleth
sharply demonstrates that these gifts, in his view, are in-
significant if a man suffers the loss of enjoying the good which
he has, and also an ignominious death with no burial. The
prospect of death undermines all the orthodox and traditional
blessings which man might seize in order to establish some
proof of predictable and reliable reward in life.

4–5. The unborn child, so unconscious, so dark its world
and its existence, so ignorant and unaware, is better off.

6. *both*: Hebrew, 'all'. The unborn child and a man who
lives impossibly long (more than twice the age of Noah or
Methuselah, Gen. 9: 29; 5: 27) experience the same death;
therefore, Koheleth is saying, what does one 'gain' over the
other?

7. Greed and acquisitiveness have no end and no satisfaction; on the contrary, it is they which finally consume.

10. What the author says here was already set forth in 1: 4–7, that is, that there is nothing new under the sun, and that, translating more literally, mankind cannot act as judge of that which overwhelmingly surpasses him in scope and destiny.

11. *The more words one uses...:* This small phrase stands to mock Koheleth and all like him who with words try to wrestle the Infinite. Yet it is man's nature to use words in grappling with the mysteries of existence. ✳

Wisdom and folly compared

PROVERBS: SOME THINGS ARE BETTER THAN OTHERS

7 A GOOD NAME SMELLS SWEETER than the finest ointment, and the day of death is better than the day of
2 birth. Better to visit the house of mourning than the house
of feasting; for to be mourned is the lot of every man, and
3 the living should take this to heart. Grief is better than
4 laughter: a sad face may go with a cheerful heart. Wise
men's thoughts are at home in the house of mourning, but
5 a fool's thoughts in the house of mirth. It is better to listen
6 to a wise man's rebuke than to the praise of fools. For the
laughter of a fool is like the crackling of thorns under a
7 pot. This too is emptiness. Slander drives a wise man crazy
8 and breaks a strong man's[a] spirit. Better the end of anything than its beginning; better patience than pride.
9 Do not be quick to show resentment; for resentment is
10 nursed by fools. Do not ask why the old days were better
11 than these; for that is a foolish question. Wisdom is better
than possessions and an advantage to all who see the sun.

[a] strong man's: *prob. rdg.; Heb. obscure.*

Better have wisdom behind you than money; wisdom 12
profits men by giving life to those who knew her.

* In a series of proverbs, some doubtless taken from the rich
folklore of his day and some perhaps composed by himself,
Koheleth proceeds on an extensive digression that continues
into the eighth chapter. The proverbs in this section are however not selected haphazardly, but instead all relate to Koheleth's fundamental premise of 'Better the end of anything than
its beginning', that is, one cannot evaluate anything completely until one has seen its termination and therefore value
and meaning in the life of man must be weighed in considera-
tion of man's death.

In this first group of proverbs, wisdom is extolled and sage
advice is put in proverbs composed in a pattern beginning
with 'better is. . .than. . .'. The prominence of this type of
relative thinking shows that while Koheleth asserted the
ultimate futility and emptiness of everything, he readily con-
ceded that one could not therefore claim that everything was
valueless, or of the same little worth.

1. *A good name smells sweeter than the finest ointment:* an
extraordinarily pithy and memorable saying, playing skilfully
on words and sounds in Hebrew (*tob shem mishemen tob*), and
meaning that a good name is better than an elegant burial
with expensive anointing: or, it could be, better than a
wealthy man's life of luxury with fine toilet articles. The
second half of the verse, *the day of death is better...*, stresses the
satisfaction in a life completed, over and above the uncertainties of a life begun; but it may connote much more, as do
such excellent proverbs to perceptive and imaginative hearers,
such as the superiority of certainty to uncertainty in general,
or as a general lament over life. This idea was not new in
Israel; cp. Jer. 20: 14 and Job 3: 2.

2-4. The superiority of gravity and sobriety (and of wisdom, as well as of death) to hilarity and fun (and to folly, as well

as to life) is extolled in these proverbs. Three bases for that superiority appear: everyone must mourn sometime (verse 2), a mournful expression may be accompanied by a *cheerful heart* – or the Hebrew can mean, 'may make a heart cheerful' (verse 3) – and wisdom and sobriety go together just as do folly and mirth (verse 4).

6. *This too is emptiness:* perhaps the author refers to the laughter of a fool, or this may be an ejaculation which describes his own process of thinking of such things (as a man might mutter or muse to himself 'what's the matter with me?'). We do not know what the point is.

7. *Slander:* literally, 'oppression'. *breaks a strong man's spirit:* or, alternatively, the Hebrew text without emendation may be translated 'and a bribe breaks the spirit'. Thus 'oppression' and 'bribe' are paired together as corrupting evils.

8. *patience than pride:* the literalness of the Hebrew is colourful here, 'length of spirit' than 'height of spirit'.

10. No unreflecting antiquarian, Koheleth the pragmatic man finds no satisfaction in reminiscing over the glories of the 'good old days'.

11. N.E.B. here follows the many scholars who have suggested that *better than* be read here. The Hebrew says, 'Wisdom is good *with* an inheritance, and an advantage (or 'gain', in a form related to *yithron*; cp. 1: 3)...' Koheleth's vacillating position may cause problems of interpretation, but this is a characteristic of the book anyway; there is no need to emend the Hebrew text.

12. A more literal translation, attested also in the versions, would be, 'The protection of wisdom is like the protection of money; and the gain/*yithron* of knowledge is that wisdom gives life to those who possess it.' ✳

THE VALUE OF WISDOM IS NEVERTHELESS ILLUSORY

13 Consider God's handiwork; who can straighten what
14 he has made crooked? When things go well, be glad; but

when things go ill, consider this: God has set the one alongside the other in such a way that no one can find out what is to happen next.[a] In my empty existence I have 15 seen it all, from a righteous man perishing in his righteousness to a wicked man growing old in his wickedness. Do 16 not be over-righteous and do not be over-wise. Why make yourself a laughing-stock? Do not be over-wicked 17 and do not be a fool. Why should you die before your time? It is good to hold on to the one thing and not lose 18 hold of the other; for a man who fears God will succeed both ways. Wisdom makes the wise man stronger than 19 the ten rulers of a city. The world contains no man so 20 righteous that he can do right always and never do wrong.[b] Moreover, do not pay attention to everything 21 men say, or you may hear your servant disparage you; for you know very well how many times you yourself 22 have disparaged others. All this I have put to the test of 23 wisdom. I said, 'I am resolved to be wise', but wisdom was beyond my grasp – whatever has happened lies 24 beyond our grasp, deep down, deeper than man can fathom.

I went on to reflect, I set my mind[c] to inquire and 25 search for wisdom and for the reason in things, only to discover that it is folly to be wicked and madness to act like a fool. The wiles of a woman I find mightier[d] than 26 death; her heart is a trap to catch you and her arms are fetters. The man who is pleasing to God may escape her, but she will catch a sinner. 'See,' says the Speaker, 'this is 27

[a] find out. . .next: *or* hold him responsible.
[b] can do. . .wrong: *or* prospers without ever making a mistake.
[c] *Prob. rdg.; Heb. adds* to know and.
[d] *Or* more bitter.

28 what I have found, reasoning things out one by one, after searching long without success: I have found one man in a thousand worth the name, but I have not found one 29 woman among them all. This alone I have found, that God, when he made man, made him straightforward, but man invents endless subtleties of his own.'

8 Who is wise enough for all this? Who knows the meaning of anything? Wisdom lights up a man's face, but 2 grim looks make a man hated.*a* Do as the king commands you, and if you have to swear by God, do not be 3 precipitate. Leave the king's presence and do not persist in a thing which displeases him; he does what he chooses. 4 For the king's word carries authority. Who can question 5 what he does? Whoever obeys a command will come to no harm. A wise man knows in his heart the right time 6 and method for action. There is a time and a method for 7 every enterprise, although man is greatly troubled by ignorance of the future; who can tell him what it will 8 bring? It is not in man's power to restrain the wind,*b* and no one has power over the day of death. In war no one can lay aside his arms, no wealth will save its possessor.

* Smaller sections can be identified within this large portion of the book. The material however seems to be collected quite aimlessly, and the reader can trace no thread of argument or development of issue throughout these verses. Koheleth is repeating himself now from time to time, and we wait for something decisive to be said.

13. *who can straighten what he has made crooked?* What was said in 1: 15 is now repeated here.

[a] make...hated: *prob. rdg.; Heb. obscure.*
[b] *Or* to retain the breath of life.

14. Here the thought in 3: 11 is reiterated.

15. Previous complaints about unjust fortune (3: 16) are sharpened; like Ps. 73 the author laments the fact that it happens that righteous men die young and the wicked sometimes enjoy long life, the opposite of what one might imagine if God were pre-eminently fair.

16–17. Under these circumstances it does no good to seek one's gain (cp. 7: 11) in wisdom or righteousness, and obsessively to pursue them.

18. *will succeed both ways:* better, 'will emerge from them all', that is, 'will not be fettered by anything', or more colloquially perhaps, 'will get by'.

20. *do wrong:* a finite verb-form of a word often translated as 'sin', and bearing the sense of 'to miss the mark', 'to make a mistake'. Passages in the Old Testament which relate specifically to a doctrine of universal sin are few, and the reader may be surprised to discover one here; the cool and somewhat detached perceptions of the wise man however reach the same conclusions as the passionate thoughts of a prophet or psalmist with respect to the evidence for the fact that all men are sinful.

21–2. *disparage:* or 'curse'.

23–4. Even wisdom itself, when put under the relentless and baleful scrutiny of Koheleth's tests, proves to be elusive and unattainable. In Koheleth's world, where disappointments crowd around in all things, where nothing is controllable by man for the ensuring of his own value and achievements, not even the wisdom which reveals such insights can be perfect or fully mastered.

25. In a way by now familiar to the reader, Koheleth turns his thoughts around, or back, to familiar issues; the identical words in Hebrew (here translated *I went on to reflect*) are found in 2: 20 (there translated 'Then I turned'). *only to discover...* *madness to act like a fool:* otherwise translated, 'and to know wickedness, stupidity, foolishness, and madness'.

26–8. The disillusionment of the author with mankind is attested here. The *woman* described in verse 26 must be the kind of person described in Prov. 7: 6–27, who deliberately sets out to entice and catch the unwary youth; but the wisdom literature contains numerous references to this theme of the unwise man who is trapped by the loose woman, or to a more general warning about woman's wiles and weaknesses, to such an extent that Ecclesiasticus says, 'Woman is the origin of sin, and it is through her that we all die' (Ecclus. 25: 24). The theme is developed in the attempted seduction of Joseph by Potiphar's wife (Gen. 39: 7–20), or Samson's betrayal by Delilah (Judg. 16: 4–21).

29. *man invents endless subtleties of his own:* God should not be blamed for man's faults. And whereas Gen. 3 tells of mankind's fall through disobedience, Koheleth pictures the defection as a perversity of human reasoning and thinking.

8: 1. *but grim looks make a man hated:* better, 'and his grim look is transformed'. The last half of the verse seems to answer the first half, and call to mind at least a practical benefit to be derived from wisdom. For all of wisdom's ultimate short-comings, it does at least brighten a person's appearance.

2–4. Reference to the *king* is an interpolation of material which was popular and important in wisdom circles and tradition, and which therefore belongs in a collection of wise man's thoughts. Behaviour and etiquette in the royal court were matters of importance to the ancient wise men who themselves were functionaries there.

Verse 2 in Hebrew must be added to or subtracted from in order to make sense; the N.E.B. ignores the first word, 'I', which stands alone in the text.

5. Good advice continues, and reference to *time and method* known by the wise men probably points to the times characterized in 3: 2–8 as examples. The wise man, who studies life and experiences carefully, and who remembers the knowledge accumulated in the past, may be presumed to know better what to expect in life and how to interpret events.

6–8. The wise man's dilemma is nowhere better stated than here. Over the years it was the wise man's role to collect and to organize the communities' folklore, common sense, folk wisdom, and axioms for guiding good behaviour, just as much as to preserve elements of technical knowledge such as histories, legends, names of things, art of writing, mathematics, and other 'school subjects' from that day. But Koheleth points out that *ignorance of the future* undermines the desired effect of such activity, and makes the wise man wonder why he goes to such trouble. The vaunted and confident activity of gathering and applying learning is made trivial by the vastness of natural elements no more solid than the *wind*, and by the stern and immutable fact of *death* which terminates and dissolves all human pretensions and aspirations to conquer life's mysteries and control their meaning. ✳

THE ROOTS OF EMPTINESS

All this I have seen, having applied my mind to every- 9 thing done under the sun. There was a time when one man had power over another and could make him suffer. It was then that I saw wicked men approaching and even 10 entering*ᵃ* the holy place; and they went about the city priding themselves on*ᵇ* having done right. This too is emptiness. It is because sentence upon a wicked act is not 11 promptly carried out that men do evil so boldly. A sinner 12 may do wrong*ᶜ* and live to old age, yet I know that it will be well with those who fear God: their fear of him ensures this, but it will not be well with a wicked man nor 13 will he live long; the man who does not fear God is a mere shadow. There is an empty thing found on earth: 14 when the just man gets what is due to the unjust, and the unjust what is due to the just. I maintain that this too is

[a] approaching. . .entering: *prob. rdg.; Heb. obscure.*
[b] priding themselves on: *so many MSS.; others* forgotten for.
[c] *Prob. rdg.; Heb. adds an unintelligible word.*

15 emptiness. So I commend enjoyment, since there is nothing good for a man to do here under the sun but to eat
and drink and enjoy himself; this is all that will remain
with him to reward his toil throughout the span of life
16 which God grants him here under the sun. I applied my
mind to acquire wisdom and to observe the business
which goes on upon earth, when man never closes an eye
17 in sleep day or night; and always I perceived that God has
so ordered it that man should not be able to discover what
is happening here under the sun. However hard a man
may try, he will not find out; the wise man may think
that he knows, but he will be unable to find the truth of it.

9 I applied my mind to all this, and I understood that the
righteous and the wise and all their doings are under
God's control; but is it love or hatred? No man knows.
2 Everything that confronts him, everything is empty,[a]
since one and the same fate befalls every one, just and
unjust alike, good and bad,[b] clean and unclean, the man
who offers sacrifice and the man who does not. Good man
and sinner fare alike, the man who can take an oath and
3 the man who dares not. This is what is wrong in all that
is done here under the sun: that one and the same fate
befalls every man. The hearts of men are full of evil; madness fills their hearts all through their lives, and after that
4 they go down[c] to join the dead. But for a man who is
counted among the living there is still hope: remember,
5 a live dog is better than a dead lion. True, the living know
that they will die; but the dead know nothing. There are
no more rewards for them; they are utterly forgotten.

[a] *So Sept.; Heb.* all.   [b] and bad: *so Sept.; Heb. om.*
[c] they go down: *so Vulg.; Heb.* after him.

For them love, hate, ambition,[a] all are now over. Never 6
again will they have any part in what is done here under
the sun.

* In this portion of his book the author manages to draw
together the by-now-familiar reasons for his conclusion that
everything is emptiness. His arguments are fundamentally
these three: (1) there is a quality of unfairness in life so that
wickedness is not always appropriately punished and injustice
is often rewarded; (2) man's knowledge is limited, and in-
competent for the high goal of mastering fundamental or
ultimate questions; and (3) the fact that death levels all creatures equally makes nonsense of man's efforts, and death
abolishes all hope of 'gain/*yithron*' in life.

9–14. Koheleth spins out more fully his contention that the
problem of sin is aggravated simply because wickedness and
sinfulness are often left unpunished, and in fact may prosper.
Cp. 3: 16–17.

9. *There was a time when:* this translation misleads by sug-
gesting a particular past occasion. The text, like the passage in
ch. 3, means that there is a time, or an occasion, or a situation,
when one person dominates (the root is related to the word for
'sultan') another.

10. This verse is better translated, 'And so I saw wicked men
now buried, and, as men came and went from the holy place,
they were praised in the city where they had operated. This
too is emptiness.' The concern expressed here is very similar
to that in Ps. 73: 1–12; the wicked prosper, and even in death
their evil deeds often fail to be recognized and suitably repaid.

11. Punishment is delayed, and that encourages wrong-
doing.

12–13. Here are two verses which seem to express exactly
the opposite of what Koheleth is trying to say. There are two
explanations: either these verses were added by someone who

[a] *Or* passion.

137

wanted to assert the more standard and traditional conviction that *those who fear God* are properly rewarded, or else these verses are simply added by Koheleth to represent the old point of view which he challenges but which must also be included in his reflections in the catalogue of knowledge which he is in effect assembling in his book. The latter explanation is to be preferred. *nor will he live long; the man who does not fear God is a mere shadow:* or literally, 'his days will not stretch out like a shadow, that is, he who does not fear God'.

15. The answer which Koheleth has found is repeated once more. See 9: 7–10.

8: 16 – 9: 2. Again Koheleth turns to the argument, his second in this series, that ultimate truth is impenetrable and that man cannot attain it; this is the issue argued earlier in 3: 11. By dint of no amount of effort, even with ardent dedication and intensive struggle, can man uncover the secret of the ultimate meaning of what is happening; even when we think we know, we delude ourselves.

9: 1. *love or hatred:* the phrase refers either to *God's control*, whether benevolent or malevolent, or to man's deeds, and no doubt the former is the preferable interpretation; Koheleth understands much about human motives, but it is the mystery surrounding God's work and will for man which puts all human understanding in question.

2. *empty:* the word may have been in the original Hebrew text, was translated into Greek, and then for some cause was overlooked and left out of manuscripts.

3–6. Finally Koheleth reintroduces the argument produced already in 3: 19–21, that the same death and extinction occur to all creatures, and that death nullifies life's meaning.

4. *a live dog is better than a dead lion:* an old proverb is quoted to show that an ignominious life is better than a noble death. Death indeed destroys every plan and ends every man's personal aspiration. The verse seems to contradict the sentiment of 4: 2, where Koheleth counted the dead as more fortunate than the living. But if we are to understand Kohe-

leth we must come to terms with the force of what he says, and not pursue every possible inconsistency. In 4: 2 he is in despair of the hopes and worth of living; here he returns to lament that death makes everything absurd.

5. At least some knowledge exists with the living; but the dead possess neither reflection nor remembrance.

6. *part:* the word is translated as 'lot' in 5: 19 and is discussed under 5: 18. Nothing is left for the dead to feel, or want, or enjoy; for the living, chance provides at least something, but the dead lack even this. *

IN THIS PREDICAMENT THERE IS VALUE

Go to it then, eat your food and enjoy it, and drink your 7 wine with a cheerful heart; for already God has accepted what you have done. Always be dressed in white and 8 never fail to anoint your head. Enjoy life with a woman 9 you love all the days of your allotted span here under the sun, empty as they are;[a] for that is your lot while you live and labour here under the sun. Whatever task lies to your 10 hand, do it with all your might; because in Sheol, for which you are bound, there is neither doing nor thinking, neither understanding nor wisdom.

* Koheleth sets down in this section the last and fullest affirmation of what he conceives to be the only sensible way for a person to carry on in life, under all the circumstances. He has often before spoken of this answer, but here in ch. 9 he develops his position, picking up the issues from previous statements (for instance, 2: 24; 3: 12–13, and 5: 18–20) and joining them into one forceful declaration.

7. Words which before (2: 1–2, for example) were used to describe the madness and emptiness of a life given to gross

[a] *Prob. rdg.; Heb. adds* all your days, empty as they are.

acquisition and lavish enjoyment are now applied to the simple pleasures of life – *eat your food and enjoy it, and drink your wine with a cheerful heart* – in which is to be found the only satisfying way to spend one's life.

for already God has accepted what you have done: this phrase, more than any other, holds the key to Koheleth's solution of his problem. He has explored many avenues of getting the most out of life and trying thereby to insure his future and to establish some sense in all that he was doing; but all such efforts ended in emptiness. He finds instead that the simple daily and transitory activities of man can be satisfying if one proceeds under the assumption that it is God who has already *accepted* what one has done. Man's effort to establish his own acceptance in life is folly; nothing that he can do will endure. But God has accepted us already; the word *already* is late Hebrew, and in the Old Testament found only in Ecclesiastes. Here, as in 5: 19, Koheleth reveals that he has a powerful insight into God's grace, and a sure grasp of its significance; he cannot achieve sufficient meaning for his life, and cannot control his life's consequences. But God has *already. . .accepted* him and his deeds, and he is enabled to enjoy small experiences, and, in other words, to receive his 'daily bread'. *accepted:* the word contains the implication of 'approved', 'been pleased with'.

8. *Always:* literally, 'every time'; in all the 'times' and occasions of human existence, like those in 3: 2–8, be ready to enjoy and to be satisfied, says Koheleth. *dressed in white:* the symbol of celebration or festivity; ancient cultures generally regarded white or gaily coloured garments as appropriate for happy and positive moods. *anoint your head:* anointing the head with perfumed and pleasing ointment was another sign of happy living (cp. Matt. 6: 17, 'But when you fast, anoint your head and wash your face').

9. *a woman you love:* although one cannot be certain, the most probable interpretation is that Koheleth did not mean 'any woman', but rather 'the woman whom you love'. *woman* in Hebrew is also the usual word for 'wife'.

days of your allotted span: literally, 'days of your empty life'. This reference in the midst of the author's affirmation of life reasserts his claim that ultimately life is empty, so far as he can tell; eating, drinking, and enjoying does not alter that fundamental fact, and one must accept it as a premise to that which can genuinely and indisputably be enjoyed. *all the days of your allotted span here under the sun, empty as they are:* the Hebrew text reads, 'days of your empty life which he has given to you under the sun, all the days of your emptiness'. By insisting that the truth of life appears when one recognizes that it is given, Koheleth repeats his idea in 3: 13 that one can enjoy life when one discovers that it is given and not taken by us; no one can create or give his own life to himself. The mystery in life's meaning lies in the fact that it is given.

your lot: 'lot' is discussed under 5: 18. The nature of the *lot* is also that it comes to one as something given; the meaning of chance and accident in life is tied to Koheleth's concept here, for their function is to guarantee that man must live in the uncertainties of providence and giving, rather than under the security and absolutes which his own craving for control may attempt to supply.

10. The author's counsel is offered here, and finally again in the last sections of the book (11: 7 – 12: 1); in other words, what God has given you to do, *do it with all your might*, for this is the sense and ultimate vindication of life, insofar as you can ever know it. You cannot live in your dreams or aspirations, or in the world of what you think ought to be; you cannot postpone finding sense in life until your death, and you cannot imagine some celestial levelling of accounts after death. While it is good not to press too hard to establish yourself in goodness or evil (cp. 7: 16), in the sense of making that the obsessive pursuit of your life, do what is given you to do as energetically and forcefully as possible.

Sheol: the underworld, and residence of the dead (cp. 3: 20, 21 and 6: 3), Sheol was conceived in ancient Israel as a dark and dismal place inhabited by the dead 'souls' of men, in a manner very similar to other ancient ideas about the abode of the dead. In Sheol existence was quiet and separated from God and from human activity or memory ('Will thy wonders be known in the dark, thy victories in the land of oblivion?', Ps. 88: 12). No life was imagined for Sheol, and as the place where all the dead go it certainly provided no means for Koheleth and his contemporaries of solving the issues of death, mystery, and unfairness through reliance upon some grand recompense at the end of time. In the religion of the Old Testament, Sheol signified neither a last judgement, nor heaven or hell; it was not a place where people either suffered for wrong-doing or were rewarded for good.

All of this was of course taken for granted by Koheleth. But as an old wise man, he found most distasteful about the notion of going to Sheol the fact that there would be no chance in that place for wisdom, knowledge, reflection or action. His life's work as a wise man would be ended, and he could look forward to being still, and perhaps bored.

Even more important then is his advice – do with all your might whatever task lies to your hand! ✳

MUCH IS UNCERTAIN, AND WISDOM IS IGNORED

11 One more thing I have observed here under the sun: speed does not win the race nor strength the battle. Bread does not belong to the wise, nor wealth to the intelligent, nor success to the skilful; time and chance govern all.

12 Moreover, no man knows when his hour will come; like fish caught in a net,*a* like a bird taken in a snare, so men are trapped when bad times come suddenly.

13   This too is an example of wisdom as I have observed it
14 here under the sun, and notable I find it. There was a small town with few inhabitants, and a great king came

[a] *So Vulg.; Heb.* an evil net.

to attack it; he besieged it and constructed great siege-
works[a] against it. There was in it a poor wise man, and he 15
alone might have saved the town by his wisdom, but no
one remembered that poor wise man. 'Surely', I said to 16
myself, 'wisdom is better than strength.' But the poor
man's wisdom was despised, and his words went un-
heeded.

✶ Koheleth's strong statement of advice in 9: 7–10 does not
conclude his deliberations; instead he turns back once again to
add to his book some wisdom material which was probably
part of his heritage, just as he did at ch. 4. This material in the
rest of ch. 9 and in ch. 10 adds nothing to the argument of the
book.

Verses 11–16 return to the problem of inequity in life's
rewards, the futility of human efforts, the capriciousness of
recompenses in man's life-span, and the irony in the fact that
wisdom is ignored.

11. *One more thing:* the Hebrew text does not speak of 'one
more thing', as though it were an afterthought. Rather, the
phrase which begins 4: 1 and 4: 7 is repeated here, to begin
this section, and should be translated, 'I turned', or 'I returned'; in other words, 'I went back to observe again', a
characteristic manner of the wise man who is always ready to
reflect again on some important issue, to handle once more
some old and familiar wisdom, and to re-examine a question
for some possibly new insight.

Neither *speed* nor *strength*, wisdom nor intelligence nor skill
guarantees success; life affords too many exceptions to believe
that they do. *time*, or 'occasion' (cp. 3: 1), which might mean
'the combination of circumstances', and *chance* (literally, 'what
a person happens to meet') *govern* (literally, 'happen to') *all*
(literally, 'all of them'). The uncertainties and unpredict-

[a] *So Sept.; Heb.* fortifications.

abilities dominate life; man neither knows nor can manipulate and control everything, and God's control and design (cp. 3: 11) are beyond human knowledge.

12. For man does not even know *his* own *hour* (literally, 'his time', the word used in the preceding verse); we are all the victims of uncertainly known events, and times beyond our ken.

13–16. This homely illustration shows both the value of wisdom and its uselessness; wisdom is better than strength, but mankind is not wise enough to use its available wisdom, and so disaster stalks human enterprises while wise men are despised. Some scholars have unconvincingly posited that an actual event lies behind this illustration; but there is no direct or specific evidence to support such hypotheses. ✴

OBSERVATIONS AND PROVERBS

17 A wise man who speaks his mind calmly is more to be heeded than a commander shouting orders among
18 fools. Wisdom is better than weapons of war, and one mistake can undo many things done well.

10   Dead flies make the perfumer's sweet ointment turn rancid and ferment; so can a little folly make wisdom lose
2 its worth. The mind of the wise man faces right, but the
3 mind of the fool faces left. Even when he walks along the road, the fool shows no sense and calls everyone else[a] a
4 fool. If your ruler breaks out in anger against you, do not resign your post; submission makes amends for great
5 mistakes. There is an evil that I have observed here under
6 the sun, an error for which a ruler is responsible: the fool given high office, but[b] the great and the rich in humble
7 posts. I have seen slaves on horseback and men of high

[a] calls everyone else: *or* tells everyone he is.
[b] but: *prob. rdg.; Heb. om.*

144

rank going on foot like slaves. The man who digs a pit 8
may fall into it, and he who pulls down a wall may be
bitten by a snake. The man who quarries stones may strain 9
himself, and the woodcutter runs a risk of injury. When 10
the axe is blunt and has not first*a* been sharpened, then one
must use more force; the wise man has a better chance of
success. If a snake bites before it is charmed, the snake- 11
charmer loses his fee.

A wise man's words win him favour, but a fool's 12
tongue is his undoing. He begins by talking nonsense and 13
ends in mischief run mad. The fool talks on and on; but 14
no man knows what is coming, and who can tell him
what will come after that? The fool wearies himself to 15
death*b* with all his labour, for he does not know the way
to town.

Woe betide the land when a slave has become its king, 16
and its princes feast in the morning. Happy the land when 17
its king is nobly born, and its princes feast at the right
time of day, with self-control, and not as drunkards. If the 18
owner is negligent the rafters collapse, and if he is idle the
house crumbles away. The table has its pleasures, and wine 19
makes a cheerful life; and money is behind it all. Do not 20
speak ill of the king in your ease, or of a rich man in your
bedroom; for a bird may carry your voice, and a winged
messenger may repeat what you say.

* Branching out from initial observations about the advantage of wisdom, Koheleth brings together in this section a
collage of proverbs and observations, after the manner of other
collections of wisdom such as the Book of Proverbs. No theme

[a] first: *prob. rdg.; Heb.* face.
[b] fool. . .death: *prob. rdg.; Heb. obscure.*

or central structuring principle for the material is apparent, and no argument is spun out. Sufficient for the task was the purpose of gathering and preserving wisdom from the past; perhaps these are some of Koheleth's favourite proverbs.

18. *one mistake:* or, one 'sinner' (in the sense of 'rogue', or 'bungler').

10: 1. A little saying from the life of the ancient apothecary, or druggist, who prepared the cosmetics of the day, makes negatively the same point found in 1 Cor. 5: 6, 'A little leaven leavens all the dough.' Wisdom, like beauty and gentleness and quiet, is fragile and can be ruined and vanquished by just a small amount of folly (or, in turn, evil or brutality or noise).

2. *right* and *left* have for long and in many cultures symbolized good and bad, right and wrong, received and rejected. Cp. Matt. 25: 33, 'and he will place the sheep on his right hand and the goats on his left'.

6. Koheleth betrays a bias for *the rich*; one might have expected him to worry rather about wise men in low places, while fools are given high office!

6–7. These proverbs express what Koheleth has steadily contended: that deserts and recompenses in life are not fairly or equally distributed, and circumstances and situations do not conform to what wisdom might dictate.

8. A well-known proverb referred to elsewhere (cp. Ps. 7: 15, 'and he himself shall fall into the hole that he has made'), this sentence highlights the unexpected consequences of man's action, which are sometimes self-destructive.

10. *the wise man has a better chance of success:* a most difficult passage; it may have been textually damaged over the years of tradition, or else was a succinct combination of words that packed together a meaning that eludes us today. It could even mean something like, 'gain/*yithron* makes wisdom succeed', that is, wisdom is complemented and 'looks good' when it is lucky.

11. *fee* in Hebrew is the by-now-familiar 'gain/*yithron*'. The proverb may mean, 'If the snake bites and was not charmed, what is the use in having a snake charmer?'

14. This passage implies that Koheleth regarded as a fool the person who believed that his wisdom enabled him to penetrate the future and ultimate mysteries.

15. Otherwise translated, 'the toil of fools wearies him who does not even know his way to town'.

16. Feasting in the morning is a sign of dissolution, profligacy, and self-indulgence. Cp. Isa. 5: 11, 'Shame on you! you who rise early in the morning to go in pursuit of liquor.'

19. *is behind it all:* literally, 'has the answer for everything'. The proverb sounds cynical to sensitive ears, but nevertheless describes aspects of life as they seem sometimes to be.

20. *in your ease:* literally, 'in your thoughts'. *

LIVING REQUIRES EFFORT AND ENTAILS UNCERTAINTY

Send your grain across the seas, and in time you will **11** get a return. Divide your merchandise among seven ven- 2 tures, eight maybe, since you do not know what disasters may occur on earth.[a] If the clouds are heavy with rain, 3 they will discharge it on the earth; whether a tree falls south or north, it must lie as it falls. He who watches the 4 wind will never sow, and he who keeps an eye on the clouds will never reap. You do not know how a pregnant 5 woman comes to have a body and a living spirit in her womb; nor do you know how God, the maker of all things, works. In the morning sow your seed betimes, and 6 do not stop work until evening, for you do not know whether this or that sowing will be successful, or whether both alike will do well.

* After the excursion into familiar proverbs in ch. 10, Koheleth returns to the theme of the book by devoting his

[a] *Or* on land.

attention to the combination of two issues: (1) take the opportunities which are afforded to you, take the chances with
which an unpredictable and, from the human standpoint, uncontrollable universe is vested, risk and try and seize the
moment; (2) for man is not the master of nature, and cannot
know her secrets.

1. *Send your grain across the seas.* . .: the N.E.B. translation
with the figure of international maritime trade is not the only
possible way to interpret the verse. Many parallels have been
adduced to show that the text can mean, more simply and
traditionally, 'Throw your bread upon the waters, and after
a while you will find it again.' Of course the point is clear:
life does not offer many certainties, so one must take a chance,
trusting in grace and in gift, not in grabbing and in securities.

2. Good advice is, don't put all your eggs in one basket.

3. What happens, happens; one cannot argue with events
as, or after, they occur.

4. *He who watches the wind.* . .: a beautiful proverb expressing Koheleth's advice exactly, these words remind the hearer
that waiting in order to insure the future produces nothing;
just looking at the future is a waste of life, for accomplishments must be undertaken now in the present, not in a future
of uncertain contingencies.

5–6. Questions raised so many centuries ago have since
been answered, and modern science possesses answers to
ancient mysteries. But Koheleth's philosophical frame of mind
may raise similar puzzles about nature and the future for us.
Koheleth says, one cannot wait to act until one has all the
answers. ✻

Advice to a young man

TAKE ADVANTAGE OF YOUTH,
AND FRESH OPPORTUNITY

THE LIGHT OF DAY IS SWEET, and pleasant to the eye 7
is the sight of the sun; if a man lives for many years, 8
he should rejoice in all of them. But let him remember
that the days of darkness will be many. Everything that is
to come will be emptiness. Delight in your boyhood, 9
young man, make the most of the days of your youth; let
your heart and your eyes show you the way; but remember that for all these things God will call you to account.
Banish discontent from your mind, and shake off the 10
troubles of the body; boyhood and the prime of life are
mere emptiness.

* The matter of the previous section is pursued here, with an
accent upon the nature of the opportunities of youth. Seizing
and taking advantage of the present moment (cp. 11: 1–6) do
not transform that moment into some final victory over
emptiness; everything, even youth, is emptiness. Man's hope
lies not in changing or in challenging emptiness, but in simple
satisfactions and accomplishments in the face of it.

7–8. The present may be light, but the future is darkness, in
Koheleth's world view. One must rejoice therefore in the
present bright moments, and count them as worth the effort
of life; for the future may not be able to provide as much
satisfaction.

9. Following such encouraging advice does not relieve one
of the responsibility for one's actions; enjoy life, he says, and
follow one's impulses, but know that God requires an account

and makes a judgement. Koheleth's advice, given the circumstances of life as he sees them, is liberating, but it is not reck-
less. It may seem to cancel the thought in 9: 7 that God has
already accepted what you have done; however, the two concepts are not incompatible, for God's acceptance does not
eliminate the need for a sober and responsible spirit in man's
youthful heart. Koheleth here is not far from Paul, for
example, who later said that 'all stand before God's tribunal'
and that 'each of us will have to answer for himself' (Rom.
14: 10, 12).

10. *prime of life:* an unusual word in Hebrew, which has
also been taken to mean 'the dark hair' of youth. ✳

POEM ON DEATH;
IN ITS PRESENCE, ALL IS VANITY

12 Remember your Creator in the days of your youth,
before the time of trouble comes and the years draw near
2 when you will say, 'I see no purpose in them.'*ᵃ* Remember him before the sun and the light of day give place to
darkness, before the moon and the stars grow dim, and
3 the clouds return with the rain – when the guardians of
the house tremble, and the strong men stoop, when the
women grinding the meal cease work because they are
few, and those who look through the windows look no
4 longer, when the street-doors are shut, when the noise of
the mill is low, when the chirping of the sparrow grows
5 faint*ᵇ* and the song-birds fall silent;*ᶜ* when men are afraid
of a steep place and the street is full of terrors, when the
blossom whitens on the almond-tree and the locust's
paunch is swollen and caper-buds have no more zest. For

[a] *Or* I have no pleasure in them.
[b] grows faint: *prob. rdg.; Heb. obscure.*
[c] *Prob. rdg.; Heb.* sink low.

man goes to his everlasting home, and the mourners go about the streets. Remember him before the silver cord is 6 snapped*a* and the golden bowl is broken, before the pitcher is shattered at the spring and the wheel broken at the well, before the dust returns to the earth as it began 7 and the spirit*b* returns to God who gave it. Emptiness, 8 emptiness, says the Speaker, all is empty.

✻ The conclusion of the book is now at hand. All arguments are registered, and even repeated, and ch. 11 has developed some areas of the positive word from Koheleth.

The enemies of his dreams and desires have been identified: unfairness, ignorance, and death. But death is clearly the major problem, which intensifies and exacerbates all others; the spectre of death mocks the brave plans of the living. Man cannot argue with this spectre, and cannot combat it. It will win in the end.

1. *Creator:* the Hebrew text contains a problem in that the word is plural; recently there has been strong support also for altering the text to read 'grave' instead of 'Creator'. It is true that God has not been referred to as creator earlier in the book. However, Ecclesiastes does contain frequent references to God's working and making. The versions also agree with the N.E.B. translation. *time of trouble:* literally, 'days of evil'. *purpose:* the same Hebrew term in 3: 1 is translated as 'activity'; it can also connote 'pleasure', as the N.E.B. footnote indicates.

The message is the same as that in the rest of the book, but here it is muted and darkly coloured, under the ominous shadow of death, the subject of this closing section. One cannot depend on promises of the future, or on what coming days might bring, for they are going to be dark.

[a] is snapped: *prob. rdg.; Heb. unintelligible.*
[b] *Or* breath.

2–6. This lovely and haunting poem which speaks of the end of a human life has been interpreted in many different ways, for example, as a description of an approaching storm, or the mourning which occurs after a death, or the failing of the several parts of the human anatomy as old age and finally death come upon man. It is better not to insist on too much uniformity, or on the presence of just one dominant figure of speech, in this section. Koheleth was never tightly restrained before in his utterances by any compulsion to rigorous logical progression and exclusion of diverting thoughts and images. The passage contains many expressions which are extremely difficult to translate; doubtless some were phrases the meaning of which is long forgotten and lost.

2. The end of man is portrayed as a gathering tempest, darkening and threatening. The image is given already in 11: 8, for to the author the thought of the future cannot be separated from the thought of death.

3. The picture is an impressionistic one; with a few deft strokes the artist describes a whole drama. *guardians* (i.e. 'watchers of the house') *tremble*, strength is bent down and made crooked, daily activities cease, and the silent and barely noticed watching of the passing scene through lattice windows is over; so it is with advancing age, and the coming of death – trembling for what one sees, bending and bowing, ceasing, and the ending of one's own private observation of the world.

4. *grows faint:* older translations tend to retain the Hebrew word 'rise up', and translate to the effect that 'they rise up [are startled?] at the sound of a bird'. The phrase probably meant something like, 'the sparrow starts at a slight sound'. *song-birds:* or, alternatively, 'singers'. The doors close, and silence falls, as death approaches.

5. Figures concerning the withering of desires and the shrivelling of vitality are wrapped around the mention of *terrors* in the street and grey hair symbolized by the white almond blossoms. *caper-buds* were associated with sexual energy and virility. *everlasting home* means Sheol (cp. 9: 10),

habitation of all the dead for ever, according to the concept in ancient Israel.

6. Perhaps the author imagined *the golden bowl* of a fine lamp, hung from a *silver cord*, which when the cord breaks will fall and shatter. *wheel:* the word may better be translated 'bowl' or 'vessel for water', a more customary article used at the well in those days.

7. In Gen. 2: 7 the LORD God formed man from the *dust* of the ground. The body of a man returns to the earth as dust (cp. 3: 20), and the elemental cycle goes on, just as Koheleth described it in 1: 4–7. Migration from dust to dust, with a brief moment for wisdom and striving and reflection, is the fate of man.

In 3: 21 the question is raised regarding what happens to a man's spirit at death. Koheleth's opinion here is obviously settled, and his goal is not to raise problems but to offer the sober closing picture from his view of life. For him, no consolation or compensation is attributed to the expectation that the *spirit* will return to God. In his culture one did not think of a spirit dying; there were no dead spirits. But the spirit (Hebrew, *ruaḥ*) was simply the vital force in a person, and not his personality as the soul (Hebrew, *nephesh*) was. Therefore at death a person's identity and personhood remained where the soul went, and did not go with the spirit.

8. In the end, under the doleful pall of death, everything is empty. Ecclesiastes ends as it begins. ✶

THE EPILOGUE

So the Speaker, in his wisdom, continued to teach the 9 people what he knew. He turned over many maxims in his mind and sought how best to set them out. He chose 10 his words to give pleasure, but what he wrote was the honest truth. The sayings of the wise are sharp as goads, 11 like nails driven home; they lead the assembled people,

12 for they come from one shepherd. One further warning, my son: the use of books is endless, and much study is wearisome.

13 This is the end of the matter: you have heard it all. Fear God and obey his commands; there is no more to 14 man than this. For God brings everything we do to judgement, and every secret, whether good or bad.

* After the book was written by Koheleth, it undoubtedly provoked misgivings and disaffection in people who were offended by its viewpoint. Therefore words were appended to offer some more justification for the book and a defence of its author, as well as to add a few other sentiments from a person or persons in the stream of tradition. Written in the third person, the epilogue is itself a kind of miniature commentary on Ecclesiastes, although it completely ignores, or misses, the central point which Koheleth so painfully made.

The epilogue consists of several parts, and may have been attached over the years by as many as three persons.

9. More literally translated the verse reads, 'And in addition Koheleth was a wise man, and went on teaching knowledge to the people; and he weighed, and examined, he arranged many proverbs.' The word for 'in addition' is related to the term 'gain/*yithron*' used in Ecclesiastes, and begins verse 12 as well.

10. *He chose:* actually in Hebrew, 'Koheleth chose'. How much pleasure Koheleth's words were meant to give may be a matter of dispute; but quite likely his fellow wise men did indeed appreciate and respect his efforts, and enjoy his approach, which was very like their own.

11. *like nails...one shepherd:* another translation is, 'like nails driven home are those who master the collected sayings given from one shepherd'. This might hint at a situation in which the writer refers to one religious leader, or teacher, who has followers or disciples. Such a situation might have ob-

tained at many times and circumstances, and perhaps reflected the writer's own position.

12. Here is a peculiar thing to add to a book; it may well have been the whimsical thought of another wise man, or the tired comment of a student which he copied into the scroll, or even a waspish remark by an unsympathetic reader.

13–14. Verses 13 and 14 seem like the superfluous last bars of an already over-extended finish of a symphony. The book of Ecclesiastes ended with verse 8; these are editorial comments from some who could not leave well enough alone. This passage, although not fully and flagrantly countering everything that Koheleth said, as some scholars allege it to do, nevertheless represents a theology and theological concerns far distant from those of Koheleth's central problems; they are peripheral, like 5: 7 (N.E.B. text and footnote), which does exhort the fear of God in the same words as 12: 13. While still of wisdom character, these verses exhort the reader to keep commandments and to live conscious of God's judgement. The lonely and agonizing resignation of Koheleth to be satisfied with doing joyfully what God gives him to do, seems remote and probably not even understood any longer. ✶

✶   ✶   ✶   ✶   ✶   ✶   ✶   ✶   ✶   ✶   ✶   ✶   ✶

THE MESSAGE OF ECCLESIASTES

Ecclesiastes has provoked resentment, frustration, dislike, and disdain in the hearts of some of its readers. The book has been charged with being boring, repetitious, aimless and disorganized, blasphemous, wrong-headed, and heretical. Readers have fretted over its pessimism and low level of expectation.

But on the other hand, in recent years many readers have found Ecclesiastes to be speaking directly and persuasively to them. It has a potent word which reaches into the marrow of problems and experiences shared widely in our time. Koheleth's perception of the emptiness of life, and the absurdity of man's attempts to wrest out meaning forcibly from a grudging existence, appeal to those who themselves see no hope in what they do and get no pleasure from what they see around them.

Koheleth boldly sallies out against what he considers to be false and hollow ambitions, and the arrogant assumptions of men who desperately long to establish some guarantees and controls for their future. In his view, the world simply was not made as a place where God's justice is always manifest and where God's fairness can be demonstrated; he finds on the contrary that the world is full of inequity, injustice, and undeserved loss. It is impossible to count on even-handedness in the world of God's creation; its cornerstone is not fairness.

He also disputes vehemently the hopes of his colleagues, and of all men who share their hopeful curiosity, that enough study and piling up of wisdom will unlock the mysteries of the universe. He contends that God has in fact made the world so that man apprehends something of the nature of the mysteries without being able to penetrate to their secret solutions. Trust in the future, therefore, and in any anticipated blessings or rewards in the future, is bound to be disappointing, both because man cannot know what lies in the future and because what lies there is dark and unhappy.

Finally, and we may say most importantly, Koheleth grappled from start to finish with the problem of death. Coming unexpectedly, often suddenly, death mows down creatures with ruthless finality. All must die, and all die the same death. Death plants the ultimate stamp of futility and emptiness on man's efforts to get his own existence under control and to be in command of his fate.

Koheleth's observations were correct, also. As far as he went, we must agree that he had a rough-hewn but clear-eyed appreciation for what he could observe and contemplate as a wise man.

His solution too is a proposal which is readily understandable. One must avail oneself of the opportunities at hand, for this is what God gives to man and what man will obtain from life. To build upon these moments is to do the only thing of which one can be sure in this life.

Constructed out of a bleak world-view, Koheleth's theology is nevertheless stout and unwavering. He has no doubt of God's mighty presence and deeds, and he displays a fine perception of God's grace. The reader encounters no references to Israel's history and to the mighty acts of God in it, and reference to the classic theological terms of the Old Testament religion are sparse, when they are found at all. Using a different, and for the student of the Old Testament a fresh, terminology, Koheleth still outlines a conviction that is rich in ideas for coming to grips with that part of God's creation which we call 'nature'.

For him, nature does not afford man the means to understand the meaning of his own existence. That meaning is disclosed only in facing the thought of God's gift to man, and the conclusion that God has already accepted man. The gift and the acceptance are valid and adequate for each person. If a comparison is made with the fate of other persons in an attempt to pry out some deeper secret or principle behind God's dealings, one finds that all is emptiness, but in one's acceptance of God's gift and in the fact that one is oneself accepted by God, one is able to enjoy the benefits of creation.

The modern western mentality may be dissatisfied with this book. Not only does it not reach very optimistic conclusions in a logical way, but it also does not achieve and then retain whatever conclusions are reached. We might wish for at least the brightest possible ending, for example. But Koheleth relentlessly holds to his tenets, and will not permit the fine and simple enjoyments which he has laboriously defined to be weakened by a creeping optimism or contrariwise to undermine his own hard observations. Man can enjoy life; but that does not make the world less empty, the future less uncertain, or death less final.

It might be claimed that the revelation of resurrection to

Koheleth would have changed his entire message, but that is to jump to a conclusion. Would that make things seem fairer, or the future in world history more predictable, or death less certain? It would to be sure have altered his life by conferring a new dimension on it; his hopes would have been different, richer and broader, and his spirit could have been lighter. But his experience itself would not have changed.

Koheleth stands at the threshold of Pharisaic Judaism and of the New Testament, with a word that through the centuries has been aggravating but nevertheless profoundly compelling.

THE
SONG OF SONGS

✣ ✣ ✣ ✣ ✣ ✣ ✣ ✣ ✣ ✣ ✣ ✣ ✣

WHAT KIND OF BOOK IS THE SONG OF SONGS?

'All the writings are holy, but the Song of Songs is the Holy of Holies (*shīr hashīrīm qōdesh qodāshīm*).' So spoke Rabbi Aqiba ben Joseph almost 2000 years ago, paying the Song of Songs a word of ultimate tribute. But the rabbi said it in the midst of a controversy in Judaism about whether the Song of Songs and Ecclesiastes were holy at all, whether they 'defiled the hands' (see p. 3), and whether therefore they should be included in the collection of holy writings.

Since that day most reactions to the book have shared the extravagant quality of Aqiba's remark. Sermons by the score have been preached to demonstrate the manifold richness and infinite edification of the book's contents; commentaries were poured out by the doctors and fathers of the Christian Church to exhibit the profundity of their own scriptural perceptions. Yet in Rabbi Aqiba's day and in our own the debate goes on about the meaning and value of this book.

For although some people regard it as most precious and worthy, others frankly consider it to be barren of any qualification for Holy Writ and its presence in the Bible as an embarrassment. It is on the very border of the canon of the Old Testament, and counted outside by some. Nowhere in the book is God mentioned; the reader searches in vain for any proclamation of religious insight and truth, or for an exposition or understanding of the people of God or indeed of the world of God. There is no shred of ethical consciousness or social concern in the book, and no hint of worship. The Song of Songs is not a serious or sober statement of faith. For many people it does not meet the standards of what a biblical book ought to be.

The Song of Songs is a book of love – sexual, erotic love. It is not written to tell about that love; it celebrates it. In language which is allusive but very specific, the book expresses the enjoyment of physical passion. The songs seem to be collected together for the sake of variety and mood instead of development of argument or sequence of scene.

HOW THE BOOK HAS BEEN INTERPRETED

With such a document one may expect to find among its readers a great variety of interpretation. As a matter of fact, there is an enormous amount of scholarly literature written on the Song of Songs, and from very different points of view.

Allegorical

Early Jewish literature already shows evidence of interpreting the book allegorically, that is, taking words and passages to bear a so-called deeper level of meaning, or a symbolical resemblance to some other truth which does not originate in the words or phrases themselves. The use of the book in lusty popular celebrations in the taverns ('houses of drinking') of Aqiba's day (A.D. 100–35), about which the old Rabbi complained, may have helped to lead to other means of explaining its message and importance. So in the apocryphal book 2 Esdras (5: 24, 26) the lily and the dove are interpreted to mean 'Israel'. Rabbinical literature in the Mishnah and the Targum (the Aramaic translation of the Old Testament) dealt with the book as an allegorical statement of God's relationship with Israel throughout her history (see notes on 1: 6 and 4: 1–3). Christian commentators from the third century onward expounded the Song of Songs as an allegory of Christ (the groom) and his church (the bride), and of the Virgin Mary (the maiden), and the allegorical interpretation not only flourished but came to be normal. The writings of the great Syrian church father Theodore of Mopsuestia, from about A.D. 400, whose opinions tended generally to be critical and realistic, were condemned at the Second Council of Constantinople in 553. One of the reasons that Sebastian Castellio was banished from Geneva in the days of John Calvin was for holding to a natural interpretation of the book. Some scholars even today, maintain the position of interpreting the Song of Songs allegorically, or at least defending such interpretation as a valid way of understanding what the book has to say.

Literal

As old as the allegorical approach, the so-called literal way of interpreting the book attracted some scholars and other people from time to time throughout history. Presumably the young people in Aqiba's day used it with that understanding. Theodore of Mopsuestia thought that it described Solomon's relationship with his Egyptian bride. Since the eighteenth century a growing number of scholars have read it as a collection of human love lyrics.

The literal interpretation enables the reader to take seriously what he sees and to reflect upon it according to the meaning of the words and their immediate allusions. It has also increased the opportunity to observe both differences between the songs and the distinctive characteristics of each song. Accordingly one important view of the book is that it is a collection of unrelated, or in some poems loosely related, love lyrics, coming from various times and places.

It has been the great contribution of this approach to open the readers' eyes to the beauty of the poetry and the human emotions in literature, and to esteem the art of religious writing for its naturally human qualities, spiritual, emotional, and physical.

Dramatic

A cursory reading of the book discloses that through the songs more than one person is speaking, and that in fact the entire book consists of such speeches or songs. Consequently, two of the major Septuagint manuscripts – Codex Sinaiticus, found at the monastery of St Catherine on Mount Sinai in 1859, and written by about A.D. 350, and Codex Alexandrinus, written in the fifth century – added to the text a series of character headings, indicating now the bride, now the groom, now the companions, as speakers. The Sinaiticus contains the more elaborate of these indications and headings of parts, or roles. In the N.E.B. translation used in this commentary, the text has been furnished with these headings.

Later application of the dramatic interpretation sought to discern a more complicated plot, and to distinguish two maidens – a noble beauty from the city and a country girl – or, more commonly attempted, two men – Solomon, and a shepherd boy, who vied for the affection of the beautiful lass (the shepherd boy winning, cp. 8: 11–12). These efforts pressed the matter too far, however, and opened the gates for criticism on the basis of the claims that the Hebrews totally lacked a drama form or theatre in Old Testament times, that there is no plot in the book, and that the book is not a unit. (The book of Job has also been held to be drama, though this is not really the best way of describing it.)

But the idea should be kept simpler. The Septuagint manuscripts accurately saw that there are at least three speaking parts in the book. Although it is misleading to insist that this constitutes drama, any interpretation must explain this fact of alternating speakers.

Wedding Cycle

In 1873 the Prussian consul in Damascus published an article on 'The Syrian threshing-floor', in which he reported his observations of village wedding customs and folk poetry among the Syrian peasants, and offered suggestions for the light which they might shed on the Song of Songs.

What he was able to observe was an intricate and elaborate style of wedding celebration. On the wedding day during a sword-dance by the bride, a song (in Arabic, *wasf*) was sung in description of her beauty. After the wedding night the feast continued for a whole week, with dancing and singing of the characteristic songs. The bride was ceremonially crowned (in a previous era the groom was crowned also), and she was addressed as queen, he as king. There were various types of special dances for the occasion, and sports were played. A special contingent of young men accompanied the groom, perhaps in ancient times for the purpose of defending the party.

Numerous parallels with ancient Jewish wedding customs have been pointed out, and the reader will note through the following text and commentary the applicability of this wedding cycle motif to the book.

Cultic

Recent decades have witnessed an attempt at interpreting the Old Testament through a better appreciation of the part played by organized worship in the life of the Hebrew community. This new appreciation of the cultic life of Israel inspired scholars to envisage Old Testament materials used and transmitted in cultic settings, where religious rites and activities expressed the consciousness of the people.

Scientific disciplines like archaeology opened doors never known before, leading into the histories and cultures of antiquity. The comparative study of ancient religions and civilizations revealed points of contact, similarities, and differences, which have been invaluable for a better understanding of the Old Testament. Among other things, archaeological work in Palestine and Syria uncovered cultic materials – myths and legends, hymns, forms of worship – very similar to those in Israel, or similar to the remnants of Canaanite religion that could be detected in the Old Testament texts. (See notes on 1: 13.) The question was no longer: how much of Canaanite religion endured in Israel? but instead: to what extent did Canaanite religion and thought penetrate Israel's religion and thought?

Documents in many languages and artefacts of various cultures from the ancient Near East demonstrate the existence through the eastern Mediterranean area, and in Mesopotamia, of cults based on myths of the sacred marriage of gods, of a dying and rising god, and of the endangering of fertility or its loss, and of seasonal weather change which were linked to the death of a god. Scholars have tried to interpret the Song of Songs as a liturgy, or a collection of liturgical pieces, which originated in the Canaanite cult of fertility, and of the dying–rising god, in which the period of death would be accompanied by periods of drought and the threat of sterility on earth. Thus the bride in the Song would be the goddess seeking her lost lover, who is in the underworld; in sexual union with him, she restores fertility and well-being to the world.

HOW THE BOOK MIGHT BE INTERPRETED

Each of these types of interpretation has advantages, and of course encounters difficulties. The allegorical interpretation really needs no defence, and does not benefit from critique; boundaries in allegorizing seem to be a matter of conviction and of taste. Literal interpretation forces one to stay with the text; and it should of course be used in any of the remaining types of interpretation, and need not be limited to a particular theory about love lyrics.

It is in a combination of several of these interpretations that the closest approximation to the truth may be reached. Each method has suffered limitations because it was too narrowly applied and pursued, and each has been criticized when it or its implications were exaggerated.

We cannot identify specific individual songs in the book

which may have originated in the cult of the dying and rising god, or in fertility rites. Lush vocabulary and erotic imagery do not prove cultic origin. Heroic dimensions (the lover 'bounding over the mountains', 2: 8) can be poetic hyperbole, and not necessarily divine proportion. We find no names of the gods (on Dod, see 1: 13; on Nergal, see 6: 4) or other clear references to the pagan cult. There are not many passages where one can even suspect cultic forms or ritual patterns. Thus there is no proof at all of the cultic origin of the songs. But the biggest problem for a defence of the cultic origin is claimed to be the difficulty for such cultic material ever to be accepted by the Hebrews. Yet we know (see under 2: 8 – 3: 5) that pagan rites were still going on in the Jerusalem temple as long as it existed; obviously the cultic material was accepted by many Israelites, perhaps even by most (cp. Jer. 44: 15–28, where the Jewish refugees in Egypt speak of the general practice of sacrificing to the 'queen of heaven' in Jerusalem).

It may be concluded that even though pagan cultic liturgical material undoubtedly was used in Jerusalem for centuries, there is no certain evidence that such material forms the basis for the Song of Songs. All the data in support of the argument lie in the categories of the hypothetical, the not-impossible, or the suppositional in the face of the weakness of other theories to supply satisfying explanations.

For what purpose then, we must ask, were the songs composed? They employ common figures of speech, repetitions are encountered in the book, and there is reason to believe (cp. on 4: 1–3 and 8: 5) that some continuity in authorship, or at least in the presence of traditional thought-patterns and types of literary expression, existed. Was there then such a thing as a language of love in ancient Israel? Is it not more likely that the songs were cast out of a core of common experience? And that common experience would most probably have been the wedding celebrations, and the singing of love songs in that context. Cultic imagery from pagan sources might easily have been adopted for many expressions, however, and have remained to puzzle commentators ever after. The unusual number of rare words and curious expressions (see notes on 4: 4; 6: 4; 6: 12) in the book points to sources which were no longer understood after a few centuries. New songs (such as those in 8: 6–14, for example) may have been composed from time to time, and added to the main collection.

The most serious objection to the 'wedding cycle' theory stems from the fact that nineteenth-century Syrian customs cannot illuminate very well the situation in Old Testament Israel. Parallels have however in fact been noted. And the strength of the theory lies not in the number of similarities with Syrian weddings 2000 years later, but in the suitability of the theory to explain the present book, and whether this theory can provide more satisfying answers than other theories.

The role headings in the Septuagint manuscripts were written in the days, and if these two manuscripts came from Egypt, even in the place, in which allegorical interpretation was at its zenith, and we might suppose therefore that these headings fit the allegorical approach. Yet there is nothing in them to make us think so. They seem to provide just a simple guide to help the reader see who is speaking in the text. And their presence in what are two of the oldest manuscripts suggests a still older origin for the headings, perhaps in some Septuagint copy even from before the days of the New Testament.

It must be acknowledged that there is no drama at all in the book; but the speeches and the speakers could well match an extended wedding celebration, and the book could be a collection of songs used at various times throughout the event. The very lack of connection between the songs, which causes some to believe that they come from various times and places, makes this association with the wedding cycle feasible. The groom is hailed not only as king, but as Solomon, the richest and the greatest lover of all; the name Solomon is hard to explain as an element in some old pagan cult piece, in any case. Whether the songs actually follow some order for all or a portion of the wedding cycle cannot be established without knowing more about the wedding customs and celebration.

WHEN AND HOW THE BOOK THEN CAME TO BE ACCEPTED

The songs were probably written at different times in Israel's history, beginning as far back as the days of Solomon or shortly thereafter. Composed by various authors, and moulded by countless others, they perhaps absorbed words, phrases, and even whole songs from pagan cultic sources; but they originated in a folk setting, receiving all the richness and artistry that the folk singers could provide.

By about the first century A.D. the book had deep and strong roots in the national consciousness, and was associated with the other books that represented and fed that consciousness. But over the centuries its use seems to have been detached from the wedding customs and its meaning became more vague and obscure. Therefore the rabbis and teachers began to interpret its language allegorically, instead of following the more direct and physical allusions from earlier times, and by A.D. 400 Theodore of Mopsuestia could say that neither Jews nor Christians read it in public. Its acceptance into the canon of the Old Testament was no doubt assisted by the fact that, named the Song of Songs (cp. 1: 1), it had become closely identified with Solomon. Nevertheless rabbinic opinion held that, like Isaiah, Proverbs, and Ecclesiastes, it had been written by 'Hezekiah and his group'.

In the early Middle Ages, it came to be read in the Jewish communities on the festival of the Passover, perhaps because its allegorical interpretation suited it then for the historical commemorations of the great holy day.

OTHER QUESTIONS ABOUT THE BOOK

Of other outstanding questions about the book not yet mentioned here, the leading one is the relation of the Song of Songs to the wisdom literature and thought of ancient Israel (on wisdom, see pp. 91–3). Wisdom thinking, and wise men, were occupied with matters of order, information, experience, and common sense, but also with beauty and nature. Prov. 5:18–19 describes the good wife both in terms of her beauty and of her good sense and counsel; a document discovered in the Dead Sea materials compares the beauty of Sarah, Abraham's wife, to her wisdom. There can be no question that lovely and attractive things, as well as natural features and functions, were contemplated by the wise men, and that wisdom thinking flourished among the common people just as the Song of Songs was sung by them. However, this is about as far as the comparison can go: common concerns and common usage. Other features of wisdom are not present in the Song, and the erotic language and exclusively sexual interest and content of the Song are not found in existing wisdom literature in the Old Testament.

Remarkable similarity between the songs and the erotic love literature of ancient Egypt has been noted. Not only were the liturgies of the Egyptian Osiris–Isis cult the first to be compared with the Song of Songs, the Egyptian secular love lyrics are also very similar. The following is a good example:

> My brother, my beloved,
> My heart pursues the love of thee,
> All that thou hast brought into being.
> I say to thee: 'See what I am doing!'
> I have come from setting my trap with my (own) hand;
> In my hand are my bait and my snare.
> All the birds of Punt [a land south and east of Egypt],
>   they alight in Egypt,
> Anointed with myrrh.

The first one comes and takes my worm.
Its fragrance is brought from Punt,
And its talons are full of resin.
My wish for thee is that we loose them together,
When I am alone with thee,
That I might let thee hear the cry
Of the one anointed with myrrh.
How good it would be
If thou wert there with me
When I set the trap!
The best is to go to the fields,
To the one who is beloved!

(from *Ancient Near Eastern Texts*, ed. J. B. Pritchard, p. 467f.; translation by John A. Wilson).

Other features of Egyptian art have also been compared with those of Israel, especially the art of literary description, since from the Hebrews' sculpture and painting little has remained and is known. What this comparison shows, however, is not the dependence of the Song of Songs upon Egyptian literature, but rather the universality of such literary types and features in the ancient Near East, for examples of erotic expression can also be found in Mesopotamian materials.

✻   ✻   ✻   ✻   ✻   ✻   ✻   ✻   ✻   ✻   ✻   ✻

THE BRIDE BEGINS HER LOVE SONGS

Bride[a]

I will sing the song of all songs to Solomon   **1**
that he may[b] smother me with kisses.   2

Your love is more fragrant than wine,

[a] *The Hebrew text implies, by its pronouns, different speakers, but does not indicate them; they are given, however, in two MSS. of Sept.*
[b] I will...that he may: *or* The song of all songs which was Solomon's; may he...

3   fragrant is*[a]* the scent of your perfume,
and your name like perfume poured out;*[b]*
for this the maidens love you.

4   Take me with you,*[c]* and we will run together;
bring me into your*[d]* chamber, O king.

Companions

Let us rejoice and be glad for you;
let us praise your love more than wine,
and your caresses*[e]* more than any song.

Bride

5 I am dark but lovely, daughters of Jerusalem,
like the tents of Kedar
or the tent-curtains of Shalmah.

6 Do not look down on me; a little dark I may be
because I am scorched by the sun.
My mother's sons were displeased with me,
they sent me to watch over the vineyards;
so I did not watch over my own vineyard.

7 Tell me, my true love,
where you mind your flocks,
where you rest them at midday,
that I may not be left picking lice
as I sit among your companions' herds.

---

* These introductory songs have in one interpretation of the
book been attributed to two different maidens, the first song

[a] *Or* more fragrant than.
[b] poured out: *prob. rdg.; Heb. word uncertain.*
[c] Take...you: *lit.* Draw me after you.
[d] *So Pesh.; Heb.* his.
[e] your caresses: *so Pesh.; Heb.* they love you.

supposed to reflect an urban setting, the second a rural scene
and a country girl. But those Septuagint manuscripts which
contain headings assigned the whole section to one girl, the
'bride', although the manuscript Codex Sinaiticus attached
the last half of verse 4 to the role of the 'companions' as the
N.E.B. indicates.

1. Verse 1 is the title of the book, literally translated 'The
Song of Songs, which is of Solomon'. The term 'of Solomon'
is like the superscription in many Psalms, 'of David', which
was traditionally taken to mean 'written by David', but we
know that the 'of' might also signify simply 'possession', or
relation to.

4. *king:* a commonly used title for the bridegroom, and
found in popular Arabic poetry and wedding celebration down
to modern times. *and your caresses more than any song* is a difficult reading which involves a change in the Hebrew text; most
translations read something like, 'rightly do they love you'.

5. *Shalmah:* a much-disputed passage, this text is better
translated as 'like the curtains of Solomon', and the parallelism
maintained between *dark* – the black tents of Kedar – and *lovely*
– the curtains of Solomon. It is a type of curtain which is
meant, and not curtains belonging to King Solomon.

6. The meaning of this verse has been transformed by
commentators to such an extent as to imply some morality
teaching like 'be concerned about your own problems', or
some allegory such as Israel's hard labour in Egypt before the
exodus or Israel's defection from obedience to the law. It more
probably was intended to explain why the young maid was so
swarthy; she was a kind of Cinderella.

7. *be left picking lice:* this rather humorous reading may in a
vivid way suggest the wearisomeness of being left alone. It is
an acceptable alternative to another translation, 'be like a
veiled harlot' who would be waiting for someone to come
along (cp. the story of Judah and Tamar, especially Gen. 38:
14, 16). The more customary translation, 'like a wanderer',
assumes a change in the Hebrew text. ✳

DESIRE IS WHETTED

Bridegroom

8   If you yourself do not know,
             O fairest of women,
         go, follow the tracks of the sheep
   and mind your kids by the shepherds' huts.

9   I would compare you, my dearest,
           to Pharaoh's chariot-horses.

10   Your cheeks are lovely between plaited tresses,
          your neck with its jewelled chains.

Companions

11   We will make you braided plaits of gold
          set with beads of silver.

Bride

12   While the king reclines on his couch,
         my spikenard gives forth its scent.

13   My beloved is for me a bunch of myrrh
         as he lies on my breast,

14   my beloved is for me a cluster of henna-blossom
         from the vineyards of En-gedi.

Bridegroom

15   How beautiful you are, my dearest,
         O how beautiful,
           your eyes are like doves!

Bride

16   How beautiful you are, O my love,
         and how pleasant!

Bridegroom

Our couch is shaded with branches;
the beams of our house are of cedar,   17
our ceilings are all of fir.

Bride

I am an asphodel in Sharon,   **2**
a lily growing in the valley.

Bridegroom

No, a lily among thorns   2
is my dearest among girls.

Bride

Like an apricot-tree among the trees of the wood,   3
so is my beloved among boys.
To sit in its shadow was my delight,
and its fruit was sweet to my taste.
He took me into the wine-garden   4
and gave me loving glances.
He refreshed me with raisins, he revived me with   5
apricots;
for I was faint with love.
His left arm was under my head, his right arm was   6
round me.

Bridegroom

I charge you, daughters of Jerusalem,   7
by the spirits and the goddesses*ᵃ* of the field:
Do not rouse her, do not disturb my love
until she is ready.*ᵇ*

[a] by...goddesses: *or* by the gazelles and the hinds.
[b] until...ready: *or* while she is resting.

❋ Although it is impossible to identify a topic or theme which is central to this section, the obvious shift in the material to form a tightly oscillating kind of dialogue, as indicated in the N.E.B. and the Greek manuscripts, sets these verses apart. Without wishing to suggest a development of theme or of action in the book, we may still attempt to define the effect of the ardent exchange in speeches with such a heading as given above, that amorous desire is thereby whetted.

8. Recent commentators link verse 8 together with the preceding verse; but the present text nevertheless correctly reflects the shift in speaker, as Codex Sinaiticus notes, 'the bridegroom to the bride'.

9. This is the first occasion in the book for the use of the Hebrew word translated as *dearest*; this word is found nine times in the book as the designation for the bride, five of the nine being in chs. 1 and 2. Comparison with *Pharaoh's chariot-horses* was a great compliment (the Hebrew properly reads 'mares') inasmuch as the horse was highly esteemed and valued; the image was that of a noble, high-bred steed, not a draft animal. One remembers that Solomon in particular traded with Egypt for chariots and horses, according to 1 Kings 10: 29; but the fame of them could have provoked this reference at some much later time than Solomon's day.

12. Codex Sinaiticus introduces this section with the appropriate heading, 'the bride (speaking) to herself and to the groom'.

13. Translated here and usually, throughout the book, as *beloved*, the singular form of the Hebrew word *dod* first appears in the Song in this verse. *dod* has been a cause of perplexity and argument for interpreters of the book; the singular of the word is translated everywhere in the Old Testament as 'uncle' (cp. Esther 2: 7, 15) except in the Song and in Isa. 5: 1, but in this book it clearly does not mean 'uncle'. It is similar in spelling to the name, 'David'; in 2 Chron. 20: 37 it is part of a proper name, Dodavahu, meaning 'beloved of Yahu (God)'. Some scholars maintain that Dod was the name of a

god worshipped in Canaanite Jerusalem, before the Hebrew conquest of it, in the fertility cult of the sacred marriage of the gods, and in the rites of a dying and rising god. According to this theory Dod would be the lover in the sacred marriage of the gods. Thus the name in 2 Chron. 20: 37, Dodavahu, might have represented an effort to relate the cult of Dod to the religion of Yahweh, god of the Hebrews, by naming that person 'Yahweh is Dod' (much as the name Joel makes a parallel profession, 'Yahweh is God [El]'). David as a name would be simply a title, and Saul's 'uncle' in 1 Sam. 10: 14f. would actually have been the 'Dod', or priest-king, of Jerusalem (one notes that according to 2 Sam. 21: 19, it was Elhanan from Bethlehem who killed Goliath of Gath; was then David's real name Elhanan, and 'David' the title by which he was known and always remembered?); the title used in Jerusalem, Dod, would have been applied to both the god and to his high priest who was also king. Upon conquering Jerusalem the Hebrews might have absorbed Canaanite religious and cultic songs and materials, and transformed their meanings to suit the worship of Yahweh. The mixture of the old Canaanite religious elements with the Yahweh-religion would cause problems and confuse people, and provoke the urgent concerns and exhortations of the prophets against worship of other gods. That worship through the elements and ideas of the Canaanite religion took place in Jerusalem is certain, because of the frequent attacks by the prophets upon it, and because of signs of it in other Old Testament literature; there is no question that Canaanite religion survived, not only in Palestine but even in the temple in Jerusalem, down to the fall of Jerusalem in 587 B.C., and perhaps in Israel even beyond that time.

According to this mythological theory of interpretation verse 13 would be translated, 'Dod is for me a bunch of myrrh', and verse 16 would begin, 'How beautiful you are, Dod.' See the notes on 2: 8 – 3: 5; 4: 8; 5: 2 – 6: 3; 6: 4, and 6: 10.

myrrh: a fragrant resin, highly prized, coming chiefly from south Arabia, and imagined here as a small pouch (*bunch*) between the breasts.

14. The *henna* flowers, growing in thick clusters, are even today well known and are noted for a particularly fragrant aroma. *En-gedi* is down to our own day an oasis on the west side of the Dead Sea; surrounded by a harsh, bleak wilderness, it was famous for its palms and vineyards.

15–16. The aptness of the Septuagint manuscripts' dialogue headings is supported in that *dearest* is the word for the bride (cp. 1: 9), and *my love* is the word for the lover or groom (cp. 1: 13) which is usually given as 'beloved'. Verse 15 is repeated at 4: 1.

2: 1. *asphodel in Sharon:* well known from earlier translations as the 'rose of Sharon', the identification of this flower is disputed, but may be the 'crocus'. The word is found also in Isa. 35: 1.

3. *apricot-tree:* like other terms in the book, the meaning of the Hebrew word behind this translation is not clear. Earlier translations read 'apple-tree', and many modern commentators have continued that tradition. But apples were scarce, and of poor quality in Palestine, and do not match the descriptions of this fruit. The apricot was on the other hand not native to Palestine and may not have been introduced as early as the Song was composed.

4. *wine-garden:* the Hebrew reads, 'house of wine', which is generally interpreted as 'banqueting house'.

5. Although the images may seem to the modern reader at first glance to be nothing more than references to pleasant food, the deeper connotations of 'raisin', 'apricot', and 'apricot-tree' are subtly and powerfully erotic.

6. This verse is repeated at 8: 3.

7. The consummation of love is reflected at this verse, to be repeated in 3: 5 and 8: 4. *the spirits and the goddesses:* literally, 'the gazelles and the stags', interpreted to mean the supernatural powers and presences in nature which were dimly

recognized by the people and perhaps in some cases not even named; this is an oath similar to the English, 'by all that is holy'. *ready:* or, 'until she is pleased', or 'until she is satisfied'. ✶

THE BRIDE IN SEARCH

Bride

    Hark! My beloved! Here he comes,   8
bounding over the mountains, leaping over the hills.
    My beloved is like a gazelle   9
      or a young wild goat:
    there he stands outside our wall,
peeping in at the windows, glancing through the
      lattice.
My beloved answered, he said to me: 10
    Rise up, my darling;
    my fairest, come away.
    For now the winter is past,   11
    the rains are over and gone;
    the flowers appear in the country-side;   12
    the time is coming when the birds will sing,
    and the turtle-dove's cooing will be heard in our
      land;
    when the green figs will ripen on the fig-trees   13
    and the vines[a] give forth their fragrance.
    Rise up, my darling;
    my fairest, come away.

Bridegroom

    My dove, that hides in holes in the cliffs   14
      or in crannies on the high ledges,

[a] *Prob. rdg.; Heb. adds* blossom.

let me see your face, let me hear your voice;
for your voice is pleasant, your face is lovely.

Companions

15 Catch for us the jackals, the little jackals,[a]
that spoil our vineyards, when the vines are in flower.

Bride

16 My beloved is mine and I am his;
he delights in the lilies.

17 While the day is cool and the shadows are dispersing,
turn, my beloved, and show yourself
a gazelle or a young wild goat
on the hills where cinnamon grows.[b]

3 Night after night on my bed
I have sought my true love;
I have sought him but not found him,
I have called him but he has not answered.[c]

2 I said, 'I will rise and go the rounds of the city,
through the streets and the squares,
seeking my true love.'
I sought him but I did not find him,
I called him but he did not answer.[d]

3 The watchmen, going the rounds of the city, met me,
and I asked, 'Have you seen my true love?'

4 Scarcely had I left them behind me
when I met my true love.
I seized him and would not let him go

[a] *Or* fruit-bats.
[b] on...grows: *or* on the rugged hills *or* on the hills of Bether.
[c] I have called...answered: *so Sept.; Heb. om.*
[d] I called...answer: *so Sept.; Heb. om.*

　　until I had brought him to my mother's house,
　　　to the room of her who conceived me.

Bridegroom

　　I charge you, daughters of Jerusalem,　　　　　　　　　5
　　by the spirits and the goddesses*ᵃ* of the field:
　　Do not rouse her, do not disturb my love
　　　until she is ready.*ᵇ*

* This group of songs is brought together here because of a
certain symmetry in the order of speeches; 2: 7, which most
commentators attach to its preceding material, marks the
separation from this passage, and is repeated in 3: 5. The section is composed of two major songs by the bride, divided by
a brief song from the bridegroom; the first song of the bride
(2: 8–13) describes the lover coming and enticing her away
with an enchanting song, while the second (2: 16 – 3: 4),
related to the first by repetition of the phrase 'a gazelle or a
young wild goat' (2: 9 and again in 2: 17), deals with the
bride's search for the bridegroom.

　　In the Sumerian and Babylonian myths of the descent of the
goddess (Sumerian – Inanna; Babylonian – Ishtar) into the
underworld, some scholars have claimed to see this search for
the bridegroom; however, in those myths the goddess goes
for other reasons than to seek her true love. (In Sumerian he
is called Dumuzi, in Babylonian he is Tammuz – according to
Ezek. 8: 14 women in Jerusalem were wailing for Tammuz,
presumably in participation of the rites in the Ishtar–Tammuz
cult; so we know that these foreign religious practices were
used in Jerusalem, cp. on 1: 13.) The 'gatekeeper' in the
Sumerian–Babylonian myth was a stern and demanding figure,
who stripped the goddess, thus humbling her, as she entered
his city; the 'watchmen' (3: 3) in the Song here seem

　　[*a*] by…goddesses: *or* by the gazelles and the hinds.
　　[*b*] until…ready: *or* while she is resting.

harmless enough, but in 5: 7 they strike the bride and wound her, stripping her of her cloak (or, large veil).

10–13. This lovely poem evokes the soft image of the gentleness of early spring, and is framed by the delicate refrain at the beginning and the end, *Rise up, my darling*...(verses 10 and 13).

14. The figure of *crannies on the high ledges* suggests the high, remote caves in the wilderness near the Dead Sea, where for centuries fugitives took sanctuary and where the scrolls from the wilderness have been found in our day.

15. *jackals:* this translation is probably right (cp. Lam. 4: 3, N.E.B. footnote), although 'foxes' has also been used, and 'fruit-bats' (N.E.B. footnote) has recently been proposed. The figure of speech is intended not to say something agricultural, but rather to refer to young lovers who have designs on the bride (she is the 'vineyard', cp. 1: 6).

16. The sentence, turned around somewhat, appears again in 6: 3.

3: 1–2. The search is described with a refrain at the end of each verse, thus connoting continued effort and duration of search.

4–5. As this section ends, one does not have the languid feeling from 2: 5–7; here one rushes to the end, and the refrain in verse 5 is sung in a context of greater passion. ✳

A WEDDING PROCESSION

Companions

6   What is this coming up from the wilderness
            like a column of smoke
            from burning myrrh or frankincense,
            from all the powdered spices that merchants
                bring?
7   Look; it is Solomon carried in his litter;
        sixty of Israel's chosen warriors

    are his escort,
    all of them skilled swordsmen,   8
    all trained to handle arms,
  each with his sword ready at his side
    to ward off the demon of the night.
The palanquin which King Solomon had made for   9
    himself
    was of wood from Lebanon.
Its poles he had made of silver,   10
    its head-rest of gold;
    its seat was of purple stuff,
and its lining was of leather.

Come out, daughters of Jerusalem;   11
you daughters of Zion, come out and welcome
    King Solomon,
  wearing the crown with which his mother has
    crowned him,
  on his wedding day, on his day of joy.

---

* A song, or a piece of a larger work, from the royal wed-
ding-ceremonies perhaps; the origin of this segment of the
Song is much debated. It would appear to be something sung
at the procession of Solomon on his wedding day; comparison
with Ps. 45, which is a royal wedding song describing at the
end the procession of the bride, makes one think that this segment may have been used at other royal nuptials. If not from
Solomon's reign, the song may have been composed as a
separate song, or as a piece for the bridegroom at the wedding
festival. Although it may seem that *Companions* should be
singing this song, and the similar passage in 8: 5 is ascribed in
detail to the companions and members of the royal retinue,
the Septuagint manuscripts made the bridegroom the speaker
at this point.

8. *demon of the night:* a phrase found also in Ps. 91: 5 (translated there in the footnote as 'a scare by night'), this probably refers to some evil spirit or fearful presence which was believed to inhabit the night, terrorizing, or at least threatening, ancient men who feared the darkness and its unknown dangers.

9. *palanquin:* a Hebrew word traced by some scholars to a Greek term, and therefore indicating a later date for the book, but by other scholars to a Sanskrit, an Akkadian, or even an Egyptian source. The matter has not been finally decided.

10. *was of leather:* it has been proposed that the Hebrew translated here as 'leather' was based upon an Arabic term; another proposal is to change the Hebrew and read 'ivory'. Still another, more traditional, rendering follows the Hebrew, 'was lovingly fit together by the daughters of Jerusalem', inasmuch as the Hebrew of verse 10 includes that last phrase, 'by [or, "from"] the daughters of Jerusalem', included in the N.E.B. translation in verse 11. ✳

THE BRIDE IS A GARDEN

Bridegroom

4   How beautiful you are, my dearest, how beautiful!
Your eyes behind your veil are like doves,
    your hair like a flock of goats streaming down
        Mount Gilead.

2   Your teeth are like a flock of ewes just shorn
    which have come up fresh from the dipping;
each ewe has twins and none has cast a lamb.

3   Your lips are like a scarlet thread,
    and your words are delightful;[a]
your parted lips behind your veil
    are like a pomegranate cut open.

[a] *Or* and your mouth is lovely.

Your neck is like David's tower,   4
   which is built with winding courses;
a thousand bucklers hang upon it,
   and all are warriors' shields.
Your two breasts are like two fawns,   5
   twin fawns of a gazelle.^a
While the day is cool and the shadows are dispersing,   6
   I will go to the mountains of myrrh
   and to the hills of frankincense.
You are beautiful, my dearest,   7
   beautiful without a flaw.

Come from Lebanon, my bride;   8
   come with me from Lebanon.
Hurry down from the top of Amana,
   from Senir's top and Hermon's,
   from the lions' lairs, and the hills the leopards
     haunt.

You have stolen my heart,^b my sister,   9
you have stolen it,^c my bride,
with one of your eyes, with one jewel of your
     necklace.
How beautiful are your breasts, my sister, my bride!   10
   Your love is more fragrant than wine,
   and your perfumes sweeter than any spices.
Your lips drop sweetness like the honeycomb, my   11
   bride,
   syrup and milk are under your tongue,
   and your dress has the scent of Lebanon.

[a] *Prob. rdg.; Heb. adds* which delight in the lilies.
[b] stolen my heart: *or* put heart into me.
[c] stolen it: *or* put heart into me.

13*ᵃ*   Your two cheeks*ᵇ* are an orchard of pomegranates,
         an orchard full of rare fruits:*ᶜ*

14   spikenard and saffron, sweet-cane and cinnamon
         with every incense-bearing tree,
            myrrh and aloes
         with all the choicest spices.

12   My sister, my bride, is a garden close-locked,
         a garden*ᵈ* close-locked, a fountain sealed.

Bride

15   The fountain in my garden*ᵉ* is a spring of running
               water
            pouring down from Lebanon.

16   Awake, north wind, and come, south wind;
         blow upon my garden that its perfumes may pour
               forth,
            that my beloved may come to his garden
               and enjoy its rare fruits.

Bridegroom

5   I have come to my garden, my sister and bride,
         and have plucked my myrrh with my spices;
         I have eaten my honey and my syrup,
         I have drunk my wine and my milk.
         Eat, friends, and drink,
            until you are drunk with love.

✻ With this section the language of the Song becomes more
erotic and explicit, to such a degree as to press beyond the

[a] *Verse 12 transposed to follow verse 14.*
[b] Your two cheeks: *prob. rdg.; Heb.* Your shoots.
[c] *Prob. rdg.; Heb. adds* henna with spikenard.
[d] *So many MSS.; others* cairn.
[e] my garden: *prob. rdg.; Heb.* gardens.

bounds of credibility all claims that the book was meant to be interpreted allegorically. Why would anyone describe erotic, physical love in such lush, sensual terms and expect the reader to think pious metaphysical or historical thoughts? In this section, as before, the text moves smoothly onward until the consummation of love is reached. The language is voluptuous. The passage radiates physical pleasure and sexual gratification.

1–3. Portions of these verses (1c, 2a, 3cd) are repeated in 6: 5–7, indicating the likelihood of some connection, such as common authorship, between these parts of the book. The various parts of the body have been identified with attributes or things, according to the commentator's basic interpretation of the book, for example, objects of natural or pastoral interest (like sheep, or mountains), or traits of character and religious life (the *two breasts* in 4: 5 were interpreted as Moses and Aaron, or as the two Messiahs who were popularly awaited around the time of the New Testament; *beautiful without a flaw* in 4: 7 was taken to refer to the Virgin Mary). Verse 2 projects an image very serious to men of long ago, before the days of dentistry: the bride has all her teeth, as well as having beautiful ones!

4. *winding courses:* a difficult, obscure passage in Hebrew. This passage reminds us that there are words and phrases in the Old Testament whose meanings have through the years been forgotten; without new information, all any scholar can do is make an educated guess.

6. *While the day is cool and the shadows are dispersing:* a phrase written also in 2: 17.

8. *Amana:* a peak in the Anti-Lebanon range, running parallel with and east of the *Lebanon* mountains which lie along the Mediterranean coast. *Senir* is another, an old, name for Mount *Hermon*, in the Anti-Lebanon range. The geographical distances give heroic proportions to the poem, and this is used as support by those who argue for a mythological interpretation.

12. Reasons for moving verse 12 to the end of the

bridegroom's song do not seem adequate; the passage makes
sense in its original order.

    5: 1. *Eat, friends...*: this passage must be directed to the
companions, as some marginal notations in Codex Sinaiticus
already interpreted it. ✴

THE BRIDE LOVES THE GROOM, AND DESCRIBES HIM

Bride

2   I sleep but my heart is awake.
       Listen! My beloved is knocking:

    'Open to me, my sister, my dearest,
        my dove, my perfect one;
      for my head is drenched with dew,
        my locks with the moisture of the night.'

3   'I have stripped off my dress; must I put it on again?
    I have washed my feet; must I soil them again?'

4   When my beloved slipped his hand through the
          latch-hole,
      my bowels stirred[a] within me.

5   When I arose to open for my beloved,
      my hands dripped with myrrh;
   the liquid myrrh from my fingers
      ran over the knobs of the bolt.

6   With my own hands I opened to my love,
      but my love had turned away and gone by;
      my heart sank when he turned his back.
      I sought him but I did not find him,
      I called him but he did not answer.

7   The watchmen, going the rounds of the city, met me;
      they struck me and wounded me;

                [a] *Lit.* rumbled.

the watchmen on the walls took away my cloak.
 I charge you, daughters of Jerusalem,   8
if you find my beloved, will you not tell him[a]
 that I am faint with love?

Companions

 What is your beloved more than any other,   9
  O fairest of women?
 What is your beloved more than any other,
  that you give us this charge?

Bride

 My beloved is fair and ruddy,   10
  a paragon among ten thousand.
 His head is gold, finest gold;   11
  his locks are like palm-fronds.[b]
 His eyes are like doves beside brooks of water,   12
  splashed by the milky water
  as they sit where it is drawn.
 His cheeks are like beds of spices or chests full of   13
   perfumes;
 his lips are lilies, and drop liquid myrrh;
 his hands are golden rods set in topaz;   14
 his belly a plaque of ivory overlaid with lapis lazuli.
 His legs are pillars of marble in sockets of finest gold; 15
 his aspect is like Lebanon, noble as cedars.
 His whispers are[c] sweetness itself, wholly desirable.   16
Such is my beloved, such is my darling,
  daughters of Jerusalem.

[a] will you...him: *or* what will you tell him?
[b] *Prob. rdg.; Heb. adds* black as the raven.
[c] *Or* His nature is.

Companions

6 Where has your beloved gone,
O fairest of women?
Which way did your beloved go,
that we may help you to seek him?

Bride

2 My beloved has gone down to his garden,
to the beds where balsam grows,
to delight in the garden[a] and to pick the lilies.
3 I am my beloved's, and my beloved is mine,
he who delights in the lilies.

☆ This whole passage has been called a dream-song, and the first part of it, the bride's first song, has been termed a nocturnal intermezzo. Whether there is a special dream-like quality in this passage the reader will have to judge. These poems however offer the bride's descriptions of the groom and her portrayal of the act of love, whereas the preceding segment of the book contained the groom's point of view. The images are richly sensual and specific.

The departure of the lover and search for him have been explained according to the mythological interpretation as the appearance of the common theme of goddess seeking the lover god who is gone, some would say to the underworld, and is now dead.

6. Does this verse indeed speak of a dream, in which such things happen as consummated love which is suddenly broken off?

6–8. The bride seems helpless and forlorn without her lover. The watchmen are brutal and mean, mistaking her for a harlot; or else, in the mythological interpretation, they carry out the

[a] *Prob. rdg.; Heb.* gardens.

188

role of the gatekeeper in the myth of the descent of the
goddess to the underworld (see under 2: 8 – 3: 5).

9. Like a similar passage in 6: 1, the companions' questions
are static and formal, like words from the chorus in the old
Greek plays.

6: 3. This sentence is found also in 2: 16. ✻

DESCRIPTION OF THE BRIDE

Bridegroom

> You are beautiful, my dearest, as Tirzah,   4
> > lovely as Jerusalem.[a]
>
> > Turn your eyes away from me;   5
> > > they dazzle me.
>
> Your hair is like a flock of goats streaming down
> > Mount Gilead;
>
> your teeth are like a flock of ewes come up fresh   6
> > from the dipping,
>
> each ewe has twins and none has cast a lamb.
>
> > Your parted lips behind your veil   7
> > > are like a pomegranate cut open.
>
> > There may be sixty princesses,   8
>
> eighty concubines, and young women past counting,
>
> but there is one alone, my dove, my perfect one,   9
> > her mother's only child,
> > > devoted to the mother who bore her;
> > > young girls see her and call her happy,
> > > princesses and concubines praise her.
>
> Who is this that looks out like the dawn,   10
>
> beautiful as the moon, bright as the sun,
> > majestic as the starry heavens?

[a] *Prob. rdg.; Heb. adds* majestic as the starry heavens (*see* **verse** *10*).

11 I went down to a garden of nut-trees
>to look at the rushes by the stream,
to see if the vine had budded
>or the pomegranates were in flower.

12 I did not know myself;
>she made me feel more than a prince
reigning over the myriads[a] of his people.

Companions

13[b] Come back, come back, Shulammite maiden,
come back, that we may gaze upon you.

Bridegroom

How you love to gaze on the Shulammite maiden,
>as she moves between the lines of dancers[c]!

7 How beautiful are your sandalled feet, O prince's
>daughter!
The curves of your thighs are like jewels,
>the work of a skilled craftsman.

2 Your navel is a rounded goblet
>that never shall want for spiced wine.
Your belly is a heap of wheat
>fenced in by lilies.

3 Your two breasts are like two fawns,
>twin fawns of a gazelle.

4 Your neck is like a tower of ivory.
Your eyes are the pools in Heshbon,
>beside the gate of the crowded city.[d]

[a] *Prob. rdg.; Heb.* chariots.
[b] 7: 1 *in Heb.*
[c] as...dancers: *lit.* as in the dance of two camps.
[d] *Or* the gate of Beth-rabbim.

Your nose is like towering Lebanon
    that looks towards Damascus.

You carry your head like Carmel;   5
    the flowing hair on your head is lustrous black,
    your tresses are braided with ribbons.

    How beautiful, how entrancing you are,   6
    my loved one, daughter of delights!

You are stately as a palm-tree,   7
    and your breasts are the clusters of dates.

I said, 'I will climb up into the palm   8
    to grasp its fronds.'

May I find your breasts like clusters of grapes on the
      vine,
    the scent of your breath like apricots,

and your whispers*a* like spiced wine   9
flowing smoothly to welcome my caresses,
gliding down through lips and teeth.*b*

✻ The Song continues with two word-pictures of the bride,
the first one containing numerous phrases used early in the
book and expressions rather more indirect than those employed earlier for the bride, the second one describing the
bride in her dance. The intensity of the erotic imagery from
preceding passages is absent, and the portraits of the bride are
more objective, drawn by one who is an observer more than
an immediate partner in love.

4. *Tirzah:* capital of the northern Hebrew kingdom during
its first fifty years, after the death of Solomon and before King
Omri built Samaria and moved his political centre there. Mention of Tirzah alongside of Jerusalem, as the two principal and

[*a*] *Lit.* palate.
[*b*] through...teeth: *so Sept.; Heb.* lips of sleepers.

beautiful cities, implies that this song comes from the days when Tirzah flourished as the capital.

The Hebrew phrase noted in the footnote to verse 4 and found again in 6: 10 is a notorious problem. This phrase evidently was in its present form already when the Septuagint translators worked, and it will not do to relegate the words to a footnote, or to alter the text and read 'Nergal', Babylonian name for the planet Mars, and the god of fire, war, and weaponry. Like the case in 4: 4 we have an expression here which is no longer understood; it may have meant something like 'dreadful as an army with banners, or as some kind of flashing signal' (for example, it has been recently speculated that the ancients understood the potential for arranging many mirrors and directing them upon a given point).

Verse 5 confirms the interpretation that the bride is said to be blindingly, dazzlingly beautiful.

Parts of verses 5–7 are found also at 4: 1–3; see there.

10. *dawn:* in Hebrew *shaḥar*, name of the morning star, but also well known from a text discovered at Ugarit, an ancient city on the Syrian coast at a place called Ras Shamra, from the fourteenth century B.C. In the Ugaritic text Shaḥar and Shalim (perhaps this latter name is present in the last part of the word Jeru*salem*) are two children born to El, the supreme god; their names mean dawn and dusk, and their birth demonstrated the virility of El. This passage has also been called upon to demonstrate the mythological interpretation.

The entire verse paints a consistent picture, of one who gazes out like the dawn, beautiful as the moon, bright as the blazing sun, and terrible as flashing light (cp. verse 4; the translation here, *starry heavens*, interprets the word discussed in verse 4 to mean 'celestial constellations').

12. This verse has posed severe problems to translators and commentators, requiring alteration in order to find some meaning. But we might simply take the Hebrew words as they are and, following the lead of the Septuagint, translate: 'I did not know myself; she put me on the chariots of Amminadab.'

The phrase perhaps had an idiomatic meaning which is lost today.

13. Ch. 7 in Hebrew begins as the Shulammite maiden is first introduced. *Companions* is an interpretative heading for this translation, and does not come from the Septuagint manuscripts.

Shulammite: taken by various scholars to mean 'Solomon's woman', or a Canaanite goddess of war like the Assyrian goddess Shulmanitu, or Abishag the fabulously beautiful Shunammite who comforted David in his old age (1 Kings 1: 3ff.) and who was a subject of contention between Solomon and Adonijah his half-brother and the former heir apparent (1 Kings 2: 13–22). Most probably it was either a name signifying that the maiden came from the village of Shulem, or else a word designed to remind the hearer of the beautiful Abishag and to compare the bride to her.

Verse 13 has been interpreted in the following way. *Companions* call for the beautiful Shulammite; she responds with the question (in N.E.B., *How you love to gaze...maiden*), 'What will you see in the maid of Shulem?', and the companions respond, 'The counter-dance' (reading the Hebrew for the last line of N.E.B. verse 13 as a proper name for a kind of dance). In other words, they call her, she replies 'What do you want?', they say 'Dance for us.'

7: 1–9. As she dances, the description follows her body from foot to head. It was presumably the custom then, as it has been in modern times in the Near East, for the wedding to be celebrated by week-long festivities featuring the dancing of the bride and of the groom, during which time they were referred to as king and queen. In the nineteenth century the festivals observed in Syria featured the sword dance.

4. *Heshbon:* a large and important city east of the Dead Sea, first connected with the Amorite king Sihon, and then part of Moab.

5. *your tresses are braided with ribbons:* or, 'a king is held captive in the tresses'. ✻

BRIDE AND GROOM CONTEMPLATE LOVE

Bride

10 I am my beloved's, his longing is all for me.

11 Come, my beloved, let us go out into the fields
       to lie among the henna-bushes;

12   let us go early to the vineyards
and see if the vine has budded or its blossom
       opened,
    if the pomegranates are in flower.
There will I give you my love,

13   when the mandrakes give their perfume,
and all rare fruits are ready at our door,
fruits new and old
which I have in store for you, my love.

8   If only you were my own true brother
      that sucked my mother's breasts!
Then, if I found you outside, I would kiss you,
      and no man would despise me.

2   I would lead you to the room of the mother who
      bore me,[a]
bring you to her house for you to embrace me;[b]
I would give you mulled wine to drink
   and the fresh juice of pomegranates,

3 your[c] left arm under my head and your[c] right arm
      round me.

[a] to the room...bore me: *so Sept.; Heb. om.*
[b] for you to embrace me: *or* to teach me how to love you.
[c] *Prob. rdg.; Heb.* his.

194

Bridegroom

> I charge you, daughters of Jerusalem: 4
> Do not rouse her, do not disturb my love
>   until she is ready.[a]

Companions

> Who is this coming up from the wilderness   5
>   leaning on her beloved?

Bridegroom

> Under the apricot-trees I roused you,
> there where your mother was in labour with you,
> there where she who bore you was in labour.
> Wear me as a seal upon your heart,   6
>   as a seal upon your arm;
> for love is strong as death,
> passion cruel as the grave;[b]
>   it blazes up like blazing fire,
>   fiercer than any flame.
> Many waters cannot quench love,   7
>   no flood can sweep it away;
> if a man were to offer for love
>   the whole wealth of his house,
>   it would be utterly scorned.

---

* Continuing the book are songs which speak of passion, but do not assert it as forcefully as preceding songs have done. Some of the figures of speech are familiar, and whole passages (8: 3, 4) are repeated from earlier in the book.

13. *mandrakes:* a herb which produces a small berry ripening in early summer. The berry and the heavy, forked

[a] until...ready: *or* while she is resting.   [b] *Heb.* Sheol.

195

root were reputed to have aphrodisiac qualities, and were accordingly known as 'love apples'. Cp. their use in the story of Jacob and his two wives (Gen. 30: 14–17). The plant grows wild along the eastern part of the Mediterranean Sea.

8: 1. Embraces and gestures of affection might be shown in public between brothers and sisters.

3. This verse occurs also at 2: 6.

4. Reminiscent of the charge in 2: 7 and 3: 5, this passage omits the phrase, 'by the spirits and the goddesses of the field', although the phrase is retained in a few manuscripts of the Hebrew.

5. Similarity between the opening words of this verse and 3: 6 is highlighted by the fact that 8: 5 and 3: 6 have preceding verses which are the same; even 2: 8, after the same charge in 2: 7, speaks of the groom coming up. No doubt some pattern of order, or even steps in celebration, dictated this coincidence in such varying poems.

6. *cruel:* a bit too severe; 'hard' or 'strong' catches the intention of the word. *grave:* see on Eccles. 9: 10 (p. 142) for a discussion of Sheol, the place of the dead. *fiercer than any flame:* the Hebrew word is unique, and may be so divided as to produce the reading, 'flame of Yahweh', which would then be the only place in the book where God is mentioned.

6–7. The material in these verses seems so dissimilar from the rest of the book as to cause one to ask whether it was not either added by a writer of far different personality or else was intended as a kind of conclusion. To consider this as the high-point or climax of the book, however, as has been done, is to miss the whole force of the erotic and passionate poems; the moralism of verse 7 does not dry up the ardour of the book or its sensual, sexual quality. Even worse, interpreters have over the centuries sought to read into the book through the channel of this verse a notion that the Song of Songs speaks ultimately of 'Christian love'; but the book patently sings neither of 'Christian love' nor of God's love. What verse 7 extols is erotic, sexually-centred human love. ✳

MORE SONGS

Companions

> We have a little sister　　　　　　　　　　　　8
>> who has no breasts;
>> what shall we do for our sister
> when she is asked in marriage?
>> If she is a wall,　　　　　　　　　　　　　9
> we will build on it a silver parapet,
>> but*a* if she is a door,
> we will close it up with planks of cedar.

Bride

> I am a wall and my breasts are like towers;　　10
> so in his eyes I am as one who brings contentment.
> Solomon has a vineyard at Baal-hamon;　　　11
>> he has let out his vineyard to guardians,
>> and each is to bring for its fruit
>>> a thousand pieces of silver.
> But my vineyard is mine to give;　　　　　12
>> the thousand pieces are yours, O Solomon,
>> and the guardians of the fruit shall have two
>>> hundred.

Bridegroom

> My bride, you who sit in my garden,　　　　13
>> what is it that my friends*b* are listening to?
>> Let me also hear your voice.

[*a*] *Or* and.
[*b*] my garden...friends: *prob. rdg.; Heb.* the gardens, friends.

Bride

14   Come into the open, my beloved,
        and show yourself like a gazelle or a young wild goat
            on the spice-bearing mountains.

✻ The poems at the end of the book provide no conclusion
for it. They appear to go on to the end, prepared to launch out
into a whole new series of love songs. However, they can be
so interpreted as to reflect the unwinding, or last stages, of a
folk wedding celebration, and the best guess is that this is what
brings them to this book.

8–9. One interpretation of these verses is that the speakers
are brothers of the bride who are concerned about the un-
married status of their little sister who is not as physically
endowed as the bride. Another and more likely interpretation
reads the speakers as suitors who now follow a time-honoured
ritual of making one last attempt teasingly to woo the bride
(who herself is the *little sister*) away from the bridegroom. In a
village wedding scene one might imagine some closing phase
wherein the attendants sport with the bride and groom,
symbolically bringing the first test to the marriage.

10. The bride's answer, raucous and bold-sounding, self-
confidently insists on the power and formidableness of her
charms.

11. *Baal-hamon*: identification is unknown.

11–12. The bride asserts her own independence; although
now married, and subject to a husband, she lets it be known
that her favours are not to be taken for granted. Doubtless
more nuances of meaning were present originally in these
words, although they cannot be traced today.

13. Playfully the groom still teases the bride; 'Are you
giving my friends something you withhold from me?' he
asks her.

14. Her reply is couched in words used early in the songs,

2: 9 and 2: 17, picking up the old themes and whirling on with them into new love. 'Come on then, beloved; let's see what you can do!'

✻   ✻   ✻   ✻   ✻   ✻   ✻   ✻   ✻   ✻   ✻   ✻

THE MESSAGE OF THE SONG OF SONGS

The attempt has been made throughout this commentary to deal honestly, openly, and sympathetically with the material in the book. Interpreters over the centuries have added layers of tradition and exposition, especially of the allegorical nature, and for that one is always appreciative; yet often those layers say more about themselves and about those who put them there, than they do about the original book.

It is fruitless to try to establish that this book teaches us about theology, or God's love, or even man's love. The book was written to celebrate, not to teach. God is not even mentioned, and although references are made to Palestinian geography, and to Solomon, there is no connection with Israel's history or with the elected people of God. In a word, this book has no message, except the implication that human and erotic love are a good and joyful part of God's creation; there is no need for us to feel that we must try to 'justify' the presence of the Song of Songs in the Bible, by inventing teachings or messages from it, or to feel that something deeply and perhaps mysteriously edifying must be in a document just because it has been included in the Bible. In this case, the message on the basis of which the Song was included in the canon was drawn out by allegory; but what has been taught from the Song by allegory can more readily and substantially be based upon other passages in the Bible.

What we may learn from it, however, is that human sexual enjoyment can be counted among holy things, as this book is counted in sacred scripture. Without ethical preachments or overtones, or any effort whatever to instruct or to influence the reader or anyone else, this book celebrates sexual love.

For admonitions, qualifications, warnings, and other reactions to the misuse and abuse of sex and one's fellow human beings, one must turn elsewhere in the Bible. The freedom in sexual love which is expressed and felt throughout the Song of Songs is constantly assailed by many and great temptations; for so long as man is sinful, and subject to sin, he cannot presume to acquire untouched and uninhibited the spirit of this Song of Songs, or to suppose that his understanding of and sympathy with it justify him and prove that he is a whole man. The spontaneous and enthusiastic joy of the ancient villager at this Song gives way, under analysis of the universal human condition, to the awareness that the Song of Songs taken literally and wholly is more than we of ourselves can ever be. In this vein perhaps old Rabbi Aqiba ben Joseph was correct: the Song of Songs *is* the Holiest of Holies.

LAMENTATIONS

✳   ✳   ✳   ✳   ✳   ✳   ✳   ✳   ✳   ✳   ✳   ✳   ✳

THE NATURE OF THE BOOK

The book of Lamentations is a collection of poems written shortly after the fall of Jerusalem in 587 B.C., describing and lamenting the survivors' experiences after the Babylonians under King Nebuchadnezzar had besieged and captured the city. It is thus a very significant part of the Old Testament, documenting from an extremely critical time an expression of Israel's faith in God and its understanding of the adversities of life. The book is a monument to an indomitable trust and belief in God's presence which went hand in hand with stubborn and relentless willingness to face boldly the most brutal facts of life. Lamentations is not a book of dreary sobbing; neither is it an effort to ignore harsh truths and to focus instead on the bright side of things. The writer holds the reader's gaze to the suffering and the despair in his experience, and compels the reader to contemplate the way in which God's presence and purpose can be interpreted under such circumstances.

THE HISTORICAL BACKGROUND OF LAMENTATIONS

To understand the importance of the book, we need to appreciate the decisive events which it reflects. In Old Testament times no political event took place in Israel which surpassed in importance the fall of Jerusalem in 587 B.C. The theological consequences of the event were enormous, and it stands along with the exodus under Moses as also one of the most influential episodes in the development of Hebrew faith and religion.

Hebrews in Palestine had witnessed and had survived tempestuous times in the eighth and seventh centuries B.C. The kingdom had divided into two parts after the death of Solomon, and in 722 B.C. the northern kingdom was conquered by the Assyrian army. The southern kingdom of Judah, around the capital city of Jerusalem, felt intermittent but growing pressure from the Assyrian Empire. Jerusalem itself was put under siege or under threat of siege more than once near the end of the eighth century, and in the seventh century suffered the indignity of subjection to Assyrian influence and actual vassalage.

Nationalistic and patriotic hopes rose as the power of the great Assyrian Empire began to wane near the end of the seventh century. Kings of Judah who had had to submit to the domination and sphere of influence of Nineveh, Assyria's capital city, were succeeded by the energetic and independent Josiah. Pious and well advised, and fortunate in his place and time in the course of events, Josiah was able to exercise his political ambitions to the point of extending influence over adjacent territory in the old northern kingdom which had been under Assyrian rule until that day. He could furthermore take advantage of the disappearing Assyrian presence and power along the Mediterranean to pursue a policy of religious and cultural independence, which policy may have been partially responsible for, and certainly was built around, what is sometimes called the Josianic Reform.

Also known as the Deuteronomic Reform, this premier religious event was actually a movement of revitalization and refining which lasted several years, perhaps even as long as two decades. According to information provided in Chronicles, Josiah undertook efforts to purify the nation of alien religious rites and theology in the twelfth year of his reign, about 628/7 B.C., when he was only twenty years old. Six years later a book of the law was discovered in the temple, during or after renovating and purging activities; this book, generally considered today to be an early form of portions of Deuteronomy or perhaps even the major part of that book, was the cause of a great national revival and seems to have served as the guideline for the vigorous measures pursued by Josiah. High places were destroyed, images of other gods were removed or burned, and priests of alien deities were put away. Idolatrous centres were defiled, and the king caused foreign or pagan worship practices to cease. Of great political as well as religious significance was the prevention of the traditional worship at Bethel, established almost three centuries before by Jeroboam son of Nebat as a worship centre alternative to Jerusalem when he led the great schism of the kingdom; Bethel lay in Assyrian-controlled territory, and Josiah's deed affirmed his independence and his authority.

Perhaps the most important effect of the Deuteronomic Reform was the centralization of Judaean worship in Jerusalem. The local centres and high places located throughout the kingdom were eliminated during the reform, sacred groves were destroyed, and the priests were offered the opportunity to settle in Jerusalem. As a consequence of this reform, the temple in Jerusalem together with the outward forms of worship there and also the concepts and feelings attached to it were magnified in importance and exalted in esteem. To speak of God's dwelling in Zion no doubt became much more significant because he was no longer to be worshipped anywhere else. The temple, the ark, the sacrifices and festivals, the priesthood, and the king probably drew even more attention than they had before. The use of the book of Deuteronomy, with its promises for keeping the covenant, may have underscored the popular expectations of reward for faithful obedience, and perhaps also elevated the hopes of well-being and blessing which were connected with the king, the temple, the cult, and the promise of God's residence in Jerusalem. 'God is in that city; she will not be overthrown', sang the leaders and people in the liturgy on Zion (Ps. 46: 5) as earnestly as ever and now with more exclusiveness.

The scene in Jerusalem changed radically with the untimely death of Josiah in the battle of Megiddo in 609, against the Egyptian forces under Pharaoh Necho II who was advancing to assist the tottering Assyrian army now fighting for survival against the Babylonians. There is no record of just how successful was the Deuteronomic Reform, or how long its fruits endured, but after 609 Judah had to submit to the over-lordship of Egypt. Certainly religious hopes built on national-istic feelings and political independence had to be altered.

Only four years later the Babylonians defeated Necho at Carchemish, a site very near the Turkish border in present-day northern Syria, and pursued the vanquished Egyptians south-ward through Palestine. Political affiliation and direction had to be changed again; Judah's king, Jehoiakim, now became the vassal of Nebuchadnezzar, king of Babylon. During these years the tenor of religious life in Judah, perhaps especially among the leaders, worsened dangerously. Jeremiah accused the king of unscrupulous and immoral behaviour, and attacked the priests and prophets for unrealistically harbouring the old hopes about divine protection for Zion and the old expecta-tions of reward for merely worshipping according to the rules.

About 601 Jehoiakim tried to break away from the Baby-lonian yoke, in a conspiracy joined by neighbouring kings. Momentarily occupied with other pressures elsewhere in the empire, Nebuchadnezzar sent Syrians, Moabites, Ammonites, and Chaldeans to harass Judah, and in 598 came himself and took Jerusalem after a brief siege. Jehoiakim had died at the beginning of the siege, and his son Jehoiachin was deported to Babylon after a three-month reign. Zedekiah, another son of Josiah and half-brother of Jehoiakim, was set on the throne as a vassal by Nebuchadnezzar.

The political turbulence of the previous decade, with alle-giance vacillating from Egypt to Babylon, to efforts for independence, and back to Babylon, continued through Judah's last ten years. Zedekiah, chosen to be loyal to Babylon, joined and perhaps even led another plan to revolt in 594–593. Although this plan seems to have come to nothing, continued rebellion led to a final struggle a few years later. The Baby-lonian army moved in 589 to punish the rebels, and the

Hebrews set themselves to defend Jerusalem to the end, relying both upon military preparations and strategic position, and upon the religious hopes for deliverance which they had cultivated. The countryside was overrun and Jerusalem quickly brought under siege early in 588.

Conditions of siege for a city in that era were naturally harsh in every way. Food supplies were limited, and water was always a problem; burial of the dead, care of the sick, and removal of filth became major concerns within city walls where there was little open space and the total area did not exceed more than a few acres. A brief period of hope, when the Babylonians had to leave Jerusalem to beat off an Egyptian force that came out to help, brought relief that in the end probably only prolonged the agony. For Nebuchadnezzar resumed the siege, after smashing the Egyptians, in late 588 or early 587. The suffering for the Hebrews became intolerable; hunger and misery ravaged the city, women grew wildly desperate and killed their own babies for food, and the stench of the dead and dying hung over the walls. Jerusalem fell in the late summer of 587.

The picture for the survivors may have seemed no better after the collapse of the defence. Thousands of the leaders and those who were physically able, which may have constituted nearly all of the able-bodied persons, were led off into captivity. Young girls and women were ravished, walls torn down, leaders humiliated, the king captured and forced to watch the murder of his sons as his last view before his own eyes were put out. The survivors were left to wander amid the rubble, to scavenge for food and to remember the dead.

The religious destruction was as complete as the political and physical loss. The temple was in ruins, the priests and prophets gone and discredited; pilgrims came to worship and lament over the spot of the once magnificent edifice built by Solomon (Jer. 41: 5). The celebrations of past victories and God's mighty, glorious acts of salvation were over; the hopes of a last, miraculous deliverance were dashed.

LAMENTATIONS' THEOLOGY, AND ITS WORD

With the memory of these events, and in their aftermath, the book was written. The psalmist among the exiles in Babylon who wrote, 'How could we sing the LORD's song in a foreign land?' (Ps. 137: 4) expressed a problem which had its counterpart for the survivors in Jerusalem. What could be said now about God's power, love, and salvation? What good, and how valid, had been the old theologies with their hopes and convictions? What did these events mean for someone who believed in God?

The fundamental, and most important, point to be observed is the tough, unshaken faith in, and conviction about, Yahweh, the God of Abraham, Isaac, and Jacob. Our modern mentality immediately casts about for alternatives, questioning the premises, and raising doubts about the viability of faith in God. But whatever uncertainties the author may have had, and whether he ever wondered about the possible superiority of Bel and Marduk the Babylonian gods, no evidence of unbelief appears. His question is not whether Yahweh is God, or whether one can believe in any god at all, but rather how does one interpret God's action, and how does one discover and come to terms with God's will.

The theology of Lamentations rests upon convictions about God's presence and power, and his activity in Israel's experience. It was he who brought the power of Babylon upon Judah, and he who broods now over the frightful scene of unhappiness and torment in Zion. He is not dependent upon man's liturgical imitations of his work, and he is not subject to man's desire to manipulate him.

God's sovereignty extends to his response to man's prayer. An issue of major seriousness for Lamentations is the awareness that God does not automatically answer prayer (cp. 1: 17; 3: 8; 3: 44). But this is not couched in terms of the experience of God's absence; it is rather the experience of the mystery of his presence, when he does not fulfil man's requests and does

206

not relieve man's anxiety by dramatic manifestations of his presence.

His power is evident in the Babylonians' power. The fall of Jerusalem, the destruction of Zion, and the human tragedy of it all are due not to his inefficacy but rather to Israel's sin. The book does not grovel helplessly or aimlessly in uncontrollable impulses to feel guilty, but it firmly, deliberately, and in detail asserts the fact that the Hebrews had sinned, and rebelled against God. The leaders had misled, and all the people had transgressed his commandments and his will. God's power was therefore applied to express his wrath, and to punish the sin of his people. The richness and variety of the Old Testament vocabulary for wrath has often been noted, and this book utilizes the full range of expressions. In the day when his power is made obvious in wrath, man must acknowledge that fact, and submit to it, waiting upon the manifestation of his gracious will.

It is the manner in which God's mercy will be revealed of which the writer remains uncertain. He must wait upon God's good time and good will; he cannot induce his own deliverance and salvation. His foreseeable future remains bleak, and he is not able to predict confidently an end of the suffering in his own experience. He cannot make his faith conditional upon the enjoyment of some tokens of God's promised blessing which are delivered in advance. This is altogether an excellent illustration of what should constitute elements in human trust in God. Hope as a spiritual quality must be portrayable in these Old Testament terms if it is to be realistic and relate to all the facts in human existence and experience. Yet God's grace is also sure, as declared in the third chapter. God will bless his people and save them; but the people must learn that part of the meaning of hope is waiting, and that God shows mercy according to his own will and time-table.

Because of their realism, the theological affirmations of Lamentations are grand and powerful. They pin down the issue to the events of the day, and do not depend upon nostalgic remembrances of the dim past or upon wishful thinking about the future. There is in the book remarkably little reference to the history of Israel, and no visions of future dramatic, sudden vindication. The book chooses instead to make do with the current events, and the hopes which have been nourished out of the past. The reader is forced to confront the theme of tragic reversal – that is, briefly put, the tragic, lamentable, drastic, and not entirely equitable change of circumstances from bliss, happiness, or good fortune, to unhappiness and evil days. Israel is afflicted, through events which she cannot completely understand and by forces which she cannot control; her affliction occurs at the hands of those who may be as deserving of punishment as she is. Descriptions of such tragic reversal fill the book (cp. 4: 5, 'Those who once fed delicately are desolate in the streets') and accentuate the pathos which the reader feels. Yet grace, even in such miserable times, is sufficient; it is not a panacea, but it does sustain and fortify the waiting kind of hope which the book presents.

LITERARY FEATURES AND CHARACTERISTICS

The message of the book and the situation to which it was originally addressed are plain, and it is put in a literary style built of some remarkable and obvious features. Chs. 1, 2, 4, and 5 each contain 22 verses, the number of letters in the Hebrew alphabet; there are 66 verses in ch. 3. Chs. 1, 2, and 4 are simple acrostic poems; the verses begin, from the first verse to the last and in order, with the letters of the alphabet, so that verse 1 starts with the letter 'a', verse 2 with 'b', and so on. Many oracles and poems in the Old Testament probably originated with oral expression, but measured, careful literary power and artifice are very evident here. Chs. 1, 2, and 3 are all built upon the scheme of three units to each verse (with the rare exceptions in 1: 7 and 2: 19). But in ch. 3, which is an example of the acrostic pattern applied with rare ambition, each unit is counted as a whole verse by the framers and those responsible for the numeration of the verses in the tradition, making a total of 66 verses, because each group of 3 verses begins in each verse with its distinctive letter; verses 1, 2, and 3 therefore begin with 'a', verses 4, 5, and 6 with 'b', and so on. Obviously this chapter represents a very studied effort in composition. Why these poems were written in this manner is not clear; some scholars have supposed it to be in order to facilitate memorizing, others have credited it to an effort to create beauty, while still others explained it as some kind of form with magical or superstitious value. Such acrostic poems are found elsewhere in the Old Testament, especially in the Psalms where Ps. 119 is the example of the most extended effort. Curiously, in chs. 2, 3, and 4 the sixteenth and seventeenth letters of the alphabet are inverted, possibly indicating a different alphabetical order in those days and in some quarters of the tradition.

Many verses in the book are said to be written in the metre known as *qinah*, or lamentation; according to this form the first half of the unit contains three main beats, while the second half is constructed of only two. For example, in 2: 8*a* we might read with the following accents and pauses,

'The-LORD   was-minded   to-bring-down-in-ruins
        the-walls-of   the-daughter-of-Zion.'

This manner of scanning Hebrew poetry is however not universally accepted by scholars today, and is being increasingly questioned because of so many uncertainties and variations found in the Hebrew texts.

Ch. 5 is distinctive on formal grounds for two reasons: it is not an acrostic poem, and each verse contains only one unit as in ch. 3. Such dramatic literary differences, which are applied so uniformly chapter by chapter, immediately raise serious problems in explaining the origin of the various chapters.

Recent years have witnessed a multiplication of studies to discern formal patterns and characteristics in Hebrew literature. Contemporary literary discussions begin with the premise that distinguishing and understanding the different structures of the composition are essential for the fullest possible appreciation of the intention of the author, and of the meaning expressed through the tradition over the centuries. Identifying forms in Lamentations is not difficult, and the commentary below attempts to assist the reader from chapter to chapter. However, it is clear that forms were also mixed at times, and often the transition between forms is not sharply defined.

Distinguishable forms employed in Lamentations include the dirge (1: 1–11; 2: 1–10, 13–17; 4: 1–16), the individual lament (1: 12–22; 2: 11–12, 18–22; 3: 1–18, 48–66), and the communal lament (3: 42–7; 4: 17–20; 5: 1–22). Comparative study of other Old Testament literature, based on literary features, but also on such other factors as content and apparent use of the literary piece, indicates that these forms are all very similar; the differentiating characteristics rest principally on the use of the dirge in funeral situations, the individual lament in moments when a single individual speaks in the first person singular, and the communal lament on occasions where a whole community laments together and usually in the first person plural. Laments often end with imprecations, or curses, upon the enemy, and chs. 1, 3, and 4 all demonstrate this feature. Chs. 1 and 2 are remarkably similar in literary structure and in content (see below), as well as in other aspects noted above.

Of particular interest in the study of Lamentations is the opportunity to compare it with some remarkable Mesopotamian parallels. In the Sumerian document 'Lamentation over the Destruction of Ur', printed in *Ancient Near Eastern Texts*, pp. 455–63, we have an extensive lament over the ruins of the city of Ur, written more than 1000 years before Lamentations. The walls and gates of the city have been breached, the temple and shrines are destroyed, and the people are suffering deeply. Formal qualities of the piece are noted in the antiphons

placed at the beginning of each song, and in a long lament put
into the mouth of the goddess Ningal, whose husband is the
deity over Ur, the moon-god Nanna-Sin. In the lament the
cause of the destruction is attributed to Enlil, the father of the
Sumerian gods and great god of sky and air, and is determined
by him to take place in spite of the ardent intercessions by
Ningal. Although it has been recently claimed that the
Sumerian lament is closely parallel to, or even influential upon,
Israel's Lamentations, the similarities lie more in the common
subject-matter and ways of looking at the disaster. It is very
doubtful that the known laments in the ancient Near East
beyond Israel had a direct effect upon Lamentations, for the
book grew out of the Hebrews' own cultural patterns and
experience. Nevertheless, there is no doubt that these patterns
and experiences had many characteristics in common with
those of other nations nearby.

THE COMPOSITION OF THE BOOK

While so much about the literary structure of Lamentations is
obvious at a glance, the most important questions about its
origin have not been finally answered. Literary analysis discloses that the chapters are very different in form, and reveals
significant dissimilarities in content and tone. Chs. 1, 2, and 4,
the acrostic poems, all alike describe the situation after the fall
of the city in vivid and intimate language. Ch. 5 bears very
different literary marks, and also seems to reflect a situation
somewhat removed in time from that of the other chapters.
Finally, ch. 3 is also unique in form, and adopts a very special
theological stance; this chapter represents greater artistic ambition and theological reflection, containing thoughts and considerations not found elsewhere in the book. The unity of the
book exists therefore not in its uniformity or in the impression
of being cast in one mould, of one piece, but rather resides in
the configuration of ideas about, and responses to, the disaster,
and in the sweeping movement that goes from lament and

description in chs. 1 and 2, to hopeful reflection in 3: 19–39, to more general or universal references about human supplication and God's answer at the end of ch. 3, then back to the lament and description (chs. 4 and 5).

It seems unlikely that all the chapters were written at one time as a unit. From arguments like those just set out, scholars have proposed hypotheses concerning when the chapters were written which correspond roughly to the observations made in the preceding paragraph. Some have construed the tone in chs. 3 and 5 as such that 5 is placed several decades later than 1, 2, and 4, and 3 is dated a century or more after the fall of the city. But there is no reason to postulate so much distance from the rest of the material. Five or ten years is already a long span of time for meditation, for healing of wounds, and for adjustment to a situation. Although there are no arguments to prove, or to disprove, the theory, it seems more probable that chs. 1 and 2 were written together, ch. 4 separately but at about the same time, ch. 5 next, and finally a considerable time later – perhaps up to several years – the various parts of ch. 3 were composed. The five chapters were then fitted together to form a complete liturgy of lamentation which was used in commemorating this key event in Israel's history.

Although individual commentaries have proposed that most, if not all, the book was written in exile in Babylon, it seems rather artificial to deny the feeling of immediacy in the book, and we may accept the impression given from Lamentations itself that it was all written in or around Jerusalem. References in chs. 2 and 4 which allegedly relate it to Ezekiel, and therefore to the exile, do not in fact establish a certain connection with either the one or the other.

If the book then was written in Jerusalem, in separate sections but none of it long after 587, who was the author? In biblical and ecclesiastical traditions the usual answer has been that Jeremiah wrote the book. The Septuagint version of Lamentations begins with a preface which says that after the exile of Israel and the devastation of Jerusalem, Jeremiah sat down weeping, and 'lamented this lamentation' concerning Jerusalem. The traditions were based upon such references as Jer. 8: 21, 'I go like a mourner, overcome with horror', and 2 Chron. 35: 25, 'Jeremiah also made a lament for Josiah; and to this day the minstrels, both men and women, commemorate Josiah in their lamentations. Such laments have become traditional in Israel, and they are found *in the written collections.*' (So N.E.B.; Hebrew reads, 'in the lamentations'; Syriac reads, 'in the book of the lamentations'.) Although candidly it must be admitted that authorship by Jeremiah is not impossible, it is still most unlikely. The variations of form and content within the book, together with the facts that Jeremiah's oracles have nothing similar to Lamentations, and that the details of Jeremiah's ministry which are known after the disaster give no reason to expect the book to come from his hand, are enough to cause us to look elsewhere for the author. But there are no other data; the book itself says nothing anywhere about its author. Perhaps the best attempt to identify him, or indeed them, for we cannot be sure that everything came from the same person, was the suggestion that the book was written by survivors of the priesthood who remained in Jerusalem after the fall of the city. Without further data the question remains unanswered.

HOW WAS THE BOOK USED?

Like the question of authorship, the use to which the book was immediately put must remain uncertain. Although not incredible, it stretches the imagination too far to claim that the book was written to be a liturgy for the commemoration of the fallen city; there is just no evidence to support the theory. However, it is not impossible, in fact on the contrary it seems quite plausible, that after its composition it was used in festivals or holy days to recall and relive the experience of the disaster. Throughout the centuries it has been read on the ninth of Ab, the fifth month in the Jewish calendar, which falls in late summer, as part of the remembrance on that day of the fall of Jerusalem.

Certainly the shift in theme and tone within the book lends itself to this interpretation. It is not difficult to imagine a liturgical sequence in the emotional pitch and movement through the dirges and laments, sombrely repeating the themes but in subtle and significant variations, changing over to the individual songs in ch. 3 and the hopeful passages there, reverting back to laments with warnings directed against enemies (in chs. 3 and 4), and finally returning to the doleful lament and end in ch. 5.

✳   ✳   ✳   ✳   ✳   ✳   ✳   ✳   ✳   ✳   ✳   ✳   ✳

Sorrows of captive Zion

ALL MAJESTY HAS VANISHED

1 How solitary lies the city, once so full of people!
   Once great among nations, now become a widow;
   once queen among provinces, now put to forced labour!

2 Bitterly she weeps in the night,
       tears run down her cheeks;
   she has no one to bring her comfort
       among all that love her;
   all her friends turned traitor
       and became her enemies.

3 Judah went into the misery of exile
       and endless servitude.
   Settled among the nations,
       she found no resting-place;
   all her persecutors fell upon her
       in her sore straits.

214

The paths to Zion mourn,   4
    for none attend her sacred feasts;
all her gates are desolate.
    Her priests groan and sigh,
    her virgins are cruelly treated.
How bitter is her fate!
Her adversaries have become her masters,   5
    her enemies take their ease,
    for the LORD has cruelly punished her
because of misdeeds without number;
    her young children have gone,
driven away captive by the enemy.
All majesty has vanished   6
    from the daughter of Zion.
Her princes have become like deer
    that can find no pasture
and run on, their strength all spent,
    pursued by the hunter.
    Jerusalem has remembered   7
her days of misery and wandering,[a]
when her people fell into the power of the adversary
    and there was no one to help her.
The adversary saw and mocked
    at her fallen state.
Jerusalem had sinned greatly,   8
and so she was treated like a filthy rag;
all those who had honoured her held her cheap,
    for they had seen her nakedness.
What could she do but sigh

[a] *Prob. rdg.; Heb. adds* all her treasures which have been from days of old.

and turn away?

9   Uncleanness clung to her skirts,
and she gave no thought to her fate.
Her fall was beyond belief
and there was no one to comfort her.
Look, LORD, upon her[a] misery,
see how the enemy has triumphed.

10   The adversary stretched out his hand
to seize all her treasures;
then it was that she saw Gentiles
entering her sanctuary,
Gentiles forbidden by thee to enter
the assembly, for it was thine.

11a   All her people groaned,
they begged for bread;

11b   they sold their treasures for food
to give them strength again.

☆ The book opens with a moving dirge which describes the plight of the people and introduces the theme of tragic reversal. The author and his contemporaries could remember the happy days during the reign of Josiah, when Judah was strong and self-assertive. Through the activities in the Deuteronomic Reform of 621 and the years immediately following, in which the covenant-making days of Moses were re-enacted, religious pride and confidence increased. Then the city was beautiful and apparently secure. Now the scene is desolate and depressing.

1. To be a *widow* in ancient Near Eastern society was to share with the orphan, and the migrant or the immigrant, a state of great vulnerability. Without police or other law-enforcement agencies such as we know, that society relied upon the law of vengeance, whereby the male relatives of

[a] *So Old Latin; Heb.* my.

victims bore responsibility for avenging crimes. Such a relative was known as a vindicator, avenger, or saviour (cp. Ruth
2: 20; 3: 13; Job 19: 25). Alone, and without a husband, the
widow had no one to carry out retaliation for wrong done to
her. The *forced labour* imposed upon the survivors may have
reminded them of the slavery in Egypt (cp. Exod. 1: 11) or
of the Hebrews' own subjugation of the Canaanites in the
early days of the conquest of Palestine (cp. Judg. 1: 28). The
poignancy and power of the book derive in part from the
personal manner in which the disaster is understood and described; this is no statistical report of loss, but rather a provoca-
tive expression of human pathos.

2. The sensation of loneliness becomes acute as the author
recalls, in what the reader will note is almost a refrain in the
book, that there is no source of *comfort* for the people who are
left. The *friends* and those *that love her* refer probably to the
futile political alliances made with neighbouring nations before
the fall of Jerusalem (cp. Jer. 27: 3 for a list of them, and Jer.
30: 14).

3. The first unit of the verse can also be interpreted to mean
that 'Judah went into exile after misery and much servitude',
that is, after suffering through the siege of Jerusalem. The
entire southern kingdom did not of course go into exile; only
a few thousand persons were deported (8000 according to
2 Kings 24: 16; other statistics are given in Jer. 52: 28–30).
Others however fled to Egypt (2 Kings 25: 26), and we may
suppose that still other groups found refuge elsewhere. The
want of a *resting-place* reduced Judah to the status of migrant
(cp. verse 1). Furthermore, in Israel's traditions the concept of
'rest' or 'resting-place' played an important role in the divine
promise and the religious hope; lack of *resting-place* suggests
withdrawal of the promise, as Ps. 95: 11 puts it against the
murmuring Israelites in the wilderness, 'As I swore in my
anger: They shall never enter my rest.'

4. *cruelly treated* is an expression often used in Lamentations
but seldom elsewhere in the Old Testament. Verse 4 describes

the effect of the disaster upon the worship and cultic life. *How bitter is her fate!* literally, 'and she, she has bitterness!'

5. *Her adversaries have become her masters:* the reference is in contrast to the promise in Deut. 28: 13 that the Lord will make Israel the head in blessing. *misdeeds:* literally, 'rebellions', in Hebrew a harsh word for sin.

7. The footnote addition is found also in the Septuagint and Peshitta (Syriac) manuscripts, and is deleted in the text for reasons of uniformity in size of verse. *fallen state:* literally, cessation, or annihilation; the versions offer a number of variant readings.

8. *filthy rag:* the reference is to menstrual uncleanness. *sigh:* the same word is translated as 'groan and sigh' in verse 4; the word means a 'groaning sigh', in bitterness or mourning, and never in relief. Sexual impurity was abhorrent to the Hebrews, and many laws were devised to govern such occasions; the Hebrews felt themselves to be similarly abhorrent after the fall of Jerusalem.

9. *fate:* literally, 'future'; this word is translated by the N.E.B. in Jer. 5: 31 as 'end', in Jer. 29: 11 (where the Hebrew reads literally, 'future and hope') by 'a long line of children after you', and in Jer. 31: 17 (footnote) by 'posterity'. The Hebrew word clearly has to do with time, and not primarily with posterity; but the hopes for the future of the ancient Israelite were certainly connected with his descendants. *beyond belief:* literally, 'wonderfully', 'terribly'. *her misery:* in major textual traditions, including the Hebrew, the text shifts from using the third person previously, to the first person here, 'my misery'. As in verses 12ff. the text reflects a change such as might occur in a service of worship, where the speaker changes or otherwise refers to himself. This abrupt shift may also be explained as an interjection by the author, and an exclamation in the first person for those who later read the book.

10. Entrance to the temple by foreigners was sternly forbidden by the law (cp. Deut. 23: 3, 8), and this verse discloses

how profoundly shaken were Israelite rules and feelings; for indeed, the temple and its holiness, which represented the divinely established structure of the universe and which symbolically helped to uphold that structure, were being trespassed and violated. ✻

I WEEP OVER MY PLIGHT

Look, O Lord, and see   II *c*
 how cheap I am accounted.
Is it of no concern to you who pass by?   12
 If only you would look and see:
is there any agony like mine,
 like these my torments
with which the Lord has cruelly punished me
 in the day of his anger?
He sent down fire from heaven,   13
 it ran through my bones;
he spread out a net to catch my feet,
 and turned me back;
he made me an example of desolation,
 racked with sickness all day long.
My transgressions were bound*ᵃ* upon me,*ᵇ*   14
 his own hand knotted them round me;
his yoke was lifted on to my neck,
 my strength failed beneath its weight;
the Lord abandoned me to its hold,*ᶜ*
 and I could not stand.
The Lord treated with scorn   15
all the mighty men within my walls;

[a] bound: *prob. rdg.; Heb. word unknown.*
[b] upon me: *so Pesh.; Heb.* a yoke.
[c] its hold: *prob. rdg.; Heb. obscure.*

he marshalled rank on rank against me
    to crush my young warriors.
The Lord trod down, like grapes in the press,
    the virgin daughter of Judah.

16 For these things I weep over my plight,[a]
    my eyes run with tears;
for any to comfort me and renew my strength
    are far to seek;
my sons are an example of desolation,
    for the enemy is victorious.

17   Zion lifted her hands in prayer,
    but there was no one to comfort her;
the LORD gave Jacob's enemies the order
    to beset him on every side.
Jerusalem became a filthy rag in their midst.

18   The LORD was in the right;
    it was I who rebelled against his commands.
Listen, O listen, all you nations,
    and look on my agony:
my virgins and my young men are gone into captivity.

19   I called to my lovers, they broke faith with me;
my priests and my elders in the city
    went hungry and could find nothing,[b]
although they sought food for themselves
    to renew their strength.

20   See, LORD, how sorely I am distressed.
    My bowels writhe in anguish
and my stomach turns within me,

[a] my plight: *prob. rdg.*; *Heb.* my eye.
[b] and could find nothing: *prob. rdg.*; *cp. Sept.*; *Heb. om.*

   because I wantonly rebelled.
The sword makes orphans in the streets,
   as plague does within doors.
Hear me*ᵃ* when I groan   21
   with no one to comfort me.
All my enemies, when they heard of my calamity,
rejoiced at what thou hadst done;
but hasten*ᵇ* the day thou hast promised
   when they shall become like me.
Let all their evil deeds come before thee;   22
   torment them in their turn,
as thou hast tormented me
   for all my transgressions;
for my sighs are many and my heart is faint.

✸ The dirge in 1: 1–11 is followed by the individual lament here, whereby the action changes from communal expression to that of Jerusalem speaking as an individual, in the pattern of individual laments known so well from the Psalms.

13–14. Verse 13 accentuates the direct role of God in causing the sufferer's misfortune and torment. In verse 14 the consciousness of sin is dramatically represented as a yoke heavily and relentlessly weighing on the individual, and clinging to him. This image of the yoke might be compared to that of the albatross in the 'Rime of the Ancient Mariner' by Samuel Taylor Coleridge. *bound:* the Hebrew word found here does not occur elsewhere in the Old Testament. Perhaps the best suggestion for its meaning is that proposed a century ago, that it was a technical term for 'putting on a yoke'. The text might then read: 'My transgressions are (like) a yoke placed upon me; they are knotted (on me) by his own hand; his yoke is on my neck, he has made my strength to fail;

> [*a*] Hear me: *so Pesh.; Heb.* They listened.
> [*b*] but hasten: *so Pesh.; Heb.* thou hast hastened.

the Lord has delivered me into their hand, I am not able to stand.'

15. God is personally responsible for the humiliation of Israel's warriors, who have always before in popular theology been regarded as his own army. *rank on rank:* an ingenious translation, similar to that in Isa. 14: 31, maintaining a martial image. The older rendering 'assembly' or 'festal assembly' makes little sense in the context, even if one were to interpret it as meaning a sacrificial banquet of some sort.

17. *the LORD...to beset him on every side:* the phrase might also be translated, 'the LORD commanded, concerning Jacob, that his neighbours become his enemies'. Precisely what happened in Jerusalem after the fall in 587 is unknown; but the bitterness of Judah towards Edom especially (cp. Obad., or Ps. 137: 7) may have reflected looting of the ruins and other forms of harassment by Edom. This verse makes the first reference to what constitutes a major theological problem posed by this book, namely, the shocking awareness that God was not going to answer soon the prayers of his people for respite.

18. Carrying further the confession of guilt (cp. 1: 5, 8, 14), this lament proceeds to lay the foundation for a very realistic and constructive response to the disheartening situation. There is no effort to avert the fact of Judah's guilt and instead blame God; there seems to be no bitterness or smouldering resentment.

19. *lovers:* cp. 1: 2. *went hungry:* literally, 'perished, expired'.

20. *See, LORD:* the Hebrew is identical with 1: 11c. With this hortatory 'see' and the 'hear' in the next verse, the lament draws to a close.

21–2. The author(s) and users of Lamentations did not fail to react towards those who brought death and misery upon them. True to a customary form of the lament (cp. 3: 58–66), this section terminates with an imprecation upon the enemies of Judah. Social sensibilities about non-violent response, and Christian conscience about blessing and not cursing one's

enemies, should not prevent the modern reader from understanding the cultural appropriateness of the imprecation in the
ancient Near East. Israel incorporated into its life in Canaan
adaptations of the nomadic law of revenge. Evil-doing, for
instance murder, was avenged by the taking of the life of the
murderer, usually at the hands of the victim's male relatives.
Furthermore, from all that Israel was able to understand about
its existence under God, his justice dictated that those who
committed evil against Israel should also suffer, for in acting
as Israel's enemies they had become God's enemies. *

Zion's hope of relief after punishment

THE LORD PLAYED AN ENEMY'S PART

What darkness the Lord in his anger   2
  has brought upon the daughter of Zion!
He hurled down from heaven to earth
  the glory of Israel,
and did not remember in the day of his anger
  that Zion was his footstool.
The Lord overwhelmed without pity   2
  all the dwellings of Jacob.
  In his wrath he tore down
the strongholds of the daughter of Judah;
he levelled with the ground and desecrated
  the kingdom and its rulers.
  In his anger he hacked down   3
the horn of Israel's pride,
he withdrew his helping hand
  when the enemy came on;

and he blazed in Jacob like flaming fire
    that rages far and wide.

4   In enmity he strung his bow;
    he took his stand like an adversary
   and with his strong arm he slew
all those who had been his delight;
   he poured his fury out like fire
    on the tent of the daughter of Zion.

5   The Lord played an enemy's part
    and overwhelmed Israel.
He overwhelmed all their towered mansions
   and brought down their strongholds in ruins;
sorrow upon sorrow he brought
    to the daughter of Judah.

6   He stripped his tabernacle as a vine^a is stripped,
    and made the place of assembly a ruin.
In Zion the Lord blotted out all memory
   of festal assembly^b and of sabbath;
king and priest alike he scorned
    in the grimness of his anger.

7   The Lord spurned his own altar
    and laid a curse upon his sanctuary.
He delivered the walls of her mansions
   into the power of the enemy;
in the Lord's very house they raised shouts of victory
   as on a day of festival.

8   The Lord was minded to bring down in ruins
    the walls of the daughter of Zion;
   he took their measure with his line

[a] *So Sept.; Heb.* garden.
[b] festal assembly: *or* appointed seasons.

224

and did not scruple to demolish her;
he made rampart and wall lament,
  and both together lay dejected.
Her gates are sunk into the earth,   9
he has shattered and broken their bars;
her king and her rulers are among the Gentiles,
  and there is no law;
her prophets too have received
  no vision from the LORD.
The elders of the daughter of Zion   10
sit on the ground and sigh;
they have cast dust on their heads
  and clothed themselves in sackcloth;
  the virgins of Jerusalem
bow their heads to the ground.

✻ It has been observed that the first two chapters are very
similar in form and content. Each begins as a dirge and ends
as an individual lament, and each concentrates upon description of the city. Yet Zion is not personified quite so much in
the second chapter, and the descriptions of the ruined city and
people are if anything more vivid and specific here.
  1. The dirge begins in Hebrew with the word 'how', as in
1: 1 and 4: 1, although the word is not carried into the translation. The presence of God is in other places portrayed as a
cloud (cp. Exod. 19: 9 and 1 Kings 8: 10, 12), but there it is
in blessing or benevolence. The cloud can also however por-
tend evil; the text literally says that the Lord has 'brought a
cloud' upon the daughter of Zion and this is suitably paraphrased as *darkness*. The phrase *hurled down* is reminiscent of
the references in the Old Testament to God casting down his
enemy from heaven to earth as a punishment for pride and
arrogance (cp. Ezek. 28: 17; see also Isa. 14: 12). The last part
of the verse in Hebrew says only that 'he did not remember

his footstool in the day of his wrath'. *footstool* may refer to Zion, or even the earth (Isa. 66: 1), but here it may be an allusion to the Ark of the covenant (cp. 1 Chron. 28: 2; Pss. 99: 5 and 132: 7), which rested in the Holy of Holies in the temple, and which was probably destroyed or lost in the destruction of the city. After the fall of Jerusalem the Hebrews had to face the fact that God himself had not remembered Zion, at least in the sense of delivering it unscathed.

2. *without pity:* the phrase is repeated in 2: 17, 21, and in 3: 43. It summarizes the extreme severity of God's abandonment of Judah.

3. *horn* was a symbol of strength in Israel; in verse 17 it is translated as 'pride'. *helping hand:* in Hebrew, 'his right arm'; the right arm of God was a legendary symbol of help as in the exodus for example (cp. Exod. 15: 6; Ps. 77: 10). *far and wide:* literally 'all around'.

4–5. *strong arm:* literally, 'right arm'. *tent*, an archaism, used for the temple, connotes habitation and, by extension with reference to God's habitation, can mean Jerusalem; cp. Isa. 33: 20, 'Look upon Zion, city of our solemn feasts, let your eyes rest on Jerusalem, a land of comfort, a tent that shall never be shifted.' The images of reversal are heaped up in the first four verses of ch. 2.

It requires a strong and realistic faith to make at such a time the daring affirmation that the covenant and creator God has appeared as the enemy, and that the smouldering wreckage that once was a lovely and supposedly impregnable city is the work of God's hand.

6. *tabernacle*, or booth, was another name for the temple, like 'tent of meeting' (cp. verse 4). The people must have experienced a terrible collapse of their concepts of order and support in life when the entire worship structure and religious order – worship life, festival calendar, religious and political leadership – were overthrown.

8. Destruction of the walls and gates (verse 9) was a final act in the thorough physical humiliation of the city. Without

walls it was defenceless, and in fact remained so until the days of Nehemiah. The destruction, and perhaps subsequent depredations, so tore apart the walls that Nehemiah had to turn back from his path in tracing the old walls before rebuilding (Neh. 2: 14).

9–10. In Hebrew society, kings and rulers provided order and leadership, priests the law (torah), prophets the word (and, as here, the *vision*), and elders and wise men the advice (cp. Jer. 18: 18). Now the structures for preservation and interpretation of tradition and the creative springs for the faith were destroyed. *The elders*, who before sat in the city gates with dignity and honour (a description of such a scene is given in Job 29), deciding cases in dispute and stabilizing society, now sat about numb, with nothing to say. ✵

IS THIS THE CITY ONCE CALLED
PERFECT IN BEAUTY?

My eyes are blinded with tears,   11
    my bowels writhe in anguish.
In my bitterness my bile is spilt on the earth
    because of my people's wound,
when children and infants faint
    in the streets of the town
    and cry to their mothers,   12
'Where can we get corn and wine?' –
when they faint like wounded things
    in the streets of the city,
gasping out their lives
    in their mothers' bosom.

How can I cheer you? Whose plight is like yours,   13
    daughter of Jerusalem?
To what can I compare you for your comfort,
    virgin daughter of Zion?

For your wound gapes wide as the ocean;
    who can heal you?

14   The visions that your prophets saw for you
      were false and painted shams;
    they did not bring home to you your guilt
      and so reverse your fortunes.
    The visions that they saw for you were delusions,
      false and fraudulent.[a]

15   All those who pass by
    snap their fingers at you;
    they hiss and wag their heads at you,
      daughter of Jerusalem:
    'Is this the city once called Perfect in beauty,
      Joy of the whole earth?'

16   All your enemies
    make mouths and jeer at you;
    they hiss and grind their teeth,
      saying, 'Here we are,
    this is the day we have waited for;
      we have lived to see it.'

✻ This section shifts first to the form of individual lament, and then in verses 13–16 back to the dirge form.

11–12. The *bile*, or perhaps more literally, 'liver', was considered to be the centre of the human emotions and sensitivity; the figures of *bowels* and *bile* are combined here to convey the source of the most passionate feelings. Famine was a nearly inevitable consequence of such a terrible defeat; its awful extent is graphically set down later (2: 20 and 4: 10).

13. Consolation by means of comparison with those in great misfortune is not very substantial, and this passage

[a] fraudulent: *or* causing banishment.

reflects that fact. Other nations and cities had of course suffered equally severe desolations as had Judah and Jerusalem. Comparisons were possible; but he who has suffered deeply knows that they are fundamentally futile. *daughter of Jerusalem ...virgin daughter of Zion:* or, more correctly, 'daughter Jerusalem' and 'virgin daughter Zion', picture the city as a young woman; the picture is elaborated in the next verse to suggest mockery of one who has lost her virtuous character. The same theme is used in a dirge in Amos 5: 2 and elsewhere.

14. *painted:* this translation is preferable to others that read 'foolish', 'deceptive', etc. The word in Hebrew can mean either 'whitewashed' or 'tasteless'. The task of prophecy in Israel was that of admonition and of speaking the truth. Jer. 23: 9–40 describes prophets who spoke that which God had not given them to say. 'They say to those who spurn the word of the LORD, "Prosperity shall be yours"' (Jer. 23: 17); 'they encourage evildoers, so that no man turns back from his sin' (Jer. 23: 14). These are the false prophets, who do not understand the nature of God's will.

15–16. Clapping hands (the N.E.B. renders the phrase *snap their fingers at you*), shaking heads, hissing and whistling were gestures of mockery and scorn, and a remarkable prediction of just such an occurrence is found in Jer. 19: 8. Ruins of a city are portrayed as a dreadful place in Isa. 13: 20–2. '*Joy of the whole earth*' is the proud appellation also used in Ps. 48: 2. The mockers repeat this eulogy in derision of Jerusalem, ridiculing its fine geographical situation and its prominence in Israel's religious faith. Whether or not there were in fact visitors or travellers in Jerusalem who so mocked, the surviving Hebrews believed that it was happening (cp. the prophetic statement in 1 Kings 9: 8). '*Here we are*': this very free interpretation of what is taken to be a different root meaning for the Hebrew verb affords greater internal logical progression than do earlier translations, which nevertheless faithfully rendered the Hebrew as 'we have devoured' or 'we have swallowed'. ✶

THE LORD HAS DONE WHAT HE PLANNED TO DO

17   The LORD has done what he planned to do,
       he has fulfilled his threat,
     all that he ordained from days of old.
       He has demolished without pity
     and let the enemy rejoice over you,
       filling your adversaries with pride.*ᵃ*

18   Cry with a full heart*ᵇ* to the Lord,
       O wall of the daughter of Zion;
     let your tears run down like a torrent
       by day and by night.
     Give yourself not a moment's rest,
       let your tears never cease.

19   Arise and cry aloud in the night;
       at the beginning of every watch
     pour out your heart like water
       in the Lord's very presence.
     Lift up your hands to him
       for the lives of your children.*ᶜ*

20   Look, LORD, and see:
       who is it that thou hast thus tormented?
     Must women eat the fruit of their wombs,
       the children they have brought safely to birth?
     Shall priest and prophet be slain
       in the sanctuary of the Lord?

21   There in the streets young men and old
       lie on the ground.

[a] filling...pride: *lit.* raising the horn of your adversaries high.
[b] Cry...heart: *prob. rdg.; Heb.* Their heart cried.
[c] *Prob. rdg.; Heb. adds* who faint with hunger at every street-corner.

My virgins and my young men have fallen
  by sword and by famine;[a]
thou hast slain them in the day of thy anger,
  slaughtered them without pity.
Thou didst summon my enemies against me from   22
    every side,
  like men assembling for a festival;
not a man escaped, not one survived
  in the day of the LORD's anger.
All whom I brought safely to birth and reared
  were destroyed by my enemies.

✻ 17. This verse provides a transition from the dirge-like section in verses 13–16 to the lament in 18–22. It puts into sharp focus the historical background of the disaster. The prophetic message had contained assurances that God's words and threats would come true; the book of Lamentations stands as a witness to that fulfilment, affirming that the burden of history stored up through the years had now been released by God.

20. *Must women eat the fruit of their wombs?* The grisly consequences of extreme famine included also cannibalism among the half-crazed people in the starved city (cp. further 4: 10).

20–2. Life in the city must have been nearly unendurable for the survivors, as they first had to remove the dead from the blood-stained rubble, and then had to watch death stalk among the living. The poem relentlessly pursues its terrible theme, moving from object to object. Without any qualification, it relates this disaster to God: *thou hast slain them... Thou didst summon:* under such circumstances it is hardly an exaggeration to claim that none has escaped. *my enemies against me from every side:* in the Hebrew this is *magor missabib* ('terror on

[a] and by famine: *so Sept.; Heb. om.*

every side' or 'terror let loose' as the N.E.B. renders it). The expression appears in Jer. 6: 25 and as a mocking name for Pashhur in Jer. 20: 3 (cp. also Ps. 31: 13); it proclaims imminent and inescapable doom, and it is this that is recalled here.

In contrast to ch. 1, this chapter does not end in longing for revenge upon the enemies; it rather turns inward, digesting and reflecting upon the experience. ✶

AGAINST ME ALONE HE HAS TURNED HIS HAND

3 I am the man who has known affliction,
  I have felt the rod of his wrath.

2 It was I whom he led away and left to walk
  in darkness, where no light is.

3 Against me alone he has turned his hand,
  and so it is all day long.

4 He has wasted away my flesh and my skin
  and broken all my bones;

5 he has built up walls around me,
  behind and before,

6 and has cast me into a place of darkness
  like a man long dead.

7 He has walled me in so that I cannot escape,
  and weighed me down with fetters;

8 even when I cry out and call for help,
  he rejects my prayer.

9 He has barred my road with blocks of stone
  and tangled up my way.

10 He lies in wait for me like a bear
  or a lion lurking in a covert.

11 He has made my way refractory and lamed me
  and left me desolate.

12 He has strung his bow

and made me the target for his arrows;

he has pierced my kidneys with shafts   13
   drawn from his quiver.

I have become a laughing-stock to all nations,[a]   14
   the target of their mocking songs all day.

He has given me my fill of bitter herbs   15
   and made me drunk with wormwood.

He has broken my teeth on gravel;   16
   fed on ashes, I am racked with pain;

peace has gone out of my life,   17
   and I have forgotten what prosperity means.

Then I cry out that my strength has gone   18
   and so has my hope in the LORD.

* With ch. 3 the book changes sharply; the first section
(verses 1–18) is an individual lament, is written in the first person singular, and because it does not offer such vivid data
describing the fall of the city as in the previous chapters, may
betray a somewhat later origin than that for chs. 1, 2, and 4
(cp. p. 212). If the book as a whole was in fact used in worship
in Jerusalem after 587, one must imagine a shift in the liturgical action between chs. 2 and 3. In almost every verse in the
section, reference is made to God's immediate role in punishment; this factor makes more acute the sensation of personal
expression, and of personal wrestling and agonizing with God
in this chapter.

1. *I am the man* raises a question of identity which as yet has
not been finally answered. There is no way of knowing with
certainty who the speaker is here. Historical figures such as
Jeremiah or King Jehoiachin have been proposed by some
scholars; others have concluded that the pronoun 'I' must be
interpreted as a collective, to mean the whole people. More

[a] nations: *so many MSS.; others* my people.

233

likely it is the author himself who used the first person pronoun to express for himself and all his people their deep personal grief and agony.

2. *darkness, where no light is:* a figure rich in allusion. The Day of the LORD was darkness according to Amos (5: 18) and Zephaniah (1: 15). The residence of the dead was dark (Job 10: 21), and primeval conditions before creation were also dark (Gen. 1: 2). The mood for the piece is thereby set, and what follows closely resembles some Psalms and a few passages from Jeremiah and Job. Verses 1–18 reveal simultaneously a highly personal aspect, and the utilization of what may have been rather common and formal figures of speech or expressions in the language.

4–18. Three movements, or images, stand out in these verses: (a) the obstruction, encirclement, and abandonment of the afflicted author in an oppressive enclosure (verses 4–9); (b) the hunt, with cruelty and torment in taking the prey (verses 10–13); (c) the tormenting host (contrast Ps. 23: 5, 'Thou spreadest a table for me in the sight of my enemies; thou hast richly bathed my head with oil, and my cup runs over') (verses 15–18).

5. *he has built up walls around me, behind and before:* a still defensible alternative translation is, 'he has built against me, and surrounded me with bitterness and hardship'.

8. *he rejects my prayer:* the extremity of the separation from God is evident here; even prayers are no longer answered (cp. below, verse 44).

13. *shafts drawn from his quiver:* literally, 'sons of his quiver'.

14. Reminiscent of Jer. 20: 7, 'I have been made a laughing-stock all the day long, everyone mocks me.'

17–18. The end of the lament summarizes the downcast state. It is bad enough that *peace* (or, well-being) and *prosperity* (or, goodness) are gone. But the next statement is shocking from the mouth of one who believes in God, whose lament still shows complete certainty in God's effect upon his own life: *my hope in the LORD is gone!* The Hebrew word for hope here signifies 'to wait, to expect'. In other places in the Old Testament (e.g., Jer. 15: 10–21, Ps. 73) the believer found support in times of stress and doubt by coming to realize that hope for future deliverance and hope in God's abiding presence were firm bases for living. Here the passage would seem to reject all hope. We may compare Jesus' cry from the cross, quoting Ps. 22: 1, 'My God, my God, why hast thou forsaken me?' ✶

I WILL WAIT PATIENTLY

The memory of my distress and my wanderings	19
is^a wormwood and gall.	
Remember, O remember,	20
and stoop down to me.$^{b\,c}$	
All this I take to heart	21
and therefore I will wait patiently:	
the LORD's true love is surely not spent,^{d}	22
nor has his compassion failed;	
they are new every morning,	23
so great is his constancy.	
The LORD, I say, is all that I have;^{e}	24
therefore I will wait for him patiently.	

✶ At the lowest point of the book, after verse 18 where hope itself is given up, the author finds his way out from his despondency. The same word for 'hope' which is used in verse 18 is found in both verse 21 and verse 24, but now however it

[a] The memory...is: *or* Remember my distress and my wanderings, the....
[b] stoop down to me: *prob. original rdg., altered in Heb. to* I sink down.
[c] Remember...me: *or* I remember, I remember them and sink down.
[d] spent: *prob. rdg.; Heb. unintelligible.*
[e] all...have: *lit.* my portion.

is in verbal form and has new significance; rather than look for hope as a status, or condition, which may come or go, the author discovers that it is instead actually an action on his own part. 'I will wait patiently' is the clue. The question is therefore not, 'does hope exist?' but rather 'is anyone hoping?'

22. The ground for hoping is charted in verses 22–4. Verse 22 can be translated, 'it is because of the merciful covenantal loyalties of the LORD that we are not consumed, that his compassions have not failed'. 'The fact that we are still alive is a sign that God is gracious', the passage says, 'and therefore we may patiently wait.' Analysis of the past is made by those who have survived it, and who in this case see the long arm of grace reaching across the years.

24. *The LORD, I say, is all that I have* is the same conclusion as that reached in Ps. 73: 26: 'God is my possession (better, to translate the word as 'portion', as in Lam. 3: 24 footnote) for ever.' To hope is possible even when one is certain of nothing more for oneself.

With this part of Lamentations, the summit of the argument appears. In black despair because of the desolation around him, the author comes to quiet reverence and hope when he remembers that life has been vouchsafed to him. Jeremiah's words to Baruch, his wavering friend, reveal the same sturdy conclusion: 'You seek great things for yourself. Leave off seeking them; for I will bring disaster upon all mankind, says the LORD, and I will let you live wherever you go, but you shall save your life and nothing more' (Jer. 45: 5). In those times when the earth is winnowed in God's wrathful presence, one hopes because life is granted, but one should not expect to be spared from the misery brought upon all the rest of mankind. It is in the nature of human living to hope, to expect, to wait. ✻

THE LORD IS GOOD TO THOSE WHO LOOK FOR HIM

25   The LORD is good to those who look for him,
          to all who seek him;

it is good to wait in patience and sigh   26
   for deliverance by the LORD.
It is good, too, for a man   27
   to carry the yoke in his youth.
Let him sit alone and sigh   28
   if it is heavy upon him;
let him lay his face in the dust,   29
   and there may yet be hope.
Let him turn his cheek to the smiter   30
   and endure full measure of abuse;
for the Lord will not cast off   31
   his servants[a] for ever.
He may punish cruelly, yet he will have compassion   32
   in the fullness of his love;
he does not willingly afflict   33
   or punish any mortal man.

To trample underfoot   34
   any prisoner in the land,
to deprive a man of his rights   35
   in defiance of the Most High,
to pervert justice in the courts –   36
   such things the Lord has never approved.

Who can command and it is done,   37
   if the Lord has forbidden it?
Do not both bad and good proceed   38
   from the mouth of the Most High?
Why should any man living complain,   39
   any mortal who has sinned?

[a] his servants: *prob. rdg.; Heb. om.*

✻ In this part of the chapter, each three-verse group, beginning with its own distinctive letter of the alphabet (cp. p. 209),
makes a particular point.

25-7. In contemplating the meaning of suffering and the
attitude necessary for bearing it, *good* is the key word. *look:*
literally, 'wait'; the Hebrew word for 'wait', or 'hope', here
is different from that in verses 18, 21, and 24. These lines
sound like wisdom sayings, from ancient thinkers who were
calm, passive, optimistic, and prudential; but they also affirm
a conclusion from bitter human experience which offers a
deep insight into the meaning of suffering for man. It is good
to learn the hard truth of real living, that it means waiting,
hoping, believing, and enduring (cp. 1 Cor. 13: 7).

28-30. He who grows impatient with the passivity displayed must recall that the survivor in Jerusalem had recourse
to few possibilities except that of summoning enough strength
to endure. The reference to *hope* is the third in an important
trio. In verse 18 hope seems to be forsaken, but in verses 21
and 24 the author is in fact hoping. In verse 29, the end of the
summit plateau of the book, hope is set in the real situation.
Amid the ruins, surrounded by taunts, and tempted to doubt
any possibility of relief, the author nevertheless asserts his
willingness to hope and to wait. *there may yet be hope:* this is no
sceptic's concession, but rather the open-hearted confession of
one who is leaning towards the future, ready for what God
will bring and willing to rest upon that. He has no guarantee
and no tokens of anticipated victory except the conviction
gained from experience that God is gracious (verses 22-4).
But instead of resting with what is sure (Jerusalem is destroyed, the temple, altar, and ark are gone, God is punishing),
he is prepared to hope for what he cannot yet see.

31-3. To hope is possible under such conditions because of
faith in God who is ultimately compassionate, loyal in his
covenant, and true. God's desire, that is, the ultimate goal in
life, is not that men should suffer or be afflicted. *compassion:*
the word suggests that God feels and suffers with his people.

In Hebrew it connotes a feeling of being warm, soft, or gentle. A multitude of anthropomorphic expressions (e.g. words for divine anger or emotion) illustrates this readiness to think of God as 'suffering-with' or 'feeling-with' man.

34–6. The prophetic-sounding words cite traditional wrongs, but also apply specifically to the situation after the fall of the city. The unfortunate *prisoner* was then of all people most vulnerable. *justice in the courts:* some remnants of the former juridical process remained; there were still elders about who might hear complaints and arbitrate disputes (cp. 2: 10 but also 5: 14).

37–9. This theology, which claims that God is responsible for all that happens, is consistent with the Hebrew faith, especially that faith set down in wisdom literature and the creation hymns. Although the Hebrews may have recognized that problems were raised in affirming that God is behind both good and bad, and fortune and misfortune, they would not consign the origin of some events to a realm beyond God's power and responsibility. Amos 3: 6 and Isa. 45: 7 make the same point: 'I make the light, I create darkness, author alike of prosperity and trouble' (Isa. 45: 7). Verse 39 probably means, 'Why should a man complain, seeing that at least he has life? And why should a man murmur about his sins?' The section reinforces the way by which adjustment to the situation could be made. ✶

THOU HAST HIDDEN THYSELF

Let us examine our ways and put them to the test   40
    and turn back to the LORD;
let us lift up our hearts, not our hands,   41
    to God in heaven.
We ourselves have sinned and rebelled,   42
    and thou hast not forgiven.

43 In anger thou hast turned[a] and pursued us
       and slain without pity;
44 thou hast hidden thyself behind the clouds
       beyond reach of our prayers;
45 thou hast treated us as offscouring and refuse
       among the nations.
46 All our enemies make mouths
       and jeer at us.
47 Before us lie hunter's scare and pit,
       devastation and ruin.

＊ 40–1. The logical connection with the preceding verses, probably exercised in liturgical use of this material, is that the recital in verses 37–9 of demands made by the covenant relationship with God is followed by the call to self-examination and repentance in verses 40–1. *not our hands:* the difficult Hebrew may have been an idiom of the day, now forgotten; perhaps the Septuagint caught the meaning by reading 'upon hands'. Our translation requires the transposition of two letters, to form the word for 'not' instead of the word which means 'to' but which can also mean 'upon'.

42. As in reply to the preceding call, this verse constitutes a confession, and introduces the communal lament in verses 42–7. The meaning of forgiveness is here placed in question, and any concept of automatic or inevitable divine forgiveness must reckon with this passage. In the circumstances, forgiveness is regarded very concretely and apparently related to assuagement of suffering.

44. One of the most drastic and doleful expressions in the Old Testament, this verse challenges a keystone of traditional piety which holds that God will always be attentive to prayers. There are passages from experience which warrant this old assumption (e.g. Ps. 50: 15, 'If you call upon me in

[a] *Prob. rdg.; Heb.* hidden.

time of trouble, I will come to your rescue, and you shall honour me'). But the poet here reflects a different experience known among the people of God, although this experience of the moment must be correlated with the dominant chord of hope already expressed, namely, that 'I will wait for him patiently' (3: 24). The remainder of this chapter also shows that the community did indeed expect that God would respond. The ambivalence of the human reaction and the ambiguity of the human situation are nevertheless made clear with admirable honesty. In Hos. 6: 4–6 and in Isa. 59 there are other passages which show man's predicament and his inability in trying to find or reach God in a time when the effects of sin are being purged and God's demands for justice are being enforced. ✶

THEY TAUNT ME BITTERLY

My eyes run with streams of water   48
    because of my people's wound.
My eyes stream with unceasing tears   49
    and refuse all comfort,
while the LORD in heaven looks down   50
    and watches my affliction,*a*
while the LORD torments*b* me   51
    with the fate of all the daughters of my city.

Those who for no reason were my enemies   52
drove me cruelly like a bird;
they thrust me alive into the silent pit,   53
    and they closed it over me with a stone;
the waters rose high above my head,   54
    and I said, 'My end has come.'

[a] my affliction: *prob. rdg.; Heb.* my eye.
[b] the LORD torments: *prob. rdg.; Heb.* tormenting.

55   But I called on thy name, O LORD,
      from the depths of the pit;

56   thou heardest my voice; do not turn a deaf ear
      when I cry, 'Come to my relief.'[a]

57   Thou wast near when I called to thee;
      thou didst say, 'Have no fear.'

58   Lord, thou didst plead my cause
      and ransom my life;

59   thou sawest, LORD, the injustice done to me
      and gavest judgement in my favour;

60   thou sawest their vengeance,
      all their plots against me.

61   Thou didst hear their bitter taunts, O LORD,
      their many plots against me,

62   the whispering, the murmurs of my enemies
      all the day long.

63   See how, whether they sit or stand,
      they taunt me bitterly.

64   Pay them back for their deeds, O LORD,
      pay them back what they deserve.

65   Show them how hard thy heart can be,
      how little concern thou hast for them.

66   Pursue them in anger and exterminate them
      from beneath thy heavens, O LORD.

* The chapter closes as it began, with an individual lament, and in its total structure anticipates the form of the whole book, opening with lament and dirge, following with the section of hope, and closing with a lament. The liturgical difference between communal and individual laments is blurred by the fact that the transition to the individual form

[a] when...relief.': *lit.* to my relief, to my cry.

occurs in the middle of a three-verse alphabetical unit, after verse 47.

49. *comfort:* a reading following the Targum; most translations read 'respite', 'intermission', 'ceasing', etc.

50–1. The text is difficult. Some translators alter the verse order, to read 51, 49, 50. Others keep the present order, but translate verses 50–1, 'until the LORD looks down and sees from heaven; my eye afflicts me, because of all the daughters of my city'. This rendering is preferable since it keeps to the theme of distress, whereas the N.E.B. introduces the new idea of God's mocking of the poet.

52. *Those who for no reason were my enemies:* the conspiracies planned in Jerusalem by King Zedekiah and neighbouring rulers against Babylon, as reported in Jer. 27, were certainly breaches of trust and contract, and were sufficient cause in international politics for Babylon to respond aggressively. The author here however may be expressing the common feeling of the ordinary citizen that he had no quarrel with Babylon. Or, this may be just a conventional expression of innocence. Certainly the theologically most complicated lament is that issuing from innocent suffering. A human problem arises when the mechanical concept of cause and punishment is challenged.

53–4. The first line might be paraphrased: 'they made an end to me by throwing me into the pit alive'. *pit:* a possible meaning is the literal one, 'a cistern for water'. However, the Hebrew word could also signify the place of the dead, Sheol (cp. Pss. 30: 3 or 88: 4, 6, where it is rendered as 'abyss'), and this overtone cannot be overlooked in seeking the meaning here. Poetically, the author would then be describing his condition as a living death. *closed it over me:* following the Septuagint understanding. The figure is that of closing over the pit with a huge stone. A more literal translation, taking 'stone' as a collective plural, might be, 'and they cast stones upon me'.

Considerable literary stylization lies behind the words and

structure of this lament; *end*, literally, 'cutting off', is the expression used e.g. in Ps. 88: 5. Although one may infer that the verse describes waters in the cistern rising above the captive's head, the phrase is also used in a purely figurative sense (cp. Ps. 88: 7 footnote; Ps. 124: 4).

55. The literary stylization in form continues in the calling upon the name of the LORD, Yahweh (cp. Ps. 88: 9). Appeal to the name of God was an especially effectual resource, for it summoned God's innermost being on the basis of the intimate covenantal relationship with him ('Yet the LORD delivered them for his name's sake', Ps. 106: 8).

56f. There is an apparent contradiction with the thought in 3: 44, which may indicate a different, perhaps later, origin for this lament in 3: 48–66. In 3: 44 the author feels that God will not even admit his prayer, but here in verses 56–7 he has already received an answer. Such contradictions must simply be allowed to stand, for they set side by side different aspects of man's reaction to his experience, first in the trough of despair and then on the wave-top of hope.

58–66. The lament concludes by invoking God's wrath upon the enemies, an element familiar from many of the psalms of individual lament (cp. Pss. 5; 6; 7).

58. *cause:* in Hebrew, *rīb*; a term from the vocabulary of the judicial process. Used for example in Isa. 3: 13 (translated 'case') and Jer. 2: 9 (translated 'charge') to indict Israel for its transgression of the covenant, it is taken here to imply a change in Israel's relation to God, so that he is now taking up Israel's cause and defending her. *ransom:* the Hebrew term, *ga'al*, is familiar to us as 'redeem' or 'vindicate', or to describe the role of a kinsman (cp. the comment at 1: 1).

59. The law-suit motif is pursued in the reference to decisions delivered in favour of the plaintiff, Israel. Some time after the composition and initial use of chs. 1, 2, and 4, the law-suit motif was probably introduced into this liturgy of lament over the disaster. It adds to the liturgy the objectivity and perspective of distance from the immediate situation,

which the earliest experiences soon after 587 B.C. could not afford. It pronounces the word of divine judgement, and implies the ultimate acceptance by God of his people, despite the appearances of the moment. This perspective through a degree of detachment lends balance to the otherwise bleak scene in Lamentations, and conveys a word of final vindication to the suffering people. The tradition in its entirety can thus contain the sharp impressions freshly engraved by the disaster, and also the word of judgement over that occurrence.

60–3. The taunting, plotting, and gossiping which were a source of particular irritation and discomfiture to the author came either from neighbouring peoples and conquerors, as in Ps. 79, or reflected more general circumstances of life which might occur any time and which then were included here as part of the universal experiences preserved and set forth in the book. Taunts and scorn were especially goading in a culture of proud men where a premium was placed upon personal dignity; for examples of other complaints about mocking adversaries, cp. Jer. 20: 8; Pss. 31: 11; 79: 4.

64–6. The imprecation reaches its peak at the end of the lament. The Hebrew text in verse 65*b* is literally, 'Thy curse upon them.' The accumulation of taunt, affliction, fear, and horror created an anger that is vented in passionate raging. The numbness, introspection, and passivity in chs. 1, 2, and 5 are supplanted here by cries of calculated hatred. These words are the evidence left by a people in pain, and not a model for responsible human behaviour. *

THOSE WHO DIED BY THE SWORD
WERE MORE FORTUNATE

How dulled is the gold,   **4**
how tarnished the fine gold!
The stones of the sanctuary*a* lie strewn
    at every street-corner.

[*a*] The stones of the sanctuary: *or* Bright gems.

2   See Zion's precious sons,
        once worth their weight in finest gold,
    now counted as pitchers of earthenware
        made by any potter's hand.

3   Even whales*ᵃ* uncover the teat
        and suckle their young;
    but the daughters of my people are cruel
        as ostriches in the desert.

4   The sucking infant's tongue
        cleaves to its palate from thirst;
    young children beg for bread
        but no one offers them a crumb.

5   Those who once fed delicately
        are desolate in the streets,
    and those nurtured in purple
        now grovel on dunghills.

6   The punishment*ᵇ* of my people is worse
        than the penalty*ᶜ* of Sodom,
    which was overthrown in a moment
        and no one wrung his hands.

7   Her crowned princes*ᵈ* were once purer than snow,
        whiter than milk;
    they were ruddier than branching coral,*ᵉ*
        and their limbs were lapis lazuli.

8   But their faces turned blacker than soot,
        and no one knew them in the streets;
    the skin was drawn tight over their bones,
        dry as touchwood.

[a] *Prob. rdg.; Heb.* jackals.   [b] *Or* iniquity.   [c] *Or* sin.
[d] crowned princes: *or* Nazirites.
[e] than…coral: *prob. rdg.; Heb.* branch than coral.

Those who died by the sword were more fortunate   9
    than those who died of hunger;
these wasted away, deprived
    of the produce of the field.
Tender-hearted women with their own hands   10
    boiled their own children;
their children became their food
    in the day of my people's wounding.

* The chapter begins by reverting to the dirge form in verses 1–16. A brief (verses 17–20) communal lament, presenting the 'inside story' on the last days before the fall of the city and the capture of the king immediately after it, precedes an interesting oracle of mixed form (verses 21–2) which begins ironically with a joyful note to Edom, then sardonically turns to taunt her. The artistic force at work has brought into this chapter, as in parts of ch. 3, a relatively large number of rare Hebrew words.

1. The first ten verses deal with the fate of people in the disaster. *gold* and *fine gold* may be metaphors; Ahaz the king of Judah had many years before availed himself of temple treasure to pay a ransom or bribe to Tiglath-Pileser III of Assyria, before 732 B.C. (cp. 2 Kings 16: 8), after the Assyrians captured Damascus and were threatening to advance on Judah, and Nebuchadnezzar had plundered the temple and the palace at the first fall of Jerusalem in 598/7 B.C. (cp. 2 Kings 24: 13). What remained was probably taken in 587. *stones of the sanctuary*: possibly 'bright gems' (so footnote) or even 'holy stones'. The precise meaning is uncertain; of the possibilities – stones of the sanctuary (with the Vulgate), temple ornaments and holy vessels, bejewelled priestly vestments, choicest citizens – the most logical is that the term was meant to be a metaphor for people. Verse 2 would appear to substantiate this interpretation.

247

3. *whales:* a unique translation, supported by the Septuagint 'dragon', or sea-monster. 'Jackals' (cp. footnote) would seem to fit better the image of desert and thirst. The *ostrich* abandons its incubating eggs in the sand during the heat of the day, and leaves unhatched eggs nearby to serve as food, acquiring thereby the reputation for being cruel (cp. Job 39: 13–18). In Isa. 13: 21–2 and Jer. 50: 39 jackals and desert-owls (ostriches?) are pictured inhabiting the ruins of Babylon.

5. The gaze shifts from the calamity of starving children (verses 3–4) to the degradation of the nobles and other persons of means, including their own elegantly nurtured children. The contrast in fortune dramatically reinforces the dirge's familiar theme of tragic reversal. *dunghills:* in Hebrew, the word is also used in the name 'Dung Gate' in Neh. 2: 13; 3: 14, and 12: 31. As in 1 Sam. 2: 8 and Job 2: 8 it was a place where refuse and dung were piled, and where beggars and outcasts could be found.

6. The traditions about God's destruction of Sodom and Gomorrah in Gen. 19 stood as lasting symbols for sin as well as for punishment, and were cited widely in the prophetic literature (e.g., Isa. 1: 9f.). The Hebrew text can mean either 'iniquity' (cp. footnote) or the *punishment* of iniquity, 'sin' (cp. footnote) or the *penalty* for sin. *wrung:* an interpretation, of a line which has also been translated, 'no one laid hands upon her (Sodom)', 'no hands caused her to quake (or whirl, writhe)', or even, with textual emendation, 'and children did not suffer within her'. The passage must mean either, 'no one grieved over her', or 'she fell not by human hands'. The whole verse contrasts the sudden overthrow of Sodom with the agonizing siege and the continuous misery of Jerusalem, as a sign of the contrast between the greater and lesser sins of Jerusalem and Sodom.

7. *Her crowned princes:* the text and supporting versions make it certain that the subject is either the nobles, already suggested in verse 5, or Nazirites (cp. footnote). The Hebrew word can mean either, depending upon the context; here it

probably means 'princes'. Nazirites were Hebrew men who were consecrated and who took vows to abstain from wine, to refrain from touching the dead, and to allow their hair to grow long. Their social and religious roles changed over the years, and came to be attached to the performance of a specific sacred act (cp. the story of Samson, Judg. 13–16). After *they were ruddier*, the text is quite unclear. The word for *branching* can mean 'body', and usually means 'bone' (as in verse 8). *limbs* is a clarification based upon the Greek translation by Symmachus.

8. Darkened beyond recognition by disease, exposure, hardship, and emaciated from famine, the princes are pathetic embodiments of the tragic reversal of fortune.

9. No better summary of the dirge in verses 1–10 could be drawn than this verse. However terrible were the siege and fall, to survive and endure the torturing experiences thereafter was worse, as life drained out and the spirit grew more wretched. The dramatic power of Lamentations lies in this, that beyond the mourning over past events, however climactic, the words portray the life which everyone in Jerusalem still had to face. The questions which this existence put to their faith are obvious; perhaps this verse is even a conscious challenge or defiance of the modest confidence in 3: 22, 29, and 58, where to be living appeared as a sign of hope and a token of grace.

10. All religious, social, and personal structure and feeling were breached when women devoured their own children in Jerusalem. Jeremiah's prediction in 19: 9 thus comes true with chilling detail. The brutal and eerie reality is high-lighted because the women are presented as compassionate, or *Tender-hearted*, perhaps to underscore the contradiction in such a deed and to show how radically human beings can change (cp. 2: 20). For reference to another incident of cannibalism during a siege, cp. 2 Kings 6: 26–31. The word for *food* may have signified food or bread given especially to comfort and sustain mourners (cp. 2 Sam. 3: 35, David at Abner's death;

2 Sam. 12: 17, David at his child's death; Jer. 16: 7 refers to the custom). ✻

THEY WANDERED BLINDLY IN THE STREETS

11   The LORD glutted his rage
         and poured forth his anger;
      he kindled a fire in Zion,
         and it consumed her foundations.

12   This no one believed, neither the kings of the earth
         nor anyone that dwelt in the world:
      that enemy or invader would enter
         the gates of Jerusalem.

13   It was for the sins of her prophets
         and for the iniquities of her priests,
      who shed within her walls
         the blood of the righteous.

14   They wandered blindly in the streets,
         so stained with blood
      that men would not touch
         even their garments.

15   'Away, away; unclean!' men cried to them.
         'Away, do not come near.'
      They hastened away, they wandered among the
            nations,[a]
         unable to find any resting-place.

16   The LORD himself scattered them,
         he thought of them no more;
      he showed no favour to priests,
         no pity for elders.

[a] *Prob. rdg.; Heb. adds* they said.

* This second part of the dirge begins and ends with the affirmation that the LORD was behind the destruction of Zion, the only distinctively theological reference in this richly illustrated piece.

12. The idea of the inviolability of Zion, the complete and constant sanctuary and protection assumed for Jerusalem by its people in those days – a confidence which caused religious leaders to threaten Jeremiah's life when he spoke against it (Jer. 26: 11) – was recited in the cult and worship ('God is in that city; she will not be overthrown', Ps. 46: 5), and was reinforced by the prophecy of Isaiah (e.g. 2 Kings 19: 31, 34) and Sennacherib's subsequent withdrawal from Judah in 701 B.C. It was, however, also based on the physical fact of the city's almost impregnable strategic position, which had already caused the Jebusites to boast that they would not fall under David's attack (2 Sam. 5: 6–8).

13. *the sins of her prophets. . . the iniquities of her priests:* among the many indictments of guilt throughout the book, the religious functionaries and experts are singled out for special blame (2: 14 and here). All were guilty, but the religious leaders were particularly at fault, not only for failure to act or for dereliction of responsibility (cp. Jer. 23: 9–40), but also for overt acts of lawlessness (cp. the threat to Jeremiah's life, Jer. 26).

14–15. The intended meaning of the passage is not clear. Who are *They* who *wandered blindly*? the prophets and priests, or the blood-stained righteous ones? Most probably it is the prophets and priests, stained with the blood of their victims. *'unclean'* was the cry which was customarily raised as the lepers went along the way. The religious leaders, experts themselves on purity and righteousness, to whom the lepers had to report for a clean bill of health, are ironically reduced to the state of defilement. *

OUR END HAS COME

17   Still we strain our eyes,
       looking in vain for help.
     We have watched and watched
       for a nation powerless to save us.
18   When we go out, we take to by-ways
     to avoid the public streets;
     our days are all but finished,*ᵃ*
       our end has come.
19   Our pursuers have shown themselves swifter
       than vultures in the sky;
     they are hot on our trail over the hills,
     they lurk to catch us in the wilderness.
20   The LORD's anointed, the breath of life to us,
       was caught in their machinations;
       although we had thought to live
     among the nations, safe under his protection.

21   Rejoice and be glad, daughter of Edom,
       you who live in the land of Uz.
     Yet the cup shall pass to you in your turn,
     and when you are drunk you will expose yourself to
       shame.
22 The punishment for your sin, daughter of Zion, is now
       complete,
       and never again shall you be carried into exile.
     But you, daughter of Edom, your sin shall be
       punished,
       and your guilt revealed.

[*a*] our...finished: *prob. rdg.; Heb.* our end has drawn near, our days
are complete.

✻ 17. The *nation* awaited was Egypt, which sent an army under Pharaoh Hophra during the siege in 588; the army was routed, and the siege resumed (cp. Jer. 37: 5; 34: 21). A short communal lament begins with this verse.

18. *When we go out... to avoid the public streets:* a paraphrase. The meaning is, translating somewhat differently, 'Our steps are so beleaguered that we do not go in the main streets.' The reference is probably to the presence of bandits and ruffians who roamed the ruins unchecked, although it could be alluding to soldiers who remained for a brief time after the fall of the city.

19–20. Although possibly speaking of fugitives in general, verse 19 is more generally interpreted to be referring to the relentless pursuit of King Zedekiah, who attempted to flee the city just before it fell (cp. 2 Kings 25: 1–7; Jer. 39: 1–7). Zedekiah tried to save his life by dashing through a city gate under cover of night. He and his company raced towards Jericho, perhaps to seek refuge in Ammon, but he was overtaken, sent to Nebuchadnezzar's headquarters at Riblah in the north, and there was forced to watch the execution of his sons and nobles after which his eyes were put out. *anointed:* in Hebrew the word *māshiaḥ*, 'messiah', means 'anointed one'. *breath of life:* a phrase reminiscent of a type of royal ideology in which the king was regarded as divine; similar expressions were used in Egypt about the Pharaoh. In fact, this very phrase was used by Canaanite vassals whose communications to their lord the Pharaoh, from the fifteenth and fourteenth centuries B.C., are found among the Tel el-Amarna letters (cp. *The Making of the Old Testament*, in this series, pp. 21–5). The phrase, and perhaps vestiges of the concept attached to it, were probably absorbed by Israel, and came to reflect the place of the king in the life of Israel. He was God's anointed, recipient of the promises to David, and the one through whom God bestowed the blessings in the promises and covenant. *machinations:* literally, 'hunters' pits'. *protection:* literally, 'shadow'.

21. Oracles of woe, threat, or imprecation against national political enemies were well known in the ancient Near East, and were common in international treaties. They were especially uttered by prophets before the exile and occupy sizeable portions of those books (cp. Isa. 13–23; Jer. 25, 46–51).

The exhortation to *Rejoice* is made in sheerest irony; this is not to be a word of comfort! Edom is placed in Uz, a territory mentioned in Gen. 10: 23 as an Aramaean tribe, in Jer. 25: 20 as a nation to be cursed, and in Job 1: 1 as the dwelling-place of Job. It was a special object of Israel's wrath after 587 (cp. Ps. 137: 7; Obad. 1–14). The Edomites were held to be descendants of Esau, and the indignation at their opportunism when Judah was helpless may have been aggravated because the Hebrews counted them as distant relatives (cp. Amos 1: 11). *cup:* a vessel used in the ceremony of execration, a cultic event in which the national foes were cursed. The cup was filled with wine which symbolized God's wrath (Jer. 25: 15, 'fiery wine'), and over it the curses were said and the enemies' names were recited. The wine was drunk or poured out as the curse was dispatched in the cultic action (cp. Jer. 25: 15–26; Isa. 51: 17).

22. The gentle tone towards Zion seems to be as distant from the contemplation of the disaster as is ch. 3, and reminds one of Isa. 40: 2, 'her penalty is paid; she has received at the LORD's hand double measure for all her sins'. Within the structure of a liturgy of lamentation, and in an oracle of woe, it is a word of comfort that Zion hears, assuring the worshipper that God's wrath was measured and is still controlled. *

A prayer for remembrance and restoration

REMEMBER, O LORD, WHAT HAS BEFALLEN US

Remember, O LORD, what has befallen us;   **5**
  look, and see how we are scorned.
    Our patrimony is turned over to strangers   2
    and our homes to foreigners.
    We are like orphans, without a father;   3
    our mothers are like widows.
  We must buy our own water to drink,   4
  our own wood can only be had at a price.
  The yoke*a* is on our necks, we are overdriven;   5
  we are weary and are given no rest.
  We came to terms, now with the Egyptians,   6
  now with the Assyrians, to provide us with food.
  Our fathers sinned and are no more,   7
  and we bear the burden of their guilt.
  Slaves have become our rulers,   8
  and there is no one to rescue us from them.
  We must bring in our food from the wilderness,   9
    risking our lives in the scorching heat.*b*
  Our skins are blackened as in a furnace   10
  by the ravages of starvation.
  Women were raped in Zion,   11
    virgins raped in the cities of Judah.

[a] The yoke: *so Symm.; Heb. om.*
[b] in the scorching heat: *or* by the sword.

12   Princes were hung up by their hands,
      and elders received no honour.

13   Young men toil to grind corn,
      and boys stumble under loads of wood.

14   Elders have left off their sessions in the gate,
          and young men no longer pluck the strings.

15   Joy has fled from our hearts,
      and our dances are turned to mourning.   .

16   The garlands have fallen from our heads;
      woe betide us, sinners that we are.

17   For this we are sick at heart,
      for all this our eyes grow dim:

18   because Mount Zion is desolate
      and over it the jackals run wild.

* Ch. 5 is a communal lament, and quite unlike the rest of the book in the following respects. In some Greek and Latin manuscripts this chapter bears the title of 'A Prayer', or 'A Prayer of Jeremiah'. It is a homogeneous unit, and is not an acrostic. It has short, single-line verses, and instead of the *qinah* metre (cp. p. 209) is written predominantly in a 3:3 metre. Attempts to date the chapter precisely, or even to identify the author, exceed what can be established by the hard evidence. Nevertheless, the suggestion that he must be a priest or prophet from the temple, living in Palestine just after the fall of the city, is a good guess which does not contradict the evidence.

The lament begins with the petition that the LORD might be attentive to the suffering (verse 1); the suffering is then described (verses 2–18), and finally the LORD is again urged to answer and to restore.

2. *patrimony:* the concept is full of theological implications. It is used in the Old Testament to show how Israel belongs to God, and to designate the land of Canaan as God's gift set

aside for the Hebrews. In Deut. 10: 9 God is even described as Israel's patrimony. Palestine was a kind of seal upon God's promise of grace and presence for Israel; the fact that it was occupied now by foreigners shook the pillars of the faith, for the validity of the seal was itself now placed in question.

3. 'Widow, orphan, and sojourner' traditionally included those persons who were most vulnerable in the society at that time; they were helpless, and bereft of the protection of family or clan (cp. 1: 1). Reference is frequently made to such persons in Deuteronomy and the prophets, and, it may be added, in the Koran as well. The terrible loss of life in the siege, and the slaughter during the fall of the city, left Jerusalem without fighting men, and therefore actually as well as figuratively exposed and vulnerable, without husband and father.

5. *The yoke is on our necks, we are overdriven:* the text reads literally: 'up to our very necks we are pursued'. Most commentators emend the text, insisting that it makes no sense as it stands; the present translation requires the least emendation, but the Hebrew itself can be readily translated, as above.

6. Already Hosea had accused Israel of reliance upon political contrivance (Hos. 7: 11), rather than upon honesty and honour with men and faithfulness towards God, in the search for a solution to Israel's grave national problems. Judah had also looked hopefully to Egypt (cp. 4: 17), and the reference to Assyria may be a reminder of the faithlessness towards God on occasions as when many years earlier King Ahaz had led Judah in waiting upon Assyria for deliverance from her problems (cp. 2 Kings 16: 7). Some commentators have construed this passage to refer to the wanderings of exiles in search of a home.

7. The sins of the fathers, remembered in the previous verse, are specifically called to mind. In the years around the fall of Jerusalem the great prophets Jeremiah and Ezekiel were affirming that men might no longer be punished for the sins of their fathers, but rather suffer for their own wrong-doing.

However, it is the ancient assurance of suffering to the third and fourth generations (Exod. 20: 5) and of fathers' sour grapes setting children's teeth on edge (Jer. 31: 29), rather than the promise of individual and personally differentiated retribution (Jer. 31: 30), which the author believes to be applicable to the situation after the fall of Jerusalem.

8. *Slaves:* the reference may be to former servants who expropriated habitations and property after the fall of the city, or, more likely, the underlings whom the Babylonians placed as governor and officials over Judah (cp. 'the slave Tobiah', Neh. 2: 10).

9. The passage is literally translated, 'We risk our lives to get bread, because of the sword of the wilderness' (or, 'because of the sword of the pursuer'). Perhaps the reference is to ravaging bands, surging closer after the fall of the city, who made survival even more difficult. *scorching heat* is a translation derived from a different rendering of the Hebrew word for 'sword'.

11. The violation of women took place so often in the fall of nations and cities that the Talmud, centuries later, assumed that it occurred regularly to those who were taken captive. According to Josephus, the Jewish historian of the first century A.D., John Hyrcanus (134–104/3 B.C.) found his claim to the high-priesthood challenged because his mother had been a captive, and it might therefore be assumed that he had foreign blood.

13. Grinding corn and carrying wood, in settled times the chores for women and slaves (Exod. 11: 5; Isa. 47: 2), became under desperate conditions the work of the strong young men.

14. The city gates provided in the area just behind them roomy spaces in which many people could assemble. Consequently they were the location for public gatherings such as the pleading of cases of law and dispute before the elders, who made decisions of judgement. Such was the setting described in Ruth 4. The elders still alive in the city after the fall (cp. 1: 19; 2: 10; 4: 16) no longer performed their function, a sign

of the prevailing social chaos. Music no longer heard from the young men may have brought to mind the prophecy of Jeremiah, 'I will silence all sounds of joy and gladness among them' (Jer. 25: 10).

15. *fled:* literally, 'ceased'. The vivid depiction of the scene of sufferings ended with the previous verse, and personal sorrow is the theme.

16. *garlands:* literally, 'crown'. The reference is sometimes related to political power and the throne, but in this context probably means wreaths of flowers donned in festivity.

18. Cp. 4: 3 (footnote). *

THOU HAST UTTERLY REJECTED US

O Lord, thou art enthroned for ever,   19
    thy throne endures from one generation to another.
Why wilt thou quite forget us   20
    and forsake us these many days?
O Lord, turn us back to thyself, and we will come back;   21
    renew our days as in times long past.
For if thou hast utterly rejected us,   22
    then great indeed has been thy anger against us.

* 19–22. The chapter as well as the book closes with a moving appeal to the Lord. It is worth noting that the book does not close with the theme of revenge and hatred, nor in blithe anticipation of solution and hopeful optimism. Instead, honesty and openness to the facts of the situation in Jerusalem are combined with a faith that will not surrender and a plea that awaits fulfilment.

19. Before the fall of the city it had been customary to speak of God enthroned figuratively within the temple; the ark was probably even regarded as the throne in a symbolic sense. The whole Zion–Jerusalem theology operated around this envisaging of the reign of God. The fall of the city and the

destruction of the temple were therefore crushing blows to this whole way of thinking. That the faithful were able to re-think their position radically is indicated by the continued reference, this time in a more figurative sense along the lines of the theology in 1 Kings 8, to the LORD's enthronement. The destruction of a city could not topple God's power nor undermine confidence in its endurance.

20. But such confidence in God's reign did not dispel the agonies of the day and the questioning they provoked. God reigned, but Judah lay helpless and subject to doubts and despair. Although not predicting or in that sense 'foreshadowing' a later event, this passage springs out of an experience like that of Jesus on the cross in saying, 'My God, my God, why hast thou forsaken me?' Life in God's presence does potentially contain such moments, and faith would be different without this possibility.

21. *O LORD, turn us back to thyself:* the instinctive hopeful-ness of the faith of Israel flashes over the entire book as the lament draws to a close with this petition. The nation lies as God first found it, helpless and abandoned (cp. Ezek. 16: 3–6; Deut. 26: 5).

22. Any bitterness in this closing verse is shrouded in recent translations, which understand the first concept as '*For if*' (as in the present translation), as a question in general – 'or hast thou' (many recent translations) – or even as a denial – 'thou canst not have utterly' (Jewish Publication Society of America, 1917). The Jewish version in fact retains the custom of repeat-ing verse 21 after verse 22 is read, a custom obtaining also for Ecclesiastes, Isaiah, and Malachi. This closes the book on a positive note, but hides the true impact of the conclusion.

The Hebrew text can just as correctly and perhaps more appropriately be translated, 'But thou hast utterly rejected us, thy wrath against us has been very great.' The book then does not end in conditional optimism, but in a statement on the truth of the moment: beneath a pitiful prayer for deliverance, a situation in despair and a feeling of lonely lament. The book is therefore not finally a proclamation of a word that transforms life; it is rather a statement by and about transformed lives in distress, which are nevertheless on the way to surviving and overcoming that distress. ✻

✻ ✻ ✻ ✻ ✻ ✻ ✻ ✻ ✻ ✻ ✻ ✻ ✻

THE MESSAGE OF THE BOOK

After the calamitous fall of Jerusalem in 587 B.C. and its dreadful aftermath for the survivors in Jerusalem, theological questions were raised which required an answer. A few years previously Jeremiah the prophet had firmly asserted that those who were left in the city of Jerusalem, after the Babylonians had carried off into exile in 597 B.C. hundreds of the Jewish leaders after the 'first fall' of the city, should be compared with bad figs, in contrast to the exiles who were like good figs (Jer. 24). The people left in Jerusalem then had assumed that they were the fortunate ones. Now, after the destruction of the city, it must have appeared that Jeremiah was totally correct. What could the 'bad figs' say for themselves?

The theological lessons from the experience, and much of the message of Lamentations, dealt with the meaning of, and the confrontation with, God's wrath. The surviving Hebrews had indeed endured the fearsome 'day of wrath' of the LORD, as Zephaniah (cp. 1: 15) had depicted it, and demonstrated in their own bodies and memories the old warnings of Amos that the 'day of the LORD' would be a day of wrath and gloom (Amos 5: 18–20). God had shown that he was no respecter of persons, and that in the terrible day of his anger all would suffer. The book is remarkable in that this theological insight is accepted so calmly and unhesitatingly; no effort is made to avoid tracing the catastrophe to God. Similar problems of dealing with the issue of God's wrath were faced by Job over against his friends; however, there the question differs in that it treats undeserved suffering. In Lamentations the suffering is clearly deserved. The relationship between cause and calamity is that of sin and punishment.

In such a time the affirmation of faith and hope is difficult. Relying both upon the hopeful traditions and experience of the past, and also upon the fierce, unquenchable convictions of the present, the book roots the believer in the problems of the moment but with hope for the future. Hope is not a static posture, or a quantity or measure; it must be an activity and a way of living. Hope is patient and persevering; it endures quietly and walks softly, making modest and unobtrusive claims about faith. This style of hope supplies an essential and entirely compatible component in the categories made famous by Paul in 1 Cor. 13, 'faith, hope, and love'.

The message of the book meets us directly as we engage in life's difficult and often painful experiences. There is indeed an element of innocent suffering here present, simultaneous with the guilty. For this author represents part of a guilty system; at the same time he was most probably not someone who could and should feel personal leadership responsibility for the advance of the foreign army, and the carnage that followed. But he vents no feeling of self-righteous indignation, and makes no accusations of unfairness against God. The world of our experience is full of innocent suffering, and of relatively uninvolved guilt, and we are reminded of this as we read Lamentations. Every day there are poor innocents who suffer; every day there are well-meaning citizens who walk guilty of that suffering.

A NOTE ON FURTHER READING

For the book of Ruth helpful material explaining the institution of the family is given in *Ancient Israel: Its Life and Institutions*, by Roland de Vaux (McGraw-Hill, London, 1961, paperback edition 1973), especially pp. 20–40. A stimulating study of the tradition and message of Ruth is that by Ronald M. Hals, *The Theology of the Book of Ruth*, Facet Books Biblical Series – 23 (Fortress Press, Philadelphia, 1969). He devotes special attention to the comparison of Ruth with other stories in the Old Testament. A new commentary is E. F. Campbell, *Ruth*, The Anchor Bible (Doubleday, New York, 1975).

An excellent recent commentary on Esther is that by Carey A. Moore, *Esther*, The Anchor Bible (Doubleday, New York, 1971). *The Book of Esther*, International Critical Commentary (Edinburgh, 1908), by L. Paton, is very old, but still a useful mine of information. Helpful material on Purim can be found in the *Jewish Encyclopedia*, and in H. Schauss, *The Jewish Festivals From Their Beginnings to Our Own Day* (Cincinnati, 1938).

The student interested in pursuing the study of Ecclesiastes would do well to read *Koheleth – The Man and his World*, by Robert Gordis (New York, 1955). The rich and thoughtful judgements offered nearly a century ago by E. H. Plumptre in the earlier Cambridge Series, *Ecclesiastes* (Cambridge, 1887), still retain their value.

A very useful commentary on the Song of Songs is that by Robert Gordis, *The Song of Songs: a Study, Modern Translation and Commentary* (New York, 1954). Helpful on a more popular level is the brief treatment in the Layman's Bible Commentaries Series, by J. Coert Rylaarsdam, *Proverbs to Song of Solomon* (S.C.M. Press, London, 1965).

Excellent commentaries on Lamentations which deal more thoroughly with textual problems are by D. R. Hillers,

Lamentations, The Anchor Bible (Doubleday, New York, 1972) and B. Albrektson, *Studies in the Text and Theology of the Book of Lamentations*, Studia theologica Lundensia 21 (Lund, 1963). Background information for the period is expounded in P. R. Ackroyd, *Exile and Restoration: a Study of Hebrew Thought of the Sixth Century B.C.*, S.C.M. Old Testament Library (S.C.M. Press, London, 1968). A fine study of the theology and meaning of the book is provided by N. K. Gottwald, *Studies in the Book of Lamentations*, Studies in Biblical Theology, Old Series 14 (revised edition, Allenson, 1962).

INDEX

INDEX

INDEX